Over The Teacups

Over The Teacups

Edited by Dulcie M. Ashdown

An anthology in facsimile
Published by Cornmarket Reprints
1971

© Cornmarket Press Limited 1971
42 Conduit Street
London W1R 0NL

ISBN 0 7191 7191 1

Printed in England by
Kingprint Limited
Richmond

Contents

How to read the face: *The Housewife, February 1890* 1
What people are wearing: *The Housewife, March 1890* 3
Things we throw away: *The Housewife, March 1890* 4
Cui Bono: *The Housewife, August 1890* 5
The mother's page: *The Housewife, September 1890* 7
American candies: *The Housewife, December 1890* 9
House-wife's corner: *The Mother's Friend, January 1891* 11
When shall we marry?: *The Mother's Friend, January 1893* 12
Christmas gifts made at home: *The Woman at Home, December 1893* 12
Original fashion designs: *The Woman at Home, January 1894* 16
Mothers and children: *The Woman at Home, April 1894* 17
Receipts: *The Mother's Friend, August 1894* 18
Women's employments: *The Woman at Home, September 1894* 18
Cookery: *The Woman at Home, September 1894* 20
Reminiscences of Royalties: *The Woman at Home, November 1894* 22
Dress and fashion: *The Woman at Home, February 1895* 33
"A very up-to-date girl": *The Woman at Home, August 1895* 37
Love, courtship and marriage: *The Woman at Home, October 1896* 49
Life and work at home—over the teacups: *The Woman at Home, October 1896* 51
Dress and fashion: *The Woman at Home, October 1896* 54
Health and personal appearance: *The Woman at Home, October 1896* 59
Cookery: *The Woman at Home, October 1896* 60
The glass of fashion: *The Woman at Home, October 1896* 61
Incomes for ladies: *The Lady's Realm, November 1896* 65
Dress and fashion: *The Woman at Home, November 1896* 68
Wrinkles: *The Woman at Home, October 1897* 73
"Master Waller, diplomatist": *The Woman at Home, October 1897* 74
Life and work at home—over the teacups: *The Woman at Home, October 1897* 78
Dress and fashion: *The Woman at Home, October 1897* 80
Love, courtship and marriage: *The Woman at Home, October 1897* 85
Simple homes, and how to make them: *The Woman at Home, October 1897* 87
The Queen of Italy: *The Lady's Realm, November 1897* 92
"An incidental man": *The Woman at Home, November 1897* 100
What to do with our daughters: *The Lady's Realm, November 1897* 105

Royal etiquette: *The Lady's Realm, November 1897*   110
Decorations for the season: *The Lady's Realm, December 1897*   112
The cuisine: *The Lady's Realm, December 1897*   116
London Society in the Diamond Jubilee Year:
    The Woman at Home, December 1897   117
The children's own corner: *The Lady's Realm, January 1898*   133
The Mirror of Venus: *The Lady's Realm, January 1898*   134
The home beautiful: *The Lady's Realm, January 1898*   135
Games for winter evenings: *The Lady's Realm, January 1898*   138
"Lady Lavender's three chances": *The Lady's Realm,*
    February 1898
    141
The children's own corner: *The Lady's Realm, March 1898*   149
Spring fashions: *The Lady's Realm, April 1898*   150
"A spring idyll": *The Lady's Realm, April 1898*   155
Women prisoners: *The Lady's Realm, October 1898*   165
Simple homes, and how to make them: *The Woman at Home,*
    February 1899
    172
"Taken at her word": *The Housewife, July 1899*   177
French fashion-land: *The Woman at Home, July 1899*   185
What we women owe our Queen: *The Lady's Realm, July 1899*   195
Some hats for the summer: *The Lady's Realm, August 1899*   198
Round the shops in September: *The Housewife, September 1899*   200
Advertisements from *The Woman at Home,*
    October 1896 and October 1897
    208

Preface

A late Victorian scanning a modern women's magazine would find herself quite at home with much of the material she saw there. She might be shocked at the frank advertisements for underwear; she would certainly be appalled at modern advice on sex and manners. But the format of the magazine would be nothing new to her.

By the end of the nineteenth century a well-tried formula had emerged for women's journalism. The dry essays on academic subjects common in periodicals of the earlier part of the century had long since given way to features of more domestic interest. Fashion had its place in almost every magazine, with fiction, household hints and cookery, advice columns, high society gossip, and information about the personal lives of European royalty. By the eighteen-nineties women's magazines had taken on a shape which is still recognisable in the more conservative women's magazines of the nineteen-seventies.

The last two decades of the century saw an unprecedented expansion in periodicals aimed at women. One reason for this was the Education Acts of the 1870s which provided for elementary state education available to, then compulsory for, all children. As previously women had been educated at home or in private seminaries, few below the middle classes had been literate. Now a new market was opened up and the artisan class, if not the labouring poor, were ripe for publishers' exploitation. However, the full effects of this were not to be seen before the turn of the century. The bulk of women's magazines were aimed at the villa and the vicarage, and only slowly turned to the back-of-the-shop parlour and the working woman's teashop. Maid and mistress might not yet subscribe to the same magazine, but the seamstress, the shopkeeper, and the stenographer would soon be able to discuss the latest editions "over the teacups".

The four magazines reproduced here are a fair sample of the women's magazines of the 1890s, other than the purely fashion or fiction periodicals. All were variants of the formula evolved by publishers and editors over the past fifty years or more. "The Woman at Home" was one of the most popular: edited by the novelist Annie S. Swann, a large proportion of its content was fiction, though it included all the aspects general to contemporary magazines. "The Housewife" was more intent on imparting domestic advice, though of a rather superficial kind, and in later numbers had a good section on English towns and the countryside (an interesting reflection on the increased mobility of the population and the general enjoyment of "bank-holiday" trips). In contrast, "The Mother's Friend" attempted a more uplifting tone, though it was certainly emancipated from the accounts of edifying lives and pious deaths rife in its mid-century issues. "The Lady's Realm" was one of the "glossies" of its day. With its many photographs, the occasional coloured cover (still an expensive rarity), social features in abundance and emphasis on high fashion, it was a prestige magazine aimed at the professional and higher commercial market.

By the eighteen-nineties most magazines had admitted advertisements to their pages, though they were usually confined to endpapers (often a large block of the magazine) away from the text and pictures. These significantly increased the income of the magazines of course, but at the same time many editors found their control of advertising material slipping away: where once even the most tasteful pictures of underwear and the most discreet mention of cosmetics had been taboo, now the need for advertising revenue dictated submission to such vulgarities. The publication of women's magazines had become big business.

Of the wide assortment of matter contained in the magazines consulted, any choice of a cross-section of material—not only from differing sources, but from a time span of a whole decade—necessarily has its faults. Six main categories have emerged: fiction (excluding serials, some of which ran for many months), fashion, royalty and society, household hints and cookery, advice and reader participation, and general features. The individual pieces have been reproduced in chronological sequence. Fascinating in themselves, these extracts also serve to illustrate a period of social history when some women, like many of our own day, were breaking the bonds of domestic "servitude", but when many more still rejoiced in the traditional role of their sex.

Dulcie M. Ashdown

How to Read the Face.

By ALFRED T. STORY,

Author of " The Face as Indicative of Character," etc.

THERE are several points, which in reading the face, must be taken into account in the outset. They are the indications of strong or weak stomachs, strong or weak lungs, strong or weak heart. These are very important, because on these things character depends very much. Perhaps very few have thought of it before, but it will only require a little thought to convince them how important are the effects on the mind of weak or strong digestive power, poor or good lungs, bad or good circulation.

Let us take digestion first. The part of the face which is most in sympathy with the stomach is situate about half way between the corners of the mouth, and the lower part of the ears, opposite the molar teeth, or in the middle of the cheeks. Those who are full in that region have naturally good digestive powers, while constitutional dyspeptics fall in there, that is, are hollow cheeked, or, as it is often popularly expressed, lantern-jawed.

The accompanying portrait (fig. XI.) indicates a dyspeptic condition. This is a condition of health very often present in literary men, and brain-workers generally, and arises in great measure from nervous strain on the system, together with the sedentary habits

FIG. XI.

of this class of persons. A dyspeptic person like (fig. XI.) is not generally characterised by great amiabilty, but on the contrary by excessive irritability. The opposite condition is seen in (fig. XII.,) which is a portrait of Meissonier, the great French artist, who is evidently not much troubled by digestive difficulties. A similar condition of stomach and temper is indicated in the face shown in fig. XIII.

The part of the face which is in sympathetic connection with the lungs is obviously that where the hectic flush appears in consumption, and where the rosiest tint appears in health. That this hectic flush is caused by lung inflammation is demonstrated by its always

FIG. XII. MEISSONIER.

accompanying it. That this particular portion of the face is in sympathy with the lungs is proved by its being always pale whenever they are inert ; red and rosy whenever they are vigorous and healthy, and hectic whenever they are inflamed.

FIG. XIII.

In constitutional consumptives the face at this part is always sunken. The larger, when we laugh, the muscular ridge running across the face from the nose to the cheekbones, the less tendency to consumption there is; and the thinner and smaller this muscle, the greater is the predisposition to consumption. This sign is infallible, whether in those from a consumptive stock or not. Those persons having a hollow beneath the eyes, where the hectic flush appears, and falling in just above or below the cheek-bone, and between it and the middle of the nose, are predisposed to phthisis. Those, on the contrary, who are full in there are strong-lunged. These signs usually go along with a narrow chest, a stooping posture, long neck, sharp features, very fine hair and cold hands and feet. Where these signs exist the nature is not so warm, ardent, and emotional as in those in whom the opposite characteristics prevail.

A strong heart or good circulation is indicated by the chin, the size, width, and downward projection of which betokens vigour in that organ. A large, long, broad, projecting chin is indicative of circulatory power and great vigour of the animal functions, and strong passions; while a small, narrow, retreating chin is a sign of feeble circulation and tameness. There is a lack of communicative force in such a chin, compare (figs. XIV., and XV.). The first is a portrait of Catherine of Russia; the other is nobody in particular. He could not be anyone in particular if he tried.

(FIG. X.V. CATHERINE OF RUSSIA.)

Persons with finely developed chins like Catherine enjoy excellent and uniform circulation, have warm hands and feet, seldom feel chilly, withstand cold and heat well, perspire freely, have an even, strong, steady pulse, and are little liable to sickness. When the chin, on the contrary is small there is a fluttering, feeble, and irregular pulse, and the person suffers from chilliness even in summer. Those so constituted are also much affected by changes in the weather, and are subject to coldness of the extremities, and to heat and pressure on the brain. They are slow to recuperate when ill, and succumb much more readily to disease than persons with a large chin. Mentally, they are not so emotional, and are much less under the control of a vivid imagination.

Old age is almost invariably accompanied by a prominent chin. The portraits of centenarians, with hardly one exception, present this sign of longevity in a marked degree. Another indication of old age is a large, long ear, and this

FIG. XV. IDIOT.

sign is all the more sure if accompanied by great length of profile from the chin to the crown of the head. It does not follow that persons having these signs of longevity necessarily live to be old. They may die a violent death, like John Brown (represented in fig. XVI.) who, it will be remembered by some, was executed in America for the part he took in instigating a rebellion to free the negro slaves. The sign, however, is very large in him.

It will frequently be found too, that persons with tolerably large heads are long livers. The explanation appears to be that, as the seat of life is primarily in the brain, the more room the brain-case affords the essential functions of life, the better are the chances for its maintenance. Large headed men like the poet Whittier, (fig. XVII.) will generally be found to have more endurance, both mentally and physically, other conditions being equal, than the small-headed. They may not wake up so soon, be so readily started, or show so much activity all at once, as smaller headed men, but they wear longer and do not tire so soon. As a man with a large heart

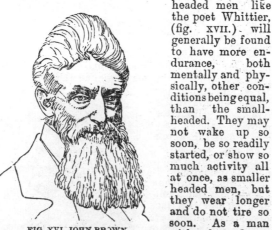

FIG. XVI. JOHN BROWN.

has a better circulation than a man with a small one, so one with a large brain possesses a more equable and constant supply of nerve force, or of that which is more essentially the life-principle than the blood, than one with a small brain. There are cases of idiots living to be old, but then they do not live much at a time.

In cataloguing the signs that indicate health and longevity we must not forget a strong nose, and especially a large nostril. A large nostril, in other words, is indicative of good lung-power.

But there are noses indicative of much more beside this, as I shall now proceed to show. The nose may be classified as follows.—

1. The Roman Nose; 2. The Greek Nose; 3. The Jewish Nose; 4. The Snub Nose; and 5. The Celestial Nose.

The Roman is the executive aggressive nose—the nose of the conqueror (fig. XVIII.) The portraits of Wellington present a good example of it, and, indeed, it is not uncommon to hear it designated the Wellington nose. The likenesses of all great military leaders, from Hannibal downwards, present strong types of this form of nose. A living example may be seen in one who is at the head of a large, though peaceful army, namely, the Salvation Army, whose originator and chief, General

FIG. XVII. WHITTIER.

Booth, possesses a strongly marked Roman nose. It is, as we shall see-by-and-by, the nose of attack, and it is Mr. Booth's mission to attack sin.

The Greek nose (fig. XIX.) indicates refinement, artistic taste, and love of the beautiful. It is the nose, as the name implies, that formed the national Greek type, in which race the instinct for the beautiful in art and nature reached its highest development. It is not uncommon to find this form of nose in both women and men. It is especially beautiful in women. The noses of poets and artists often have this form, or manifest a tendency towards it. Fig. XX. presents the ordinary form of the Jewish nose, although it is by no means confined to the Jews, who possess this form of nose in common with the Syrians. It is a marked characteristic of the Bedouin Arabs, as it was also of the ancient Phœnicians, of whom we have portraits on Egyptian monuments. This type of nose indicates a keen, apprehensive, wary, suspicious character. It is, above all, the cogitative, or deliberative nose, and

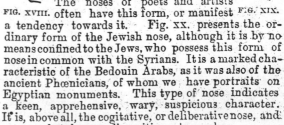

FIG. XVIII.   FIG. XIX.

betokens a disposition to make schemes and study men. The Snub nose indicates more or less a state of undevelopment (fig. XXI.) We do not find it on the faces of conquerors, nor often on the faces of artists. It has been said that it cannot be an historical nose; but this is a mistake. The

FIG. XX. Snub has made its mark in history as well as the Roman and the Greek. The nose of Socrates was a confirmed Snub, FIG. XXI. combined perhaps with a little of the Celestial type, and few historical figures stand out so prominently as he. The Snub nose is not incompatible with a good deal of insight and humour.

Alfd. T. Story

What People are Wearing.

By LUCIE COBBE ARMSTRONG.

Author of "Doll Stories;" "Hints on Pianoforte Playing," etc.

DAME Fashion is in the condition of the Sleeping Beauty, and she will not awaken until the arrival of Spring. Many new modes and colourings lie hidden in the Paris work-shops, but we shall not have a glimpse of them till the advent of the brighter weather. The fashion chroniclers are prophesying an entire revolution of style, and it is to be feared that last year's gown will be of very little good to the possessor. We are to have skimpy skirts of rich materials, and sleeves to reach the wrists both for day and evening wear, but no one is quite certain as to what particular period of costume will be selected for reproduction. The greatest novelty at present is the mania for vandykes, and the fashion is too becoming to be quickly abandoned. The velvet yoke will be cut in long narrow points, the skirt will be made with a vandyked border, and the waist will be confined by a velvet band pointed at top and bottom. The sleeves will be of velvet to match the yoke, so that the upper part of the bodice looks as though it were made entirely of velvet. Sometimes the points are embroidered in chenille or woven in the material in a lighter shade of colour.

A pretty dress of this description was in mushroom coloured cashmere, with the skirt bordered with vandykes of lizard-green velvet, outlined in shaded beads. The bodice had loose points (bordered with vandykes) over a waistcoat of myrtle-green velvet, the collar was adorned with smaller points, the cuff was trimmed to correspond. But dahlia is the favourite colour for these dresses with the trimming in velvet somewhat darker in shade.

There are many pretty novelties in evening gowns, although it is too early for change in day dresses. Flowers are used in a variety of ways—and I lately saw a panel of a pale blue satin dress covered with tiny bunches of Neapolitan violets and edged with a ruche of the same. Velvet flowers are often applied to white satin skirts, and veiled with shaded tulle, the effect is very charming, and like the centre of a valentine. I have seen huge poinsettias veiled in crimson, and velvet pansies in yellow. Prettier than all was a dress of *vieux rose* tulle, with the neck and short hip paniers edged with hyacinths of the same pretty shade.

Short jackets are always popular for young ladies wear, though the *élégante* clings to the long graceful mantle. A pretty short jacket seen at Redfern's was of dust-coloured cloth made with a high collar and three coachmen's capes, each of which was edged with a single thread of gold. *Revers* of golden-brown velvet completed this pretty design. A second jacket was in sea-green cloth with large loose sleeves gathered into a tight fitting cuff of white cloth embroidered in gold, the collar and *revers* being made of the same material. Long mantles of fancy woollen were to be seen in many colours and shapes, and I greatly admired the indefinite effect of the new patterns, which are more like a scrawl than a scroll. A pretty mantle of green and brown *broché* had a high Medici collar of pale green velvet with long *revers* extending to the shoulder seam and finishing off in a deep point at the waist. Another pretty mantle was in a soft brown woollen material figured with a pattern of foliage in a darker tint of the same. A single row of shaded silk fringe fell over the collar and edged the fronts, which were held together by means of finger pockets. Glimpses of salmon-pink lining would be revealed with every movement of the wearer.

Contrast is the principal aim in dress at present, and the most successful costume is the one which combines the greatest variety of colours. The soft tints of grey and green harmonise beautifully by the light of the coloured lamps which are used at afternoon parties, and the crimson lining to a mantle

I

4

affords a pleasant contrast to the rest of the costume. Three colours are much in use with the

milliners, and I lately saw a green felt hat which was trimmed with nothing but three *choux* of

velvet of different colours—one green, one mauve, one yellow—but only the faintest possible tints of the latter colours. Spring flowers are being worn already, and the shaded violet is the latest triumph on the part of the artificial florist. Shaded pansies may be seen on many of the new bonnets, and the crocus in three colours—purple, red, and yellow. The Spring bonnets are to be very small, a twist of velvet and a handful of flowers being all that is necessary for the purpose. Floral bonnets will be worn this year, but they will not be so formal in arrangement as those of last season. The flowers will be placed in the centre and fall downwards towards the brim. Very small flowers will be used, such as violets, primroses, and pink-tipped daisies.

The recent epidemic of weddings has even infected our quiet pages, and Miss Adams has drawn a bridal dress in case any of the readers of the HOUSEWIFE may be shortly in need of such a garment. The dress is of rich white satin, with the front of the skirt draped with lace. The neck is covered with lace to correspond, which would make the bodice look soft and becoming. The little girl wears a cloak and hat of résida serge, lined with a pinkish shade of terra cotta.

Lucie Cobbe Armstrong

Things We Throw Away.

I HAVE been told by many ladies that they never throw away anything; I have been defied by others to mention anything except dirt which they did not cling to like a rich aunt.

Now, to begin: Does any housewife ever throw away crusts and odd pieces of bread, or does she only slip them into a waste basket, when no one is looking? All ye that are liable to be tempted in this way know that crusts carefully saved can be made into griddle cakes, puddings, meat dressings, fish cakes; and when dried in the oven and ground up with the rolling-pin they can be used for thickening soups and gravies, or for any purpose for which rolled crackers are used. The pan of crusts carefully kept will save the measure of meal or crackers, and leave another little coin in the purse to be generous with, or to wear away the barriers of narrow means.

You have heard of the lady whose cake disappointed her in the very face of company coming to tea. Did you also hear that she was mad and threw it away! She did nothing of the kind. Instead, she cut it up in slices, made a delicate little custard, brought out her preserves, and triumphantly placed on the table a very palatable charlotte russe. Another lady in relating her marital experiences, said her husband objected to having rhubarb sauce brought to the table more than three times in succession! Of course she threw it away, and, of course, he twitted her with being wasteful. Oh, if one had but dared to suggest to the unhappy woman that she might have taken her rhubarb sauce, or any other sauce that chanced to offend by its too great familiarity, and have made of it a nice large tart,

with fancy twisted bars across the top, and thus she would have mollified the tyrant, man.

I wonder if every living housewife knows that apple jelly and vinegar can be made from apple parings? Save the parings in an ice chest till a sufficient quantity accumulates, wash, cover with water, and boil quickly for an hour. Strain through a jelly-bag, add half the quantity of white sugar, and boil gently two hours. Flavour with vanilla, and pour into heated glasses. For the vinegar, the parings are put into a jug, a little water is added, and they are allowed to ferment in a warm place behind the stove.

Do we throw away old clothes before all use is got out of them, and they are rags? Some do not, more do. With the scientific housewife, the shining robe of state descends in regular gradations till its lowly lot is cast in a comfortable mat beneath the feet. With the less industrious and the immature, who are constantly taking their places in the world, clothes are often thrown into the rag-bag before they are half worn out. A child's dress gets short in the sleeves, and in it goes! A skirt shrinks and demands piecing out. The demands, like the demands of an oppressed people, are consigned to oblivion, the oblivion of the rag-bag. Changing fashions condemn many garments to that pit of darkness before their time, and the point at which discretion judges best to take a stand against outside pressure must ever remain an individual matter to decide. While some may overstep the boundary on one side or the other, the woman of reflection will generally do what is best.

Character-Reading from Photographs.

By JAMES COATES, Ph.D., F.A.S. Glasgow.

"*A man may be known by his look, and one that hath understanding by his countenance.*"

Correspondents sending photographs for remarks on character must observe the following conditions:—

1st. Each photograph must be accompanied with STAMPED AND ADDRESSED ENVELOPE FOR ITS RETURN.

2nd. When possible, two should be sent, one giving a front and the other a side view.

3rd. A NOMINAL FEE OF SIXPENCE in stamps should be sent for each Delineation. For attention in the following issue they should reach the Office by the 18th of each month.

4th. The remarks on character will appear in the order in which they are received. Only a limited number can appear each month. Those not appearing will be forwarded direct to sender.

5th. When more complete details of character are required than can be given here, A FEE OF 2s. 6D. AND 5s. will be charged (or half the usual fees in private practice). All applications for character-readings, extended delineations, or other information in connection with the above, must be addressed: PHRENOLOGIST, "Housewife" Office, 20, St. Bride-street, London, E.C.

"*I look upon Phrenology as the guide to Philosophy and the handmaid of Christianity; whoever disseminates true Phrenology is a Public Benefactor.*"—HORACE MANN

CUI BONO ?

As we have always new faces and we hope new friends patronising this corner of THE HOUSEWIFE, we find it necessary to call attention to the CONDITIONS, as printed above. Friends should read these carefully before sending photographs, and save us and themselves trouble. Photographs should be sent to us as early in the month as possible, so that we may have time to write and give space to all who come. Last month many were disappointed because their characters and those of their friends did not appear. Character-reading should be as interesting now, as in winter, and it is just as easy to send a new photo from the sea-side, as from the town. To all we would say "be in time"

Delineations are only sent direct when our allotted space is filled up, unless paid for *as private delineations*. A lady in Darlington is anxious to know if "Jim" is likely to make a good husband ? All very proper and laudable, similar matters are of interest to present and prospective housewives. But we cannot answer questions like this, here. It is a matter of personal, rather than of public interest. The photographs of the two most interested should be sent to me direct for *private delineation*. For these delineations the FEES are stated on the FIFTH CONDITION.

L. H. (Sheffield) writes: "I was very much pleased and flattered with your reading of my character. I didn't know I had so many good qualities till you told me. So I have no hesitation in sending my sister's, who I think is almost perfect ; to my mind she has only one fault and I wonder if you will call it a fault. I have taken THE HOUSEWIFE from the commencement and we like it very much, particularly the Character reading, for I am sure some of it is so like people I know."

MISS A. (Darlington) writes: "Will you kindly delineate the enclosed photo, say is he likely to make a good husband ? He has fair hair and grey eyes, pale complexion. Hope I shall be favoured with reply in your next. Have taken THE HOUSEWIFE for some time and take great interest in your page."

MAGGIE SPAKE writes: "Would be so pleased to have delineation of character from enclosed photos. Your delineations of several of my friends in THE HOUSEWIFE have been *so true*. THE HOUSEWIFE is such an excellent and useful periodical."

J McH. (Dundee) writes: "I have been very much interested in the delineations in THE HOUSEWIFE, and think them so good." Sends others.

M. A. (Inverness) writes: "I have taken THE HOUSEWIFE for some time, and think a great deal of it. Will you kindly send delineation of my two boys, 'Ernest and Kenneth Inverness.' Hoping they will be in time for the next issue of the magazine."

HELIOTROPE (Hereford) writes: "My sister was delighted with the very true character you gave her : kindly examine the enclosed photograph."

S. L. (Thurgoland) writes: "Three of my friends had delineations from you a year or two ago, which were most accurate. I shall be very grateful."

E. A. R. (Devon) writes: "I thank you for your character of my sister. It is very true indeed of her, and I now send another sister and her husband for your opinion."

O. K. I. (Orkney) writes: "I was well pleased with my sister's delineation ; kindly tell me. . . ."

BLENHEIM has sharp, clear, and well-defined features, and a well-formed head ; the whole indicating refinement, adaptability, suavity, humour, as well as decision and self-reliance. He is a man of keen perceptions, vivid thoughts and prompt action. Brisk in thought and action, hates laggards, and "will not allow grass to grow on his own shoes." Versatile, humorous, and witty. Sharp, positive, and *testy*. Is also ambitious, pushing, resolute, and decided ; would be dissatisfied with a small sphere of action, and at times will attempt more than he is able to accomplish.

POPPIE (Pontypool).—Fickle, fickle, fanciful and fair. Is a little, active, coquettish body with big ideas. Her spirit, restlessness, and energy are amazing. It would be better if she had more caution, greater restraining power or more self-control. Her intensity, nervous sensitiveness, susceptibility, and approbativeness will always be getting shocks, and things occurring to upset her equanimity. She is either very depressed or very much elated; "gayness" and "graveness," according to some writers, should have a large development with her. She has a good eye for colour, likes artistic surroundings. Possesses a fair amount of order.

J. H (Sheffield) is plain, practical, and decided. She is the *generalissimo* of the domestic circle. Is there anything nice to cook, she is the one who can do it. Is there any hospitable way to make people comfortable, she is just the one to do so. She is not a slave to order, at the same time she hates to see things awry. She has a splendid memory for faces, dresses, and patterns. Has plenty to say when at home. Strong and intense affections. Splendid eye for colour—should be artistic. Capable of ardent attachment and religious intensity.

J McH. (Dundee) has an expressive physiognomy, full marked and decided features, oval face, high head; power of character resident in superior and anterior brain. She has a refined and active organisation, the nervous and muscular elements predominating. Such a woman should be spirited, energetic, self-possessed, positive, and unbending; gracious to a degree, full of mirth and mimicry. Shrewd, more secretive than cautious; tricky and youthful, strong in the love elements, romantic, a little sentimental, regardful of conventionalities, respecting authority, commanding respect, homely with those she knows, shrewd, long-headed, discriminating and decided.

MAGGIE SPAKE (Flintshire) is warm-hearted, impulsive, and fiery. She has too much energy and too little caution. So rash and headstrong, and yet so sympathetic and good-natured; dominated by two very different spirits. She is an excellent *senser* of character. She would be a good reader if possessed of more patience, given more to examine details; as it is, it is wonderful what she can see and use. Is a quick observer, ready at comparison, very intuitive, quick in sympathy. Fervent in religious feeling, warm and ardent in affections. Self-possessed, determined and resolute. Sometimes a *little too positive*. Nervous and *excitable*, must watch these points.

MY BOY (Handsworth, Birmingham) is a fine, healthy, energetic, and spirited "English lad." Restless, strong-willed, sturdy, with a good hold upon life. Square in face and square in head, he promises well for an active life—business energy and uprightness. He is affectionate and playful, a little stubborn—not intractable, but wilful—needs firm but always gentle direction. The petted and spoiled element must be avoided and "English lad" led to be manly, courteous, and *promptly obedient*. There must be no taking advantage of sympathies and affection to have his own way. There *will be* a little of this. He will learn readily; his education will not be troublesome. The question of pursuit may be deferred a little.

THURGOLAND.—Your head and face are instinct with character—personal self-respect, strong affections, broad sympathies, combined with good powers of observation and intuition. You are sharp and shrewd, fiery, active, and energetic. Your organisation is a working one, giving endurance and fortitude. Trifles may annoy, but great troubles bring out coolness, decision, and fortitude. Docile but not tame. Domesticated, economical watchful, managing, are well adapted to understand children, apprehend character, and teach.

JIM (Brooklyn) is a superior type of a young man. Fine in grain, wiry, active, ambitious, social, and genial. Possessed of high instincts, honour, nobility. Full of fun, buoyancy. The sense of the humorous may sometimes carry him a little too far. If engaged in commercial pursuits, connected with a good house in shipping, brokerage, or warehousing he should do well and succeed. He is endowed with the material which makes the enterprising merchant, the public spirited citizen.

HETTIE (Brooklyn) has a refined, active, and nervous organisation. Is quick, bright, changeable, and im-

pulsive. Has plenty of spirit but is not very discriminating; rebels easily and has a weakness for *the last word* and *snap*. Soon huffed, soon pleased. Is warm, imaginative, high-spirited, and quick in temper. She should have succeeded at school in ordinary attainments, lady-like accomplishments, music and painting. Should make a good musician and possess executive power. Literary attainments of considerable promise. Experience may perfect and mature much that is now chaotic.

O. K, I.—You have an observant, thoughtful nature. What you observe and read you reflect on and remember. You have a good all-round memory. Your geographical, localising, and historical memories are good. If you had been a man, *as you often wish you were*, you would travel. If limited in your surroundings, your desire to travel is great. Are active and buoyant, yet *subject to spells of depressions*. Should have a good ear for music; are adapted for the Civil Service, postal telegraphy, teaching, secretaryship, etc. Type of character domesticated.

MRS. FRANK.—This lady has only a fairly healthy organisation. She is only buoyant in "spurts," lacks in a measure *force*, self-reliance, and endurance. Is not, therefore, the best adapted to combat with difficulties or non-successes. She forgets that "thoughts are things," or she would prophesy evil less. She should believe, work, and pray for the best, and the best will come when the brain is cleared by these. Worry fogs the brain. Greater skill is required to steer clear in the fog of the difficulties in life Anxiety is useful, but there are times it ceases to be useful. Mrs. Frank should watch these times. She is devoted, painstaking, manner quiet and agreeable. Would enjoy business *if it was doing well.*

MR. FRANK is impulsive, spirited, pushing and energetic; quick-witted, humorous and versatile. He has a good manner and excellent business tact; he is essentially a business man—would make an excellent traveller. Is a good judge of customers, manner, style, and the thing which will suit them best. He is fond of excitement, likes to be on the move, would not do well with confining or sedentary pursuits. If business was slow, and not according to anticipation he might be too rash and do impulsive things. He is good, but does not overflow with patience. He is erratic, but easily enough led; affectionate and cheerful.

BLANCHE (W. S.) is strong-willed and reflective. Cannot be guilty of doing much without fully knowing why beforehand. Observant, orderly, pretty precise and matter-of-fact. Is very discriminating, and will act as a rule with great judgment and forethought. Without, however, being exactly aware, she is inclined to be too positive, adhering to and imposing or impressing her views on others. Men admire intelligence and judgment in women, but they fear for that which may in any way interfere with their imaginary prerogatives of lordship and superiority. "Blanche" should have a good ear for music. She would make a good teacher and disciplinarian.

MARGARET (L. C.) is endowed with a healthy and vigorous constitution, a strong love nature, warm, earnest, and devoted domestic disposition. She is merry and wise rather than merry and philosophic; practical rather than theoretical. Her will is strong, and her independence of character is marked. Buoyancy, courtesy, and high spirits sometimes hide much of her self-reliance and solid worth. She is generous, impulsive, and sensitive to praise and censure. Candid as a rule. Might be a little more guarded and discreet, and all will be well.

The following delineations have been sent direct: Emily. C. E. L. "Trudie-Heeley." "Pearl." "Kilmeny."

The Mothers' Page.

THE HOUSEWIFE devotes this page every month to matters specially intere~~ing and instructive to mothers. Many questions have from time to time been asked by young or inexperienced mothers relative to the clothing, general management, and training of their children from infancy to that period when girls and boys are expected to be capable of self-discipline. Any mother wishing for information or advice shall be answered in the succeeding issue of the magazine, provided the questions are received not later than the 15th of the month. If the information sought is beyond our experience, the question will be submitted to our wide circle of readers, amongst whom, doubtless, someone will be found able and willing to give the help required.

FINGERS AND TOES.

THESE twenty little digits and pedal appendages of baby's do require a deal of looking after, else they may cause much suffering.

The tiny nails break and tear so easily they need a close watch kept over them that no sharp little point is left to cruelly scratch baby's face, or to stab and goad the tender flesh of adjacent toes.

It is not always stomach pains that make baby scream and kick. Maybe, he is suffering from a vicious little dagger of a toe nail that with every movement of the active foot, gives a torturing prod into its neighbour.

Twice, at least, after one of our babies had cried itself to sleep with pain that I could not find to relieve, hard as I tried, I discovered a long hair tightly withed about a strangled toe, cruelly cutting into the sensitive flesh.

Another time, we found a sharp edged bit of a chip—clinging, probably, to the turned sock when baby was dressed that morning—wedged between two pink toes, jamming them till they had blistered. No wonder baby had had a peevish day.

" I don't see where my baby finds so many pins with which to scratch herself !" a young mother once said to us, again anxiously scrutinising her clothing for the pin-point she believed had so savagely drawn blood in several places on her child's face.

We looked at her baby's fingers and found just what we suspected, a needle-like nail point that had done the hurt.

As baby grows older and boots take the place of soft wool socks, care must be given that the fast growing little feet are not cramped by too small boots. Even dainty kid can goadingly pinch and chafe the tender flesh, and if the boot is too short, barbarously double the flexible, helpless toes in under themselves, causing baby much wailing distress, which we in our ignorance, try to relieve with generous doses of castor oil.

A creeping child is apt to wound its hands with splinters from floor or furniture, and they should often be examined. Only yesterday, our baby crept to me crying as though hurt. I took her into my lap and looked her over; knees and wrists as well as hands, and found in one pink palm, the sharp point of a splinter.

With a long, cold winter at our heels, constant watchful care we mothers must give, else our little creepers and toddlers will suffer with their quickly chilled hands and feet. We must keep them up from the floor and its strata of cold air as much as possible, and whatever else of the work goes, we will take time to keep baby warm and comfortable.

Many mothers will like to hear of

FOUR BRIGHT NEW GAMES.

THE BAG OF LUCK.—Fill a paper bag with sweets and tie it firmly by the top to a string hung across an open doorway. Each player is blindfolded in turn, given a long stick, and placed at a little distance from the bag, which he tries to hit with the stick. Three trials are permitted. If he has not then succeeded, he gives up his place to another. The game is not finished till one of the players makes a hole in the bag. The others have a right to all the sweets they can get in the scramble that follows. Sometimes the bag is filled with little trinkets which the guests are allowed to keep, and sometimes, as a joke, a bag of flour is substituted for the bag of sweets.

A game resembling this consists in suspending a large ring, or other object, by a long string, then, blindfolded in turn, each player endeavours to cut the string with a large pair of scissors.

THE BOUQUET GAME.—One of the players is asked to name her favourite flower ; this she does, mentioning three or four as the lily, the rose, the violet, etc. She is then invited to leave the room. When she has done so, the other players designate by the names of the chosen flowers, several friends or playmates (absent or present) of the one who has withdrawn. She is now called back and asked what will you do with the lily ?

To which she replies in any manner she pleases. Perhaps she says, " I will wear it next my heart." " The Rose?" " I will cast it aside," etc. When she has disposed of each of the flowers according to her fancy, she is told whom they represent ; then, it may be, she finds she has cast away her dearest friend, has given the place of honour to one whom she regards with indifference and so on. If she gives droll or incongruous answers, the game is rendered more lively and amusing.

THE COTTON IN THE AIR.—The players form a ring and join hands ; a small bit of jeweller's cotton or a light feather is then thrown into the air, and they try, by blowing it upward, to keep it from falling. If they blow too hard, the cotton is driven away ; if too gently it falls and the game is finished. The interest consists in directing it, if possible, to one or other of the players who pays a forfeit if it falls before her. All this must be done without letting go of hands. The game may also be played sitting round a table.

THE CURTAIN PANTOMIME.—This game can only be played in the evening. It consists in stationing one of the players in a recess of a window and drawing down the curtain (shade) in front of him. At a certain distance from the curtain, a light is placed upon a table. Each of the company then passes in turn between the light and the curtain making all manner of ridiculous gestures and grimaces, so as to render himself unrecognisable. Sometimes those who take part in this pantomime dress in grotesque garments, and change their appearance as much as possible. The person behind the curtain must guess who passes before it.

PHYSICAL TRAINING OF CHILDREN.

There are few questions of greater importance for mothers than how they shall train their children so as to secure to them the most vigorous bodily health. It would seem that nothing was more simple, yet the mass of people miss the way. The first year is, perhaps, in many respects, of the greatest importance to a child, so far as its physical education is concerned, in its entire existence. In this year the foundation is laid for good or ill-health, which, in a greater or less degree, will go with him through life. During this year good management may strengthen the powers of digestion and keep up a healthy circulation ; or these feeble powers may be injured by over-exertion to a degree from which they never can or will recover.

Where proper attention is paid to the comfort of the little one, the mother being scrupulously observant of all the sources of inquietude and guarding against them all, never suffering her babe to be unhappy from inattention when it is in her power to extend relief, the health of her children will be perfect and their disposition mild and affectionate. Many little ones acquire in the first year the rudiments of fretfulness and impatience from the food they take and from the neglect to which they are subjected, that what is erroneously supposed to be more important matters may be advanced. Yet what can be of more importance to a mother than the undying spirit committed to her care, lodged in a body that needs constant tenderness lest it injure the companion for whose benefit it was formed as entirely as the casket is formed to contain the jewel ?

There is a famous old prescription for mothers in reference to the proper mode of bringing up children, which runs, " Plenty of food, plenty of experience, plenty of sleep." We will heartily subscribe to this provided that they shall be given only such food as is suited to their weak powers of digestion, which are in the present day, with the great mass of children, so over-taxed that they are initiated into all the mysteries of dyspepsia long before they know the meaning of the term. The entire bodies of children should often be washed, thus promoting the circulation, keeping the pores of the skin open for insensible perspiration to pass off, and by this means strengthening the limbs and invigorating the entire system.

We do not make this plea for simplicity in the diet of children, and scrupulous habits of cleanliness, simply out of regard for their bodies. All the powers of the understanding and the gentle affections of the heart as well are interested in the treatment of the physical system. You have only to observe closely to find that the food of the child will affect favourably or otherwise its disposition and feelings.

A hardly less fruitful source of evil is often found in the vanity of the parent who condemns her little child to many hours of labour when she ought to be out in the open pure air or at her play, simply that she may be enabled to boast to her neighbours or visitors how " this little girl pieced an entire bed-quilt before she was four years old." And how often must the same terrible confinement be endured from the same inhuman, sinful motive that a boy at six may read Latin, when, if the needed attention had been paid to his physical education, he would hardly have been able to read his mother tongue.

Vigour of intellect is impaired when a child endures an amount of mental labour beyond its years. Body and mind reciprocally act upon each other. To perceive the truth of this does not require any great amount of learning. Let a plain, common-sense person observe the workings of his own mind, as occupied in the ordinary business of every day, and he will be sensible that all his plans which were bright and beautiful—all that were filled with vivacity and clustered with buds of promise, were the fruit of days of health when the spirits were light and elastic. With such feelings more progress will be made in one hour than, with an opposite temperament, would ordinarily be made in two.

If this be true, and who can question it, is it not clear that the vain and ambitious mother who burdens her child with labours to which his age and strength is unequal, ties a weight about him that will inevitably prevent his attaining to eminence in the future ? It is impossible for the child thus unnaturally goaded on to possess a well-balanced character to any great degree. There will be defects in bodily health reacting on the mind, or there will be painful deficiencies of disposition, soured by the unnatural process, which, sooner or later, will convince the ambitious parent that the road taken has been a mistaken one.

And why should a parent be solicitious so early to confine her little one to books, when every leaf and every bud, every insect and every shell are teeming with instruction, and the young heart, tender and susceptible, waits, like the unmoulded wax, to receive that impression on the affections which maternal love alone can enstamp ? The education of the little one begins with life, and is continually carried forward by every circumstance that comes under its observation ; but the first five years of childhood must be given to physical education if the great end of existence is to be best answered.

American Candies.

APART from the pleasure every mother must derive from preparing home-made sweets and goodies for the little ones at this season, there is a yet more important consideration in the satisfaction of knowing the sweetmeats are composed of pure, wholesome material, which is rarely the case when candies are purchased from the very best dealers.

With a little practice, any housewife can acquire the art of candy making, and by the display of good taste, can ornament sweetmeats so as to please the children, quite as much as with such as are purchased at a much greater expense.

The utensils necessary for making candy, are a porcelean lined candy kettle, which should be supplied with a tight fitting cover, a smooth candy slab, several shallow, square pans, a large wooden spoon, a pair of candy shears, a sharp knife, and a sugar sifter. Moulding trays and moulding patterns may be had for making bon-bons, gum drops, and other fancy candies, though in the absence of these, some convenient article about the dining-room or kitchen may be used.

Care should be given in selecting the sugar for making candy. Never use an inferior article; for ordinary varieties, confectioner's A sugar will answer, for toffies or dark candy the article called Coffee C, but for crystallising, and the finer candies the purest powdered sugars only should be used. The flavouring extracts also should be of the best quality, and the colouring pure, and of well known harmless material. The following recipes will be found quite economical as well as easy to prepare, and in every way satisfactory.

LEMON STICK CANDY.—Boil one and a half pounds of granulated sugar with three gills of water, add half a teaspoonful of cream of tartar dissolved in a little warm water. Keep covered, and boil over a brisk fire until the syrup threads and cracks. Flavour with lemon, and colour with grated lemon peel. Pour out to cool in a well-buttered dish, as soon as cool enough to handle, take up and pull. Cut in sticks, roll until round, and set aside to harden. Pretty fancy sticks may be made by separating the candy, and colouring each portion differently, pulling and twisting together.

TRANSPARENT CANDIES.—Make candy as for stick candy, stir as little as possible, and pour out to cool in broad, shallow, well-buttered trays. When nearly cold mark in squares. When perfectly cold turn out of the pan, and the squares may then be broken apart. Pineapple, orange, white rose, or any other colourless flavouring may be used for these candies.

ICE CREAM CANDY.—Put one pound of granulated sugar with a tin cup of water in a porcelain lined saucepan, and stir over the fire until dissolved, then boil without stirring until it hardens when dropped in water. When done, put in two ounces of butter and a tea-spoon full of extract of vanilla, also half a tea-spoon full of cream of tartar. Pour in a well greased pan (if desired to make fancy, divide and colour one pan pink), when nearly cold, pull each part separately, twist the pink and white together, cut in sticks, put in a large, deep dish, cover and let stand two hours.

CREAM BON-BONS.—Put one pound of the best crushed sugar with a tea-cup full of water in a porcelain candy kettle, boil, without stirring, until a soft ball may be formed of the mixture; remove from the fire, and let stand in the kettle a few minutes, flavour, and with a large spoon, beat until it becomes fine and creamy. With the fingers, roll portions of the cream into little round or oval balls. These little bon-bons can be dipped into melted chocolate, or cocoanut cream, and small candied fruits pressed into their centre.

AUNT DINAH'S MOLASSES CANDY.—Boil one quart of sugar house molasses over a clear fire until brittle. Dissolve half a tea-spoon full of soda in a little hot water and stir in. Flavour with cinnamon bark. Pour out to cool. When cold enough to handle pull until light. Draw out in sticks.

LEMON TOFFY.—Put one pound of yellow sugar, and two cups of water in a candy kettle, let it boil five minutes, and add two ounces of butter, boil until it hardens, but not until brittle, flavour with lemon, pour in well-buttered tins. When nearly cold mark off with a knife in squares, press nearly through. When cold turn out on buttered paper, and break the squares apart.

COCOANUT TOFFY.—Boil one pound of white sugar and two gills of water together, while boiling stir in two ounces of butter. Boil until it will pull between the fingers, add three ounces of grated cocoanut; pour out to cool, mark in squares.

CHOCOLATE CREAM CANDY.—Boil one and a half pounds of white sugar with two small cups of water, and a salt-spoon full of cream of tartar dissolved in a little warm water. Let boil until thick. Flavour with vanilla. Remove from the fire and let cool slightly before pouring out. With a wooden spoon, stir and beat until it begins to look milky. Then stir in six ounces of grated chocolate, mix well. Pour in shallow, wide tins, covered with well greased white paper. When it is cold, lift out the paper and cut in small squares or sticks.

MAPLE SUGAR CANDY.—Boil one pound of pure maple sugar, and half a pound of granulated sugar with two tea-cups full of water, add half a tea-spoon full of cream of tartar, dissolved. Let boil until it hardens, then pour in a buttered dish. When nearly cool, pull until it is light coloured. Make in little cakes, stick a whole walnut in the centre.

FIG PASTE.—Boil over a bright fire, a pound of fresh figs in a cup of water. When the figs become soft, strain. and boil the liquor down one half. Stir in a pound and a half of sugar and boil slowly until a thick paste. Line a very shallow pan with paper, put the paste on while hot, let cool, lift the paper from the pan, cut the paste in little blocks, and roll in sugar.

WHITE NOUGAT.—Blanche a pound of almonds, and chop. Pour four ounces of white honey in a clean new tin cup, set the cup in a kettle of water and boil until it will roll in a ball ; to this, add an ounce of powdered sugar, and the stiffly beaten white of one egg. Cook until stiff, and stir in the almonds. Take from the fire and pour in a little tray lined with white paper, press down firmly and let stand until cold. Then cut in thick small blocks. and dust with powdered sugar, which has been flavoured with vanilla and dried.

FRUIT GLACE.—Boil one pint of granulated sugar, and one cup of water, until brittle. Have oranges peeled and divided in quarters. Carefully dip each piece in a portion of the syrup, and set in a cool place to dry. Do not stir the syrup. Pineapples, bananas, or other fruits can be prepared in the same way.

ROSE KISSES.—Beat the whites of six eggs to a stiff froth. When light and dry, mix a cup full of powdered sugar quickly, flavour with extract of white rose. Spread oiled paper on a board. Drop a spoon full at a time of the mixture on it. Set in a cool oven and dry for nearly an hour, until a crust forms. Lift from the paper and stick them together at the bottom.

CHOCOLATE CREAMS.—Four cups full of granulated sugar, three table-spoons full of glucose, one cup full of boiling water. Stir thoroughly, put cover on, let it boil rapidly, till it will *almost* candy (but not quite). Then pour it out in a large pan so that it will cover the bottom not more than two inches deep. Set in a cool place till it is about lukewarm (try by putting the finger into the bottom): then stir with a wooden pestle until it looks white and dry, as if it was graining, then put in the hands and knead as you would bread, when it will soon be of a fine creamy consistency, and this is just what is wanted. You can if you wish, make several varieties of this cream at once, simply by dividing in several parts, and flavouring differently, say one vanilla, one lemon, and one rose —and the rose may be tinted a lovely pink. To flavour, pour a few drops of the extract on the cream and knead a few times. Cover the cream with a damp napkin and it will keep in perfect condition some time. Dust your moulding board with the least bit of flour, roll this cream on it, then cut in small pieces and form into balls between the palms of the hands, and set on paraffine paper to harden It is better to do this part the day before you fix the chocolate as they will be firmer. Put a cake of chocolate in a pan (set in another pan of boiling water) to melt. When melted cut into it a lump of paraffine the size of a small hickory nut, and a piece of butter about half as large, add a few drops of vanilla. Now roll the cream in this melted chocolate and set on paraffine paper to harden. A fork is convenient to dip them with.

Now for that which is tinted pink—first form into nice round balls the size of a halfpenny piece, and press into the top of each a blanched almond, then roll in granulated sugar. They are very pretty.

A part of the cream may be tinted chocolate by kneading in a little grated chocolate.

Now to make lovely fruit candy or " Weddin Cake " as confectioners call it : Chop up raisins, fig citron and almonds to suit you, and knead it in wit some of the plain cream. Then roll out a layer o the plain white cream about a half inch thick, the put a layer of the pink on that, then a layer of th fruit, then pink again being careful that it reache over the side to the other layer of pink, then th white again to reach over to the other layer of white Roll in the melted chocolate and lay on paraffine paper to harden. When hard, slice across as yo would a loaf of bread and you will be surprised t see how lovely the " Wedding Cake " is.

The pink colour is simply a little cochineal and aniline put in a bottle and some alcohol poured on Any druggist will put it up for a few pence.

EXCELLENT CREAM TOFFY.—Three cups of granu lated sugar, half a cup of vinegar, half a cup o water, butter size of a walnut. Boil without stirring until it will candy when dropped in cold water Flavour, and pour out on a buttered dish. Whe cool pull till white, then cut up in sticks with shar scissors.

BUTTERSCOTCH.—One cup of sugar, one cup o molasses, one cup of butter, one table-spoon ful o vinegar, pinch of soda. Boil all together till done pour in buttered pan and cut up in squares whe cold and wrap in paraffine paper.

Now glucose, I may as well mention, (which i simply corn syrup) is the *foundation* of all candies and may be procured very cheaply from any confec tioner. As to utensils, while a granite iron sauce pan with lip to facilitate pouring out, is preferable any bright tinned pan or kettle may be used.

CHOCOLATE CARAMELS.—Dissolve a pound and half of granulated sugar in a coffee cup of rich cream add a good-sized pinch of cream of tartar dissolved in a little warm water, let come to a boil, and put i four ounces of grated chocolate. Boil rapidly an stir until it is hard. Pour out to cool in a shallow dish. Cut in squares when cold. Cocoanut, lemo or vanilla caramels may be made in the same way.

GUM DROPS.—Put a pound of the best quality of gum-arabic in three gills of water, dissolve slowly over a moderate fire, strain, and add three-quarters of a pound of sugar with a cup of water. Let boil down until thick, stirring all the while ; remove from the fire and flavour with rose extract. Set aside to settle ; skim off the top, pour in little moulds, sift over with powdered sugar, and stand away to harden, for two or three days. When dry, crystallise.

CANDIED GINGER.

Make a syrup of one pound of granulated sugar, and a large cup of water. Place over the fire, let come to a boil, and skim. Cut a quarter of a pound of ginger root into small pieces, and put in some water to boil for an hour, drain off the water, pour some of the syrup over, enough to cover, and let boil an hour and a half, if the syrup cooks away, add more when the ginger is tender ; take up, drain on a sieve, let cool. and dust with granulated sugar, dip again in the thick syrup, set aside to cool, and when cold, roll in sugar again. The syrup should be boiled until it will crystallise the ginger.

AN EASY AND PRETTY PATTERN FOR A SHAWL.

(Quantity of wool required varies with the kind.)

Two long wooden needles. Cast on 301 stitches, plain knitting. In knitting, slip the 150th stitch; knit 151 and 152 together, pass the slip-stitch over the two knitted together. Repeat the slip-stitch and knitting two together every time when reaching the centre of the row. Continue this until only one stitch is left on the needle—and a square shawl will be the result.

*   *   *

FOOD FOR OUR AGED RELATIVES OR FRIENDS.

A CONTEMPORARY, in an article on diet for old people, dwells on the importance of milk, and says: "Give milk often, and always warm. Never boil it, but let it come nearly to a boiling point. By this means, the curd in the milk, not being so hard, assimilates more readily, and gives heat;" and explains that all hot things do not warm alike. The heat from tea does not remain long, but the heat from milk does.

CHICKEN MILK FOR INVALIDS.—Cut a chicken into small pieces, and see that it has been cleaned in the most careful manner, removing the skin. Put it into a china-lined saucepan, with the bones and neck, the white part of a head of celery, and the stalks (not leaves) of a fresh bunch of parsley, a few peppercorns, and a little salt. Cover the meat with cold water, and let it simmer till it is in rags and falls from the bones. Strain into a flat basin or large bowl. When cold, it should be in a stiff, clear jelly. Carefully, with a skimmer, take off the grease, and then take a soft, clean pantry towel, dipped in hot water, and gently wipe over the top of the jelly with it, so that no particle of greasy matter can possibly remain. Take equal quantities of this jelly and fresh milk, put them into a small china-lined saucepan, and let them boil together. Boil up the mixture three times, and strain into a cup. A teacupful is generally considered sufficient at a time. Tiny strips of dry toast are an agreeable addition. It can be eaten hot, or allowed to cool and form again into jelly, according to taste.

JAM PUDDING.

HALF a pound of flour, a quarter pound of dripping or beef suet, two tablespoonfuls of sugar, a little salt, half a teaspoonful baking soda; mix well with sour milk, make a nice dough, divide in four pieces, make them round like scones, then butter a basin, put in one of the scones, then a large spoonful of jam, then another scone with jam, until they are all in. Put on the lid with a cloth under it. Boil for two hours in a pan of water.

*   *   *   *

THE RAG DRAWER.

EVERY thrifty housewife should have a "rag drawer," or a shelf of her store closet or linen press set apart for this special purpose. Old linen sheets, after having passed through the darning, patching, and turning stages, should be tightly rolled up and stored away in the rag drawer, for old linen is often invaluable in cases of sickness. Discarded flannel garments, merino vests, &c., are most useful for all kinds of domestic purposes; all buttons and bands should be removed, and they should be cut into neatly shaped pieces before rolling up. Ancient socks should be saved to make iron-holders of, cutting them to the proper shape, and covering with a piece of print or chintz. Ripped open, and roughly quilted together, old socks (especially knitted ones) make excellent rubbers for polished floors. Old blankets, when too much worn for any other purpose, should be torn into squares, the edges roughly overcast, and used for scouring-cloths.

*   *   *   *

HOW TO MEND A MACKINTOSH.

PROCURE a small tin of indiarubber cement, or dissolve some strips of pure indiarubber in naphtha or sulphide of carbon, to form a stiff paste; apply a little of the cement on the surface of a strip of the same material of which the mackintosh is made, which can be purchased by the yard or in remnants from the waterproofers; also apply a little of the cement on each side of the torn part, and when it begins to feel tacky bring the edges together, and place the patch nicely over, and keep in position by putting a weight over it until quite hard, which will be in a few days.

When shall we Marry?

WHEN shall we marry? When the young man has at least thirty pounds in the Savings Bank, and the girl ten. It would be far better that they should have more than this, but unless they have saved forty pounds between them they must be content to wait till they have realised the required sum, for to attempt to marry when the means are insufficient to furnish the house properly, and after furnishing to have a few pounds to fall back upon when the rainy day comes, is to ensure trouble and disappointment.

Mothers should teach their children to lay by something as soon as possible. A penny a month is a shilling a year, and if the child begins at two years old, by the time he is twelve he will have a golden half-sovereign of his own at the very least, though in all probability he will have much more, for the habit once formed, the taste grows of choosing to wait till the thing worth getting can be bought, instead of frittering away money as fast as it comes in useless things.

We will imagine, now, he has passed his early boyhood, and has reached the age when he is earning twelve shillings a week. Let him grasp what this means by seeing how much he is making a year, and he will find it comes to £31 4s. Let him then carefully portion it out. We will say he gives 6s. a week to his parents, who undertake to provide him with board, lodging, washing, and mending. It is not easy to do it, but the father has his boy's welfare at heart, and the mother, with her sweet, uncomplaining love, consents to wash and mend still, though she gets nothing by it.

6s. a week is £15 12s. a year; and now he must reckon what his clothes will come to. Two good suits a year, with the necessary re-pairs, will cost about £5, but, unless his work is very hard, he will not want each year as much as this, so that one year he can manage to buy a great coat instead of the second suit. Then he must allow himself two pairs of strong boots, and a few shillings for mending; let him put aside £1 10s. for this, and 10s. for shirts and collars, then he may allow 10s. more for hats, neckties, and handkerchiefs, which will bring the whole amount to £7 10s., and added to the £15 12s. for board and lodging, it brings the expenditure up to £23 2s. The next question is pocket-money—and here the pence are most likely to be frittered away unless the young man will allow himself a certain sum and be resolute in not overstepping the bounds. A shilling a week and an extra pound for bank holiday expenses ought to be enough; this comes to £3 12s., and leaves a surplus of £4 10s. to be placed in the Savings Bank. In four years' time he will have laid by £18, besides the interest, and most likely his wages will have increased during that time, so that, although he will give his parents another shilling a week, he will also be able to put a little more into the Bank.

If young men and girls were willing to save in this fashion as soon as they began to receive or earn money they might marry with a fair prospect of comfort at the age of twenty-five or twenty-six; by that time the young man will have accumulated between thirty and fifty pounds, according to his wages and the self-control he has practised; the girl, if she has had good situations, will have laid by from ten to twenty pounds, or if her wages have been high she may have saved thirty pounds. Great care must be taken in buying suitable furniture; but the subject of furnishing a house is too wide to be dealt with here, and must be left to a future occasion.

CHRISTMAS GIFTS MADE AT HOME.

The season of Christmas is essentially one which makes heavy demands on the purse, and that much used article is then most of all liable to show signs of exhaustion. How, in this case, are the annual gifts for relations and friends to be contrived? There is but one answer, and that suggests itself : our Christmas gifts must be made at home. The few with unlimited means at their command may choose from the ready-made treasures on view in the shops, but the many must have recourse to their stores of scraps and pieces of various materials, and concoct with these the useful and ornamental trifles which they need.

It is for the benefit of home workers that these hints are given, and they shall be devoted to articles dainty rather than costly, simple rather than elaborate.

There is figured first a hanging case for pens and pencils. Two pieces of card are required; one for the back and a much shallower but wider section to form the pocket in front. Both sections should be covered with grey kid and lined with satin to match, or with some pretty bright colour. The holes for the ribbon are made with a very sharp stiletto, which should bore them quite cleanly through all the three thicknesses. The ribbon should be *fraise*, or to match the lining, and the cord also is grey and coloured.

The case as here pictured measures only about nine inches long by five wide, but made larger, say about twelve inches by six and a half, it may be utilised for holding a small ball of twine, scissors, a knife, one or two labels, a red or blue chalk pencil, and similar requisites for packing small postal parcels.

Or again, it may be used merely for string and scissors, the latter to be pendant down one side from a length of the cord or of the ribbon, the ball of twine to be in the pocket in a small round silk bag. This bag is easily made from a circle of silk, the diameter of which must measure three

Fig. 1.

times that of the ball of string. The silk is hemmed all round, and a running to hold an elastic made in it a third part away from the edge. Thus, if the elastic be tight e n o u g h, is formed a little globular bag, from the top of which the end of the twine escapes, but the ball cannot be taken out or in, e x c e p t b y stretching the elastic. Lastly, the silk bag is tacked into the pocket, and it is no disadvantage if the heading of it peeps out over the top.

The amateur painter or embroideress can of course find scope for her energies here, either on the back or on the pocket. By making the front section of plush or brocade, no need for further decoration will be found.

The next cut shows a rather more elaborate piece of work in the shape of a little horn, which is intended to be hung from a projecting bracket near an invalid's bed, and to hold a cup of milk or water, or a vase of flowers. The foundation is of strong card rolled round like a sugar-paper, and cut to shape; the lining is made of crimson satin quilted, so is very soft; the covering is a scrap of figured silk, which has a cream - coloured background, with a crimson pattern upon it. Nothing which can worry the eyes or tempt to i n c e s s a n t counting must be chosen. The bows are of cream-coloured satin rib-

Fig. 2.

bon, and on the lower one may be sewn a hook for the suspension of a fan. On the upper bow a hook for a watch may be added; and there is plenty of space in the intervening loop of ribbon to push a newspaper or pocket-handkerchief. The cord should be crimson and cream in colouring, and if when the horn is full the weight of the contents throws out the balance and endangers its safety, it is easy to add a second knot of cord at the point, and to secure the holder to the wall by this also. As another hint,

Fig. 3.

it may be suggested that if the card be exceedingly firm, or the silk thin, an interlining of thin flannel should be introduced, and this must be very smoothly put in, no fold or double layer being anywhere left.

This holder may be made much smaller for a tidy or spill-cup, or larger, to contain balls of wool, waste paper, or even umbrellas. By sewing a circle of card, covered with lining on both sides, into the bottom—of course first cutting off the point—the horn can be made to stand. If this is done, the lower bow of ribbon must be considerably raised. When made on a large scale, a covering of cretonne is appropriate and effective, and a lining of coloured linen or cotton.

Fig. No. 3 is a picture-easel made from the lid of a disused box, and its simplicity is its chief merit, since it is not designed to support an elaborate artistic production, but to display for a time a favourite card or photo which can be easily changed. For an invalid's room these easels will be found very useful, as they can be made to show in a few minutes as many pictures as a scrap-book could contain.

14

The way in which an easel is made is so plainly shown in the illustration that words are hardly needed. The box-lid must be a stout one, and one rim and about an inch of two others are left; all the rest is cut neatly away. The short pieces must of course be both exactly alike in size. The box is covered inside and out with Japanese paper for temporary purposes; for more lasting use with old gold satin, tan-coloured leather, or with brocade. Of course if either of these last three fabrics be chosen, the lid will have to be taken to pieces, and afterwards, when covered, sewn together again; if paper is used for it a clever worker can easily manage neatly without dismembering it, but it is advisable to strengthen all the joins with an inch-wide strip of muslin pasted over them on both sides before the ornamentation is added. Leather paper, by the way, sticks firmest when a mixture of liquid glue and paste is used for the purpose. The cord which supports the picture has hitherto passed unnoticed. It is merely threaded through two opposite holes and a knot tied in it at both ends. If the easel is covered with any material that frays easily, the cord must be sewn on and to the inside to save making the eyelet holes.

A foot or rest of cardboard about a third as high as the back, and about an inch wide, may be glued on with a muslin hinge, to serve as a support and permit of the easel being sloped to any desired angle, this piece of card being, it is

Fig. 4.

needless to say, covered to accord with the rest of the case. Then again, by adding a ring at the top, or by sewing on a loop of cord, our easel can be made to hang.

From a wooden box a book-rest can be made on this principle, the chief difference being that the back must be greatly lower in proportion to

Fig. 5.

the width. If the box is in good condition staining or enamelling is all that it will require, but if very shabby or inclined to drop to pieces it is easy to cover and line all the sections with cretonne or thin tapestry, interlined with flannel if the sharp corners show signs of poking through.

Next is shown a post-card case, which also can be made from a cardboard box. If the box just holds a packet of cards comfortably, so much the better; if it is too large it must be cut to size, or failing this, made up entirely by the worker from a piece of cardboard. Supposing that a small candle-box has been found to be appropriate, take away all four rims from the lid and take the bottom of it to pieces also. Cut a triangular-shaped piece out of the bottom, as shewn in the illustration, and keep three of the four rims. There are now five pieces of card; cut a duplicate of each in brown paper and cover the papers with pink satin. Cover the cards with brown bengaline on which, for the front of the case, you have embroidered the word "Post-cards," and a flourish under it. Sew all the pink portions each to its corresponding brown cover, then sew these doubled sections together in their proper box-like form, finally attach a loop of gold cord to the back of the case, and to one side of it an indelible pencil lashed on to a length of cord.

At the back, about half an inch from the top, a paper fastener is pushed in from the outside and opened out loosely inside. Then about two dozen pieces of paper all the same size (that is, an inch smaller each way than the back of the box), are threaded together on a fine cord and attached by a loop of this round the paper stud. These papers will often be found useful for making lists, memoranda, etc., upon. Failing them a piece of card bearing a table of postal rates or similar information may be substituted.

To make a pen-wiper (No. 5) of this shape, cut a long strip of black cloth, fine felt, or cashmere, about five inches wide, pink out the lower edge of it and pleat it up into a bell-like shape. It is better to do this than either to gather the upper edge or to roll up the strip, as these last ways of

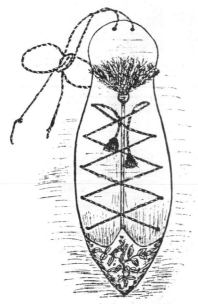

Fig. 6.

going to work make the little bundle too firm and even. When deemed the right shape, gather up closely along the upper edge with a strong thread, and add a second running about an inch lower down. Take next a strip of grey felt four inches wide, and long enough to wrap loosely once round the cashmere roll. Seam the two short edges together, run a draw-thread along the upper edge of the hoop just made, and slip it on over the black inside part, drawing it in very tightly round the lower row of gathers on the cashmere. That it may set closely, somewhat like the skirt of a doll over its petticoats tack down the lower edge of the grey here and there to the black pinking. Lastly, take a strip

of dark blue silk of thin texture and also about four inches wide. Seam this also up, and cut the lower edge of it into eight or nine scallops of alternating depths, all bordered with fine gilt gimp and lined with blue fringe, gore this sort of over-skirt slightly at the two sides and pucker it in slightly over the grey felt, running in for this purpose a draw-thread about an inch below the upper edge of the silk which now stands out round the top of the roll of cashmere. Cover this black part with the silk by turning in the latter material and pushing all folds towards the inside ; put in also snippings of flannel, cotton-wool, or anything soft, as if you were stuffing a cushion. Sew up and make neat at the top, working in a large brass curtain ring to serve as a handle ; lastly pull and knead the top with the fingers to make it a good ball-shape and firm. The monogram was not mentioned before, as it was not deemed a necessary adjunct. It should, of course, be worked on the silk before the pen-wiper is made up, and the easiest way of doing this is by tacking down fine gold thread, the ends of which are passed with a bodkin or large-eyed needle through to the wrong side of the work, and there sewn down. The silk under the monogram should be lined, to give a little extra firmness.

Lastly, we give a slipper-shaped holder for a feather broom. The foundation of the sole is of cardboard ; two similar pieces are needed, each covered with Tussah silk and sewn together all round. The pocket, or toe portion, is cut from buckram, and is a trifle wider than is the sole ; it should be covered with a piece of wash-leather richly embroidered in shades ranging from pale dull yellow to bright brown, and is brightened up with gold thread. The cord is of yellow (or tinsel) and brown silk, and does not really pass through the sole, but is sewn down to it and the stitching concealed by small flat bronze buttons. The lacing across the sole by which the broom is kept in place is similarly managed ; ten buttons being sewn on (five on each side and at regular intervals) to the front card before the two sole pieces are joined together ; the cord is then secured with the buttons, being only left free at the top where it can be knotted or tied. The tension of it must be carefully managed, as if put on too loosely it will sag, while if over tight there will be no room for the broom behind it. To those who have never tried the work we can say that embroidering upon this soft leather is by no means the unpleasant task which they might suppose it to be ; the needle chosen should be fine, and above all very sharp ; directly it becomes at all blunted and stretches instead of piercing the stuff it must be thrown aside.

ORIGINAL FASHION DESIGNS.

By Mildred Harris.

(Formerly with Messrs. Liberty.)

No. 1.—Tea gown in Liberty velveteen or cashmere. Short corsage outlined in fur fastening slightly on the left side. Drapery hanging full in front, otherwise fitting to the figure. Underdress of silk ornamented with embroidery, long hanging under-sleeves finished with plaited frills. Pointed Watteau forming train at the back.

No. 2.—Evening dress in velvet or Liberty velveteen, in a lovely shade of green. Pointed corsage, laced over under bodice of pink brocade, sleeves of the same with frills, and puffings of mousseline de soie. Train lined back with brocade. Bodice ornamented with embroidery or passementerie.

No 3.—Pelisse in grey blue cloth, with yoke, cuffs, and the large and unique revers or collar of velvet, of a darker shade of blue. Either mink or beaver would look well as a trimming. The velvet carried over the shoulders forms a large rounded collar to the cape at the back. Ornaments of passementerie.

No. 1.

No. 2.

No. 3.

MOTHERS AND CHILDREN.

A well-known lady-doctor warns mothers against undue muffling of their children, especially at the throat. "To have furs always round the neck for going out, predisposes to delicacy of the throat. I believe the best rule to be, while the child is well, leave the throat almost or quite uncovered. But never neglect even a slight cold; keep the child indoors or in bed at once, so as to get rid of it as soon as possible; and when the cold is cured and the child goes out again, mufflings should not be used except for the first one or two walks."

* * *

Mothers who live in flats or in houses to which no gardens are attached need not for that reason let their children lose the delightful education that comes from training and watching the growth of flowers. Window-boxes should be provided for every nursery. The cost is slight, and a hundred toys would not give so much pleasure to the little ones. A careful nurse or mother will know how to let the young gardeners work without risk of catching cold. London might be a far more beautiful place than it is if its windows were better cared for. That is one way in which the humblest of us can add brightness and colour to the city in which we live.

* * *

Children who are fortunate enough to have gardens of their own will find it a good plan to sow their seed in egg-shell filled with rich earth. When the little plants have got their second growth of leaves and are hardy enough to be planted out of doors, break the shells and put the lump of dirt in the ground without disturbing the roots of the plants. If you do this you will see your little garden grow very fast, for all small plants like pansies, mignonettes, nasturtiums, and sweet peas do better if they are kept in the house until they are a couple of inches high and strong enough to resist insects and garden worms.

* * *

A parent recommends 'Plain Words to Children,' by the Bishop of Wakefield, Dr. Walsham How, as an excellent book of sermons for family reading.

* * *

A correspondent of the *Parents' Review* impresses upon mothers the importance of teaching their daughters to keep accounts. She finds it a help to make at the beginning of the year a complete list of all regular payments that have to be made, such as subscriptions, insurances, etc. The account does not only check undue extravagance, but a glance at previous years enables one to see when the heavier expenses, such as school bills, taxes, etc., have to be met. "I think the simplest way for a girl to begin account keeping is the usual way of receipts on one page of her account book, and expenditure on the other, with a careful weekly balance. I would also encourage her to keep a quarterly account, and a page for the total receipts and expenditure of each year. As a girl I used to divide my allowance quarterly, and found it a great help to divide it into little packets, labelled 'Winter Jacket,' 'Gloves and Boots,' 'Stamps,' 'Charity,' etc., etc."

* * *

A mother writes:—Having had a good many little accidents in my family of late, I have resolved always to have a bottle of Carron oil in my medicine cupboard. It is by far the best application for a scald or burn, and for bumps and bruises I find it best to apply arnica or boracic ointment. Stings of wasps and ants will be relieved by the application of a strong solution of bicarbonate of soda.

* * *

A wise mother who had successfully reared a large family, was once asked by a young mother who was wholly worn out by her devotion to her children, who were fretful and troublesome to an unusual degree, for advice as to how she should deal with them. "I think, my dear, that a little wholesome neglect would benefit both them and yourself," was the reply. The answer is one which young mothers who find their children nervous and troublesome would do well to ponder.

* * *

Madam Tel Sono, when she was in England last summer, showed a family of little children how the Japanese children play with the ball. Among other interesting exercises were the following, which have been adopted by her audience and played ever since.

I. (1) Stand with feet together, left hand on hip. (2) Strike the ball on the floor with palm of right hand. (3) When the ball ascends let it alight on the back of right hand and instantly hit it down again with the palm. To be played ten times without a mistake.

II. Hit the ball on the floor with palm of right hand nine times. Hit the tenth ball harder, turn round on one's toes, and again hit it down the eleventh time. Turn round every tenth ball, and always count aloud.

III. Kneel on the ground and hit the ball down, first with the right and then the left hand. Do this a hundred times without a mistake, remaining quite stationary.

Receipts.

RHUBARB FOR WINTER USE.

SIX pounds rhubarb, six pounds sugar, quarter-pound whole ginger. Do not peel the rhubarb, but rub it with a damp cloth; cut the sticks into pieces of an inch long, and put them into a dish with the sugar and ginger. Let it stand for two days, then pour off the syrup and boil for half an hour; add the rhubarb and boil till it is clear and transparent. Put it into jars and tie down. This will keep many months.

RICE-FISH.

Boil as much rice as you require in plenty of water till perfectly soft. Take any fish that is left, or buy two or three pennyworth; boil it and break it into small pieces, care-fully removing the bones. Pour nearly all the water from your rice into a jug, mix the fish and rice together; add pepper and salt, and place it in your oven, or in the saucepan to re-heat. This is a very nourishing dish for children. It is well to pour a little of the rice-water over each plate as you serve it, because some of the nourishment has been drawn from the rice in boiling into the water.

PICKLED NASTURTIUMS.

One pint of vinegar, one ounce of salt, six peppercorns. Put this pickle into a dry glass bottle, and having wiped the ripe nasturtium pods, put them into the bottle, filling it from day to day as they ripen, taking care always to keep it well corked. Finally seal the cork down and leave it for nearly a year, when it will be found fit for use.

WOMEN'S EMPLOYMENTS.

PROSPECTS FOR WOMEN EMIGRANTS.

The information for the following interview has been kindly supplied by a lady prominently connected with the British Women's Emigration Association, to whom we shall give the pseudonym of Mrs. Vincent.

"The Association has been in existence about ten years," Mrs. Vincent informed our representative "The President is the Hon. Mrs. Stuart Wortley, and the Vice-President the Hon. Mrs. Joyce, St. John's Croft, Winchester. The object is to provide openings for working women, of good character in Canada, South Africa, and West Australia. We secure for our emigrants proper protection on the voyage, and arrange for them to be met on their arrival. It is also our aim to keep the girls in sight for a year or two after their emigration, so that they may not feel themselves altogether forsaken and forgotten by their friends at home. During 1893 the Association sent out 176 single women, besides eleven families."

"What colony received the largest number?'

"Canada stands first, with 68; then West Australia, with 42; and next South Africa, with 30. To the United States we sent 20, and to New Zealand 19. Matrons are sent out in charge of the different parties, and their fares are paid for by the Society for Promoting Christian Knowledge, except in the case of those on the West Australian ships, who are provided for by the Government of the colony. The presence of the matrons gives a guarantee that no harm will befall the young travellers on the voyage."

"Do the colonies recognise the work of the Association?"

"We have had most cordial recognition from Canada, and also from West Australia. In Canada, 20,000 circulars were issued to the various municipalities in the Dominion, recommending our Association.

"As to the prospects of colonists," Mrs. Vincent continued, "West Australia wants strong, hardy girls, who are not afraid to rough it, and who are thoroughly competent in all branches of household work. There are no actual hardships to fear in the colony, but the work is heavy. To a general servant, £2 a month is an average monthly wage in Perth; a cook may perhaps get £3. The only expense incurred by emigrants is £1 each for ship-kit. The colony pays their rail fare to London, and board and lodging at the Emigrants' Home in Blackwall, while awaiting emigration. West Australia is the only colony which grants free emigration to women, the qualifications required being good health and sound intelligence, with good character and service capacity. The travellers are usually grouped in parties of about fifty, and a large compartment in the ship is fitted up for them apart from other passengers. One great privilege granted by the colony to satisfactory emigrants is that of nomination, which allows them—after a six months' residence—to bring out relatives at a slight charge. An industrious young woman might very soon see her whole family gathered round her."

"What class of young women do you advise to emigrate?"

"Not those who are already receiving good wages, such as the highest class of domestic servants in England. Our President, Mrs. Stuart Wortley, says: 'To underpaid household servants, or overworked maids-of-all-work, sempstresses, laundresses, and general servants, these openings are a wonderful boon, and offer a far safer and wider outlook than the usual rush to overcrowded cities.' The classes rather below and rather above the usual English domestic servant are those most likely to benefit by emigration. Take, for instance, the women who go out as 'lady-helps' or 'companions.' In hundreds of little country towns there are girls who have never had the opportunity of such an education as would provide them with an income as a teacher. They are fairly well educated, active, willing, anxious to make their own living. Their relatives would not hear of their going into service, and would be distressed even to think of their standing behind the counter of a shop. Such girls would be highly valued in colonial families, specially at the Cape, if only they were willing to help in household duties. A 'lady-help,' who has secured a situation in the far North-West of Canada, writes:—

"'The work is certainly hard, but everyone works, even the wealthiest people, and it is not considered to be beneath one's dignity to turn your hand to anything. The gentlemen here light the fire in the morning and make the porridge and coffee. I get up and lay the table for breakfast, dress the little girl, who sleeps in my room, and tidy my room. Then we have breakfast and begin work seriously after, only it is apt to be interrupted by the babies. Monday is the worst day, when we wash, and the baking day is also a disagreeable day. But altogether work is made as easy as possible; there is no blacking of boots or anything of that kind. We dine at twelve or half-past twelve, and have supper at six. Everyone who has been out here any time seems to like it very much.'

"A companion help from South Africa says:— 'I live a very out-of-door life, getting up early and going for a long ride with my pupil, aged twelve; and again, after school is over, we walk and play tennis, if not too hot. You ought to impress on all the girls that think of coming out here that they will have to turn their hands to anything and everything. I had to cook, sweep, dust, any amount of needlework, scrub, act as nurse to two young children. The places that seem to be most vacant are those for nurses, and, ladies are generally preferred. One has many unpleasant things to put up with, especially at first, but if you are good-tempered and obliging, and do your duty, any girl can get on. I have been out here ten months now, and must say I am very happy and comfortable.'

"Great care has to be exercised in selecting suitable emigrants," Mrs. Vincent continued; "and unless the character is strong and self-reliant, I should hesitate before advising a young woman to leave her home. But for a girl who loves the open air and has a spice of adventure in her nature, the free life of these young colonies offers many advantages. For myself, if I had to choose between slavery for a paltry pittance in some 'shabby genteel' situation at home, and seeking my fortune in the far North-West, or in some thriving Australasian city, I should thankfully accept the opportunity which the Emigration Society offers. Those who wish further information about the openings for working women in the colonies should apply by letter or in person to
Miss LEFROY,
11, Imperial Institute,
South Kensington,
London;
or to

Miss BROMFIELD, *Hon. Sec.,*
Friary Cottage,
Winchester."

* * *

WIDOW will find a useful article on Fowl-rearing in "What our Daughters can do for themselves" (Smith, Elder and Co.). She should also consult the *Fancier's Gazette*, Imperial Buildings, Ludgate Circus, E.C.

COOKERY.

Now that September is come, we may expect the mornings to have a tiny nip of frost, and hot dishes for breakfast will not be out of place. Bacon is good, few things better, but as at some tables bacon and eggs make their appearance with unceasing regularity, we think our housekeeping friends will welcome as a variety the breakfast recipes we have arranged for this month.

BREAKFAST DISHES.

MOCK WILD DUCK.

Cut four rolls in halves lengthways, toast and butter them—a mere slight buttering will not be enough, they must be thoroughly soaked through. Cover one side with anchovy paste, or better still with pounded anchovies. Pile the rolls on top of each other, cut them again in convenient sized pieces, and pour over them a sauce made with a gill of milk, the yolks of two eggs which have been well beaten, a little pepper, salt, and chopped parsley. The sauce must be thick, but it must not be allowed to boil. Serve this dish very hot.

SARDINE OMELET.

Bone five sardines and lay them on pieces of thin brown bread and butter the same length and width as the sardines. Let these get hot in the oven. Beat four eggs, two tablespoonfuls of milk, a teaspoonful of chopped parsley, pepper and salt till the mixture is well blended. Put an ounce of butter into an omelet pan, and when it is very hot pour in half the egg mixture. When it gets firm, turn it on a hot-plate, lay the sardines and bread on it. Fry the remaining portion of the egg and lay it over the other half on the hot-plate. Place the omelet a moment in front of the fire to brown, and press it with a knife so that both pieces adhere. Any other fish may be substituted instead of sardines if their flavour be disliked.

SMOKED HADDOCK WITH RICE.

Boil three ounces of Patna rice till it is soft, skin and bone a thick Aberdeen haddock, and cut it in small pieces. Stew it in enough milk to cover it, and thicken the milk with an ounce of butter and an ounce of flour. When the haddock is cooked, place it on the rice, which must be dry and very hot, and pour the milk sauce over the fish; garnish the dish with sprigs of parsley. This may be used as a plain savoury, in which case portions of the haddock and rice would be laid on toasted bread, and the sauce poured over the fish as we have directed.

POTATO BALLS.

Mash five cold potatoes, an ounce of butter, and either two ounces of boned fish, minced roast beef or game, an ounce of breadcrumb, pepper, salt, a pinch of mixed herbs, and an egg. When this is thoroughly mixed, form it into balls the size of an egg and fry them in boiling fat. On no account let them get dark in colour, as that means that they are over cooked, hard, and flavourless. Brush each ball over with warm butter, and stick sprigs of parsley in each. These potato balls may be made without meat or fish, if a little cooked onion and chopped parsley be mashed with the potatoes.

CANADIAN SAUSAGES.

Bake a pound of pork sausages in a hot oven for a quarter of an hour. When they cool, skin them and cut them in pieces three inches long, and brush them over with egg. Cover them with mashed potatoes; egg and breadcrumb them and fry them in boiling fat. They should be a golden brown colour. Should the Canadian sausages be used as a plain dinner savoury, pour a rich brown gravy over them, and lay them on toasted cracker biscuits.

GENERAL RECIPES.

GROUSE SALAD.

Use for this salad a brace of grouse which have been nicely roasted. Wipe them, and if the skin is tough remove it, cut the flesh into two-inch pieces, and lay them in a rich, thick mayonnaise sauce (see recipe in the first number of THE WOMAN AT HOME), and let them soak in it for one hour.

Decorate the dish on which the pieces of grouse are to be laid, by edging it with

MONTPELIER BUTTER,

which is made in this way. Lay three ounces of butter in a soup plate with a tablespoonful of cream, a teaspoonful of lemon juice, two drops of white vinegar, a tablespoonful of chopped watercress, a salt-spoonful of chopped parsley and a pinch of salt. Mix these thoroughly.

When the border of the butter is put all round the salad dish, stamp it into pretty patterns with a vegetable cutter, and if possible set it on ice to get firm. Pile lettuces—break them in small pieces—cucumber cut thin in the centre of the dish, over this the grouse and mayonnaise, garnishing it with alternate strips of white of hard-boiled eggs and tomatoes. As a finish to this decorative cold entrée or lunch dish, place on the top a spray of nasturtium leaves and flowers.

GREEN PEA SOUP.

Most kinds of early peas are now getting dry and lacking in flavour, so that they are not of much value as a vegetable to be served with meat, yet they make very good soup if prepared as we direct.

To make four and a half pints of soup, boil three pints of peas, a quarter of a pound of spinach in four pints of water in which has been boiled a small piece of soda, a little salt, and a lump of sugar. Boil this one hour with the lid off the saucepan. When the peas are quite soft strain them and pulp them and the spinach through a sieve.

Take three pints of good white stock, and when it boils add to it one and a half pints of the liquid in which the peas were boiled, the pulped peas, a gill of cream, and boil ten minutes, adding an ounce of butter just at the last. Should the colour not be a good green give a few drops of Marshall's green colouring.

Serve oatmeal wafers or fried bread crumb with the soup. Should it be wished as thick as a purée, give more peas and thicken it with an ounce of corn flour.

CHILDREN'S CORNER.

For the children's breakfast vary oatmeal porridge with Floridor made in the following simple way. Bring a pint of milk to boiling point and mix into it two tablespoonfuls of Floridor which has been mixed with water till it is of the consistency of starch, boil it seven minutes, add salt and a small piece of butter. Eat hot with sugar or golden syrup.

VEGETARIAN SWEET PIE.

Boil four ounces of macaroni, and line a pie dish with three parts of it. Stew a pound of apples, a pound of stoned damsons or greengages with as much sugar as will sweeten them, and when nearly cooked put them into the lined pie dish. Cover the fruit with the remaining portion of macaroni, spread an ounce of butter and a teaspoonful of sugar on the top, so that the macaroni may make a glazed crust, and bake in the oven for half an hour, brushing it two or three times over with milk while it is baking. Serve cold or hot. This is a good and wholesome pie.

TABLE DECORATIONS.

Arrange small or large sunflowers in groups down each side of the table, and if for a stately dinner, make a centre of these grandly decorative flowers. If they are to completely cover the centre of the table, use the large single ones, and relieve their severity by putting in the middle a large pot of waving palms or feathery ferns. At the corner of the tables, and at intervals down the sides, white geraniums, or white hollyhocks with bramble leaves might be used, should so much yellow not be liked. For a simpler display use heather and oak leaves, Virginia creeper, and barley ears, purple dahlias with white and green grasses, blackberry leaves and berries, teasel and asparagus sprays, red geranium with mignonette. Use as much colour as possible, for, alas! this is our last really flowery month. The hedges are now gay with berries, the fields rich with golden grain ; gather from these while you can, not forgetting to preserve leaves, branches, berries (dip the latter in gum arabic to preserve them), haws, traveller's joy, oak leaves, heather, and oats.

* * *

A. S. should try this mode of cooking American popcorn. If it is unprepared, soak it for some time; boil it in milk till it is soft, and when it is quite cold add to it nutmeg, a very little sugar, yolk of egg, and lemon juice. Shape the flavoured popcorn into balls, cover them with yolk of egg to prevent them breaking while they are in the boiling fat, and fry them in good dripping. When they are taken out of the boiling fat, brush them over with milk, and while wet sprinkle grated cocoanut or finely chopped almonds on the balls.

FOURTEEN PLAIN DINNERS FOR SEPTEMBER.

Sunday— Roast Sirloin. Potatoes. Horse Radish Sauce. Stewed Damson and Custard.

Monday— Brown Soup from Sirloin Bones. Hash of Beef with Carrots. Potatoes. Cornflour Blanc Mange with Damsons.

Tuesday— Brown Soup with Rice in it. Cold Beef. Mashed Potatoes. Lettuce. Ginger Pudding.

Wednesday— Vegetarian Pie. Macaroni with Tomatoes. Fried Ginger Pudding with Lemon Sauce.

Thursday— Green Pea Soup. Roast Loin of Pork. Potatoes. Stewed Plums.

Friday— Green Pea Soup. Baked Haddock with Parsley Sauce. Potatoes (boiled in their skins). Tartlets.

Saturday— Cold Loin of Pork with Apple Sauce. Fish Cakes. Steamed Lemon Pudding.

Sunday— Boiled Fowl with Egg Sauce. French Beans. Potatoes. Raspberry or Damson Tart.

Monday— White Soup from the liquid the Fowl was boiled in. Cold Fowl with Salad and Mayonnaise Sauce. Mashed Potatoes. Fried Lemon Pudding.

Tuesday— White Soup with Parsley. Roast Leg of Mutton with Leeks. Potatoes. Fresh Plums (uncooked).

Wednesday— Minced Mutton with Turnips. Potatoes. Strawberry and Raspberry Fool.

Thursday— Cold Mutton. Peas. Baked Potatoes. Bread and Butter Pudding.

Friday— Hotch Potch (Vegetarian). Fried Flounders. Potatoes Plum Roly-poly.

Saturday— Stewed Steak with Parsnips. Fried Potatoes. Cheese and Rice Savoury.

IN SEASON IN SEPTEMBER.

Meat.—Beef, lamb, mutton, veal, pork.

Poultry.—Capons, chickens, ducks, turkeys, geese, fowls, pigeons.

Game.—Grouse, blackcock, teal, buck venison, rabbits, hares, partridge, plovers (golden and grey), snipe, woodcock, teal, wild duck.

Fish.—Bream, brill, flounders, cod, crab, doreys, eels, haddocks, lobsters, oysters, mullet, turbot, plaice, skate, soles, whiting, salmon (until the 7th), mackerel, perch, gurnets, trout (until the 7th), halibut, crayfish.

Vegetables.—Brussels sprouts, beetroot, beans, French beans, celery, cauliflowers, capsicums, cress, cabbages, chillies, cucumbers, chervil, scarlet runners, onions, leeks, sea-kale, carrots, artichokes, asparagus, lettuce, turnips, parsnips, peas, tomatoes, potatoes, vegetable marrows, mushrooms, herbs, parsley, horse radish.

Fruit.—Early apples, damsons, greengages, pears, green figs, filberts, grapes, melons, morella cherries, raspberries (rare), strawberries (rare), plums, apricots, peaches, quinces, small nuts, nectarines, bananas.

22

From Photo by]   THE QUEEN OF ITALY.   *[Flli. d'Alessandri, Rome.*

REMINISCENCES OF ROYALTIES.

By One who has Known Them.

THOUGH an Englishman by
birth and, during my early
manhood, a servant of the
British Crown, I spent a good
many years of life in the service of a foreign Sovereign,
and, during the long term of my residence
abroad, was brought into immediate contact
with several of those august personages who,
without any breach of the respect always due
to their exalted office, and sometimes to their
personal qualities, may aptly enough be termed
the figure-heads of State-ships commanded and
steered by persons of considerably less illus-

trious extraction than their own. In the course
of my protracted absence from England, which
endured almost continuously from the autumn
of 1857 to the winter of 1878, I was not only
officially presented to several Continental
rulers, and consequently bidden to Court entertainments without number, at which I was
frequently honoured by their particular notice,
but on more than one occasion, in times of
war as well as of peace, special missions were
entrusted to me which justified me in solicit-
ing private audiences from Emperors and
Kings, as well as Empresses and Queens.
In only one case, moreover, to the best of

VOL. III.—6

my remembrance, did a request of this kind, preferred by me through the proper channels, encounter refusal. I have partaken of many Imperial and Royal banquets, and have sat at table—I believe, a welcome guest—with a convivial gathering of four-and-thirty German Princes, regnant and mediatised, but all " born in the purple " and members of Sovereign Houses. I have "made music" with Royal ladies, consorts of monarchs and heirs-apparent, sometimes being privileged to act as

THE KING OF ITALY.

accompanist when it pleased them to sing to a few intimate friends, and sometimes to join them in a bout of sight-reading "quatre-mains," with no audience but the inevitable lady-in-waiting or *demoiselle d'honneur* on duty. Craving indulgence for the apparent egotism permeating this brief preamble, I will now address myself to the task which I have been asked to fulfil in the pages of this magazine ; to wit, to jot down a few of my personal recollections of the " Royalties " with whom, during one or another episode of a somewhat adventurous career, I have been permitted to

foregather on terms, perhaps, of greater mutual cordiality and unreserve than those which usually obtain between the porcelain and earthenware of latter-day humanity.

The King and Queen of Italy.

It was more than six-and-twenty years ago —in April, 1868—that I was presented to the lovely and accomplished lady who is now Queen of Italy, but was then Princess Margharita di Genova, own niece to the Rè Galantuomo, and known throughout her Royal uncle's realm by the affectionate *sobriquet* of " The Pearl of Savoy." I knew King Victor well, and among the many marks of favour with which he honoured me at different times not the least gratifying was his introduction of me to his eldest son, the Prince of Piedmont, and to his niece—about to become his daughter-in-law—a few minutes before they signed their marriage contract, in the grand saloon of the Duchess of Genoa's apartments at Turin, a ceremony to which I had been bidden by his Majesty's express command. As I was present at the wedding of the youthful cousins, and subsequently accompanied them throughout their honeymoon tour, which gave occasion to many magnificent festivities at Florence, Genoa, and Naples, I enjoyed frequent opportunities of admiring at leisure the rare and delicate beauty of the Princess, stamped with a distinctive German *cachet*—her mother was by birth a Saxon—but refined by a classical regularity of feature seldom to be seen in a thoroughly Teutonic face. Her Royal Highness was dazzlingly fair, with large violet-blue eyes, and a profusion of bright golden hair ; a little above the middle height, and almost ethereally slight of figure, but very gracefully formed. She spoke English, German, French, and Italian, as well as the quaint dialect of her native Piedmont, with equal fluency and elegance of diction, was an excellent equestrian and dancer, musician and needlewoman, and well versed in the poetical and fictional literature of half a dozen European nations. The prevalent expression of her beautiful countenance was one of unaffected cheerfulness ; hers was a spontaneous, not a stereotyped smile ; her laughter was that of a light-hearted child rather than of a Queen-to-be, menaced with the onerous duties and harassing responsibilities that "hedge about a throne." I remember a small incident of the wedding-day illustrative of her unconventional gaiety of disposition. As soon as Archbishop Riccardi, the Piedmontese Primate, had pronounced the nuptial benediction, several of the wedding-guests, myself among the number, managed to scurry back to the "sala di ricevimento" in the palace through a private passage connecting one of the Royal pews with the grand staircase, our object being to witness the *rentrée* of the newly-married pair, and the official felicita-

perial guests—among whom were the Crown Prince of Prussia and Prince (Plon-Plon) Napoleon—when my attention was attracted by "Madame Marguerite" whirling round a *champ-clos* of Princes and courtiers in the arms of an exceedingly handsome aide-de-camp attached to her husband's suite. During the waltz, in which several privileged couples joined, the Princess's dress caught in the spur of a revolving major of lancers, with the result that a tremendous rent was torn in the voluminous skirt, and a long wisp of gauze trailed forlornly on the polished floor. Frederick William of Hohenzollern, afterwards

THE KING AND QUEEN OF ITALY AT THE TIME OF THEIR HONEYMOON.

tions which had been foregone, by the King's wish, in the Royal Chapel. We had scarcely taken up positions of vantage when the bride and bridegroom re-entered the great saloon, and were at once surrounded by a throng of eager congratulatants. Having shaken hands with the "sposo," I hastened to pay my respects to the Princess of Piedmont, who replied, laughingly, to my briefly-worded compliment:

"I am in high spirits to-day. What a pity my dress is so long! I should so much like to dance!"

As she spoke, she jerked her train backwards with a quick sweep of her right foot.

At the grand ball given to the *nouveaux mariés* by the Philharmonic Academy of Turin on the evening of Thursday, April 23rd —the day after the wedding—I was standing in the semicircle of spectators spreading out from either wing of the Royal daïs, at the further end of the huge ball-room, and commanding a perfect view of the dancing-space reserved for the House of Savoy and its Im-

second German Emperor, was standing hard by, and before the Princess had had time to invoke the assistance of one of her damsels in waiting, he had extracted from the inner breast-pocket of his uniform a tiny morocco folding case, from which he produced a dainty little pair of scissors, and, kneeling at the feet of the bride, deftly cut away the trailing tatter. This done, he arose, bowed profoundly to her Royal Highness, and turning to her husband, smilingly craved permission to keep the *dépouille* as a souvenir of the lovely bride. To this gallant request Prince Humbert instantly acceded with a hearty clasp of the hand; whereupon "unser Fritz" deferentially solicited King Honestman's authorisation to his courtly "act of appropriation," and, having received a cordial affirmative, folded up his prize and carefully put it away in his pocket-book. Then he resumed his place at the right hand of the King amid the subdued murmurs of approval of all the ladies within the hallowed precincts of the "Royal Circle." Everyone acquainted with Italian character will at once understand the delight experienced by all present in relation to the readiness, gallantry, and fertility of expedient evinced by the Prussian prince who, but a few months previously, had covered himself with glory while defeating Italy's inveterate enemies on the sanguinary battlefield of Sadowa. The social success attending his felicitous little action was tenfold enhanced later in the evening when it came out that on Victor Emmanuel complimenting him anent the forethought he displayed in carrying a complete "trousse" about with him—even in a ball-room—Frederick William Nicholas replied, "Sire, the whole merit of the notion is my wife's, not mine. Long ago she gave me a *nécessaire de poche* with all sorts of useful things in it; needles, pins, and buttonhooks, thread, sticking-plaster, and scissors—as you saw just now—and made me promise to keep it always in my pocket whithersoever I might go. What took place just now only proved that I am a lucky fellow to have such a clever

From Photo by]   [A. Manders, late T. Edge, Llandudno.

THE QUEEN OF ROUMANIA.

wife to look after me." Grim Victor was hugely pleased with this disclosure, and went about after the next dance repeating it under his breath to all the great ladies of the Court, so that within an hour or so, I need scarcely say, "everybody who was anybody" in the room knew all about it. Madame de Gattinana told it to me, and I subsequently verified her narration by reference to the Crown Prince himself, who confirmed it in every particular. During the honeymoon festivities at Genoa "Madame Marguerita's" exuberant spirits more than once broke loose from the restraints of Court etiquette, even when the public gaze was riveted upon her. As she entered the Royal box on the night of the gala performance given in her honour—she was wearing the Crown jewels and a ravishing toilette of dark rose-coloured silk trimmed with tiny white feathers—the spirit of mischief prompted her to indulge in a bout of teasing, of which her brother-in-law, Prince Amadeo (afterwards King of Spain) was the chosen and submissive victim. After she had finished acknowledging, by profound curtsies, the storm of applause with which the audience hailed her, and was about to take her seat in the centre of the *palco reale*, the Duke d'Aosta—always *aux petits soins* with his charming kinswoman, to whom he was sincerely attached—set about arranging her footstool for her with his sheathed sword, which she persistently kicked aside with her daintily shod foot, laughing merrily all the while, until he desisted in comical despair, and bent down to settle the *tabouret* with both hands in the orthodox way. From my place in the grand tier I could see everything that went on in the Royal box, and watched this lively little episode with infinite entertainment, while King Victor looked on, smiling grimly, and twisting his formidable moustaches with one hand, his sword-hilt firmly clutched in the other.

The Queen of Roumania.

My presentation to the Queen (then Princess) of Roumania took place under circumstances which were certainly abnormal, and even to some extent embarrassing; that is, to me. In July, 1873, one broiling afternoon, I had taken refuge from the sub-tropical heat prevailing throughout the grounds of the Vienna Exhibition in the pretty cottage that had been constructed for the use of the British Commissioners, and luxuriously furnished as a specimen of English *villeggiatura* accommodation by some of our most fashionable art-upholsterers. One of the chief internal attractions of the annexe in question was a chintz-draped, low-toned smoking-room, containing an admirable English billiard-table. Of this cool resort all the chief British exhibitors, special correspondents, and friends of the Commissioners were hospitably made free by the tutelary genius of our Section, kindly, genial Philip Cunliffe Owen, *haud obliviscari!* On the occasion referred to I was playing a match with another member of the Commission, and three or four English ladies who were among the spectators of the game had permitted us to cast off coats and waistcoats and turn up shirt-sleeves in deference to the lofty demeanour of the thermometer, then recording 85° in the shade. The British *tabagie* was fragrant with the scent of Turkish tobacco, and appositely adorned with crystal jugs of iced champagne cup and Badminton, to which players and spectators alike frequently applied themselves under pressure of the insatiable thirst that was a chronic characteristic of Vienna Exhibitioners. Nothing more frankly and cheerfully unceremonious than the aspect and bearing of the Commission's guests could possibly have been imagined.

All of a sudden the folding-doors of the smoking-room swung asunder, and a tall, fair, tastefully-attired young lady appeared on the threshold. She was escorted by an illustrious British official —who paralysed us by exclaiming " Her Highness the Princess of Roumania !" —and followed by a highly ornate and got-up-to-the-nines suite of Roumanian and English ladies and gentlemen. Instinctively my adversary and myself "grounded cues" and stood at "attention"; observing which the Princess quickly approached us and said in faultless English : "Pray do not interrupt your game on my account." Then, turning to her guide, she asked him who the persons present were, and on being informed that they were friends of the Commissioners, requested that they might be presented to her, as she wished to express to each of them individually her regret at "having disturbed them so unexpectedly." Thus, in compli-

ance with her express command, I—although *en manches de chemise*—had the honour of being personally introduced to Elizabeth of Roumania.

In the spring of 1877, in obedience to a special command, I paid my respects to the Princess in her palace at Bucharest, and her Royal Highness, deigning to remind me of the above odd incident, was good enough to claim me as "an old acquaintance." Having heard from Prince Jon Ghica that I felt a lively interest in Roumanian music and

THE QUEEN OF ROUMANIA.

literature, she then took occasion to urge upon me the desirability of making the legendary ballads and folk-lore of her adopted country known to the British public through the medium of translations and imitations in the English language. "Though I speak and read English with ease," she observed, "and can even manage to write English prose with tolerable correctness, I find the composition of verse in your native tongue quite beyond my powers. But, as perhaps you know, I have paraphrased a considerable number of Roumanian popular poems in German, observing the original metre and rhythmical accents as closely as I could. There is a little romantic poem, of extraordinary beauty, by Eminescu, which I have just translated. I wish you would try to make an English version of it. If you will, I will copy it out for you myself, and send it to you; and your version shall have a place in my own personal album." I told "Carmen Sylva" that I would do my best to obey her commands, but that she must make allowance for shortcomings that would inevitably reveal themselves in any attempt to preserve metrical uniformity between original and translation in languages differing so widely from one another in construction as Roumanian and English. The Princess replied, "I am only too well acquainted with the difficulties you speak of, some of which are truly heart-breaking to a translator. They apply to German as well as to English, only not quite so irksomely, owing to the more elastic, or rather plastic, character of the Teutonic idiom. When you compare my translations with the originals, you will see that I have sometimes gone very near to a correct reproduction of the metres and rhythms, of course at the sacrifice of spontaneity, and even of ease. Nevertheless you must really try what you can do with some of our legends. Make your first experiment with the one that I shall send to you by-and-bye." An hour or two later I received a few lines from the Princess, accompanying a copy of Eminescu's poem and her German version of it, written out by her own hand. I lost no time in turning the verses into English, and while I was labouring over them it occurred to me that her Royal Highness might value an apt illustration of the subject—a romantic one—dealt with by the Dacian poet. Frederick Villiers happened to be in Bucharest at the time, so I hunted him up, told him the story of the poem—which struck his fancy—and asked him to depict its principal incident. Forthwith he set to work on a charming crayon sketch, which—together with my paraphrase of Eminescu's verses—it was my privilege to offer to Princess Elizabeth in the course of the following forenoon. The Royal poetess graciously accepted both drawing and adaptation, and I have reason to believe that they are in her 1877 album at the present day.

On another occasion, when I was permitted to pay her a morning visit in her favourite boudoir, I found her engaged upon some delicate needlework, surrounded by her maids of honour and singing-birds. The prevailing colour of the room was pale blue, and its walls were covered with excellent water-colour drawings, many of them the work of her own brush. After some desultory talk about the then imminent Russo-Roumanian invasion of Turkey, she began to question me as to my acquaintance with Dacian vocal music, and mentioned several melodies with which, at that time, I was unfamiliar. "You must hear some of them sung as they ought to be sung," she presently observed; and, sitting down to a small cottage piano near one of the windows, she called to her Mademoiselle Zoe Rosetti, a young lady attached to the household, whose sweet and flexible voice had earned for her the complimentary nickname of "O Rucinoâra" (the Nightingale) in Roumanian society. The Princess accompanied her in the old-world Moldavian ballad "Gianul," which sets forth in many couplets the achievements of a mediæval benevolent bandit, and subsequently in the quaint pastoral "Cinel," and the fervent love-ditty, "Doi ochi."

A few weeks later, war having broken out in grim earnest during the interim, I repeatedly saw the Princess in circumstances far less agreeable than those above alluded to. She had swiftly and skilfully organised a body of trained hospital nurses, several ambulances, and an association of volunteer Sisters of Mercy, to which many of the leading Boyarins belonged. Throughout the campaign she devoted the whole of her waking time, by day and by night, to tending the wounded and sick in the different hospitals administered under her superintendence in and near Bucharest. Arrayed in the plain dress of the Red Cross Sisterhood she was to be encountered, early and late, actively discharging all the harrowing duties of a "dresser," now in the Brancovanu palace, now at Cotroceni, showing the professional attendants a splendid example of nerve, gentleness, and endurance. Whenever I found time to look after some acquaintance, harboured in one or other of these institutions, I was sure to catch sight of the merciful Princess tendering comfort and consolation to some sufferer—pale with fatigue and anxiety, but never allowing her own heavy troubles to betray themselves by any outward sign of despondency. Throughout successive months the physical and psychical pressure brought to bear upon her must have been well-nigh intolerable; yet she never once forewent one of her self-appointed duties, but steadfastly carried on her work of mansuetude, saving lives and limbs by skilful ministration and, I am firmly convinced, by the benign influence of her gracious presence. From time to time I accompanied her on her rounds through the wards, and watched her as she stood by the pallets of mutilated and fever-stricken soldiers. Her smile had lost its former gaiety, her face its quick mobility of expression; but to the war-victims, who gazed upon it with grateful affection and reverence, it was as the face of an angel.

I was visiting a wounded officer of Rosciuri one morning at the extemporised hospital of Cotroceni with my lamented friend Lamson, who did splendid work as an army-surgeon during the 1877 war, and came to such a miserable end in London a few years later, when "Carmen Sylva" entered the ward and walked straight off to the bedside of a stalwart militia-sergeant who had sustained a compound fracture of the right thigh-bone from a splinter of Turkish shell, and was threatened with gangrene. The Roumanian peasant, I should mention, at that time entertained an unconquerable repugnance to mutilation of any kind, regarding loss of limb as a disgrace to which death was infinitely preferable. He had a notion that only cripples were entitled to beg their bread on the highway, and could not endure the thought of being subjected to the scornful pity with which professional mendicants were looked upon by his own class throughout the Principality. As, in compliance with the Roumanian army regulations, no soldier could be operated upon without his own consent—which the sergeant in question, even when solicited by the inspector-general of hospitals, had stubbornly refused—the surgeon in attendance had despairingly appealed to her Highness, who at once pledged herself to overcome the scruples of the wounded Dorobantsu. Standing by his pallet, she implored him earnestly to submit to amputation, but at first found him obdurate to her entreaties. Over and over he repeated his formula:

"I am not a beggar, nor will I become one. I will lose my life, but not my honour!"

"It is true," replied the Princess, "that you are not a beggar; but I am." Kneeling down, and taking his hand, she added: "Until now I have never prayed but to God. Now I supplicate you to listen to His wish and mine. Let your leg be taken off, and thus save your life for your family, for your country, and for me, and——"

"And if I consent," he interrupted, "what then, Márea Tá?"

"What then?" she rejoined, with a dazzling smile, as she rose to her feet. "Why, I shall

give you the most beautiful artificial leg that can be made in Europe. It will work with springs, and, when we get peace again, you shall come to the palace, and dance there with your sons and daughters."

"Let it be as you will," he muttered; "but you must hold my hand while they cut me."

Need I add that she complied with his pathetic stipulation? Chloroform was promptly administered, and in a few minutes the operation was successfully concluded. Moreover, the army surgeons thereafter met

From Photo by] [Russell & Sons, Baker Street, W.
THE KING OF ROUMANIA.

with no opposition to speak of when they recommended amputation to their patients "at the express wish of her Highness."

The Emperor William I. of Germany.

I was formally presented to William I., King of Prussia—afterwards first German Emperor—early in the spring of 1867, and a few days afterwards was honoured by a "command" to attend a church-parade of the First Footguards at Potsdam, and lunch with His Majesty in the Schloss immediately after the "march past." Before entering the Presence, I had been told that the King spoke English with difficulty, and did not particularly care to converse in French, though a perfect master of that tongue; so I was not at all taken by surprise when, after greeting me with, "I am glad to see you," in our vernacular, His Majesty changed his idiom to French, observing:

"I am not a good English scholar; doubtless you speak French."

I replied affirmatively, adding that I was sufficiently familiar with German to understand the King, should he deign to speak to me in his native language.

"Mir sehr angenehm," he instantly rejoined; "sprechen wir also Deutsch" ("That is very pleasant; let us speak German then").

Rarely did His Majesty omit to remind me of this circumstance, trifling in itself, whenever he took occasion thereafter to say a few words to me at Court festivities, autumn manœuvres, or casual meetings. Sometimes, while I was his guest in Pomerania and East Prussia, just a year before the great war, he would call me up to him by name, or summon me through the medium of an aide-de-camp, and open conversation with the words:

"You German-speaking Englishman, I have something to ask you."

In October, 1870, I was lunching one morning with my old friend, General von Kirchbach, at Beauregard, Madame de Bauffremont's luxurious château near Paris, then being utilised by the besiegers as head-quarters of the Fifth Corps. There were two or three foreign guests besides myself at the General's table: Hazen, of the U.S. Army, who had ridden out with me from Versailles, where his quarters were situate, to call upon the stout old Corps-Commander; Daniel Home, the spiritualist, then acting as war-correspondent for some American newspaper; and another "Special," whose name I forget. Kirchbach had shown us over the Ducal mansion, which was a veritable museum of rare china and costly bric-à-brac, and we were just sitting down to a copious *déjeûner à la fourchette* in the dining-room, when one of the staff threw open the folding-doors, exclaiming—

"The King, the King!"

A minute later His Majesty strode briskly into the room, helmet in hand and smiling benevolently. Of course, we all rose and stood in a row, as if on parade. The King shook hands with Kirchbach and Hazen, and then passed down the line of the General's guests. He came to a halt in front of Home, whom he addressed in French, alluding to the surprising performance of "white magic" which His Majesty had witnessed in Berlin and at the Tuileries Palace, and jocosely asking "Monsieur le Magicien" if he could find out from his familiar spirits "when Paris would surrender." Then he caught sight of me, and, turning round to Kirchbach, who was closely attending him, exclaimed:

"So you, too, know the Englishman who speaks German so well! He is an old acquaintance of mine."

This "interpellation" was followed by a few gracious and kindly words addressed to myself, and accompanied by a hearty grasp of the Royal hand. As an illustration of King William's tenacity of memory—a truly royal characteristic, often hereditary, and sometimes imparted by assiduous training during childhood—and ineffable tact, the little episode above narrated is not altogether devoid of interest.

Late in 1871, when Cardwell's scheme for the abolition of purchase in the British Army was on the tapis, I happened to visit Berlin, and, shortly after my arrival, wrote my name in the Emperor's book at the palace under the Linden, according to time-honoured custom. Two or three days later, as I was writing in my room at the Hotel de Rome, his Majesty's "reader," Privy Councillor Schneider, was announced. He was the bearer of a message from the Kaiser, who wished to see me, and "would be glad to receive me at ten o'clock of the following morning, if perfectly convenient to myself." When, in obedience to this "command," I called at the palace, I was at once ushered into the famous "corner-room" overlooking the Opern Platz. The Emperor was sitting at his writing-table with a pile of documents before him, and accorded me a kindly welcome, insisting that I should take a seat near his own wooden, round-backed chair. "Do you know anything about the English purchase system?" he abruptly asked. "Some of my best officers condemn it utterly, and others seem to see some good points in it. I don't think that I quite follow the 'for and against,' and when I saw your name in the visiting-book the other day it struck me as just possible that you might have studied the subject—for I know what an interest you take in military matters—and might be able to make the whole question clear to me. Can you do so?" I replied that I had fortunately paid particular attention to the system in question, and to the proposed measure for its abolition; whatever information I had collected was of course entirely at his Majesty's disposal. "That is very kind of you," he rejoined, "and just what I expected. Will you oblige me by setting down the pros and cons of the question in writing, and sending your *pro memoria* to me as soon as it shall be finished?" I promised to do my best, and took my leave forthwith, being well aware how strongly the venerable Kaiser objected to anything in the nature of delay, procrastination, or waste of time. Next morning I personally consigned to the aide-de-camp "du jour" a memorandum several pages in length, summarising the advantages and drawbacks of the purchase-system, and drawing the Emperor's attention to certain similarities between the pecuniary burdens imposed upon Prussian officers by the gift of a commission, and those devolving upon British officers through the obligation of purchase. Beyond a formal acknowledgment of the memorandum, I heard nothing about it for a fortnight, at the expiration of which his Majesty sent for me again, and after thanking me for the notes, which he pronounced "interesting, and suggestive of considerations which had not occurred to him before he read them," he added, "As you already have my portrait, I have been puzzled how to acknowledge the obligation under which you have placed me ; and it struck me only yesterday that you might like to possess a convincing proof of the value I set upon your very instructive communication. So I asked the Minister of War to return to me the autographic 'Cabinets-Ordre,' in which I had given him certain instructions respecting the memorandum ; and here it is. I have great pleasure in presenting it to you, and in asking you to keep it as a personal souvenir of me. Its text, as well as signature, is in my own handwriting, and it bears the official marks and numbers of the war ministry." It may be imagined how deeply gratified I was by the delicate thought underlying the gift, and by the gracious manner of its conferment.

That "Cabinet Order," fitly framed, hangs in my library, and will be preserved in my family as a precious heirloom after my death. In literal translation it runs as follows :

"The enclosure appears to be extremely interesting, wherefore I request you to have it translated for me in the ministry ; for it must be of importance to know the *pro*

et contra of the purchase of officers' commissions in England.—(Signed) Wilhelm. Dec. 3rd, 1871."

The Emperor Frederick.

My acquaintance with the second German Emperor extended over a period of exactly twenty years, during which I was indebted

THE LATE EMPEROR WILLIAM I. OF GERMANY.

to him for many unsolicited kindnesses and much genial hospitality, as well as for the ready granting of every request which, at one time or another, I had occasion to prefer to him. The very first time I met him he did me a great favour, altogether of his own accord and unsuggested on my part. It was on the race-course at Stargard, in Pomerania, during the "off-day" of the 1869 royal manœuvres, and Colonel Beauchamp Walker, at that time military attaché to the British

Legation in Berlin, had just introduced me to his Royal Highness, telling him that I had received the king's permission to witness the field operations of the second army-corps, and had been properly accredited to the chief of the staff, quartermaster-general, etc. The Crown Prince chatted gaily with me for two or three minutes, *de choses et autres*, and then, observing me to be on foot—for I had driven out from Stargard to the course and left my trap behind the temporary grand stand—asked me if I had been able to find anything to carry me during the three days'

"local resources," and was consequently in great perplexity as to how I was to get about. "Pray don't let that trouble you any further," rejoined the Crown Prince. "I have several spare horses here, all accustomed to stand fire, and I am very happy to place one of them at your disposal for the rest of the manœuvres. There will be nothing doing to-day; but I will give orders that it shall be at your quarters to-morrow morning, and when you send it back to the stables you will let the people know at what hour you want it next day." Thus, through H.R.H.'s generous

THE LATE EMPEROR WILLIAM I. OF GERMANY.

field-work that was still to be done. "You can't possibly follow the movements of the troops in a carriage," he added; "the country is too rough, and the area of the operations too large; besides, you would be continually getting in the way of some squadron or battery, and there is a good deal of short temper about in this frightfully hot weather. But perhaps you have prudently brought down a charger with you from Berlin. Just now, I fear there is nothing to be hired in or near Stargard." I replied that I had had no time to make any special arrangements for a mount, either at Berlin or Stettin —my latest étapes on the way to Stargard— but had been compelled to put my trust in

kindness, I rode a handsome chestnut mare, perfectly broken, and up to my weight, throughout the manœuvre, and was every whit as well mounted as any of the Royal personages or generals who took the field on that occasion.

After the close of the field operations, three days later, a "grand tattoo," was performed by the bandsmen of the Second Corps—about eight hundred in number—in honour of the King. The musicians were massed in the centre of the huge stone quadrangle fronting Stargard Castle. They formed a hollow square, and were conducted by the senior bandmaster perched upon a high tribune, and wielding a flame-tipped baton; for the performance took place after dark, by the flickering glare of torchlight, and the King's guests were grouped round him on a broad flight of flagged steps leading from the Schloss hall-door to the courtyard and illuminated by coloured lanterns. I was standing at the bottom of the massive stone staircase among a crowd of members of the different staffs and foreign officers—about eighty of whom attended the manœuvres by invitation, including twenty-seven representatives of the British army. One of the "tuneful numbers" set down on the "Zapfenstreich" programme was Mendelssohn's jubilant Wedding March. While this noble composition was being superbly rendered by the combined regimental bands and trumpeter corps the Crown Prince came up to me, laid his hand on my shoulder, and said, "That is my favourite piece of music, and I'll tell you why. It was the first tune I heard after my marriage, twelve years ago; for it was being played on the organ as I walked up the nave of the chapel with my wife on my arm. You were a youngster then, on that happy day, the happiest of my life." Englishwomen will readily understand how deeply I was touched by this graceful and affectionate allusion to my illustrious compatriot, the Princess Royal, whose union with Frederick William of Hohenzollern, the outcome of pure and mutual affection, had theretofore been one of perfect concord and unmarred felicity, and remained so to the day of his death, setting to married folks throughout the civilised world a shining example of high nobility of purpose, strenuous fulfilment of duty, and unswerving rectitude of conduct. Spontaneously proffered to a wandering Briton, far from his native land, and surrounded by total strangers or acquaintances of a few hours' standing with whom his intercourse could only be transient and superficial, the Crown Prince's observation was peculiarly

illustrative of the refined taste and exquisite tact which had in the days of his early manhood secured to him a firm lodgment in the hearts of his fellow-countrymen, and won for him the enthusiastic admiration, as well as the profound respect of every foreigner with whom circumstances had brought him into personal contact. I could quote here twenty

THE LATE EMPEROR FREDERICK.

more instances of his delicate thoughtfulness and fascinating geniality, manifested in connection with incidents that, at different times, came under my own cognizance; but that the space allotted to me for this somewhat sketchy and discursive paper is already filled to over-flowing. Some day, perhaps, I may take an opportunity to supplement it by jotting down a few more reminiscences of Royal personages other than those episodically adverted to in the foregoing pages.

DRESS AND FASHION.

The profusion of bloom in this moon of violets seems the precursor of an early spring. The purple flowerets fill our streets, adorn our garments, and crown our millinery. Their delicate perfume permeates the air, and its best imitation of Rhine parentage is adopted as the favourite scent of our fashionable women. Flowers, indeed, are more popular than they have been for years, and no ball-dress is complete without their aid; they give a gracious air of festivity to our gowns which the heaviness of passementerie was wont to abolish. For young girls they are, with the flutter of ribbons and the transparency of tulle, the most ideal frame their beauty could desire. Rose petals in satin or velvet edge our skirts. Shepherdess festoons of roses cross the low-pointed court bodice, or entwined with satin ribbons of their own colour enframe the bust, creep up the shoulders in epaulettes, or are boldly poised with an enormous bow on the left hip. Spangles mix with them, generally sewn on the dress material in a mitred pattern, for tinsel is, if possible, on the increase, and it may truthfully be said of us that we are growing daily more barbaric in our splendour! There is a marked tendency to favour the larger make of flowers, such as the double and single dahlia, the chrysanthemum, and the roses; of the smaller blossoms, violets, lily of the valley, hyacinth, etc., are the most popular. Colours run in the gamut of warmth —apricot, pinks, or vivid cerise; crude blues and reds have been fashioned into velvet poppies, and it is whispered that presently the anemone and the crocus will invade flowerdom to the exclusion of all other favourites.

* * *

Flowers have superseded wings in the toques at present so much worn; their popularity resides mainly in the fact that they are becoming and easily made up at home even by the unskilled fingers of a novice. As everything is jumbled together, even velvets of two colours, such as black and green, it will be found an easy matter to build up

a toque out of the odds and ends a woman always stows away in mysterious cardboard boxes. Sable tails and heads, creamy lace or guipure, an osprey, a paste buckle, and any pieces of velvet, cloth, or brocade to form a soft crown, a turban twist of velvet with a few crêpe rosettes, will

No. 1.

form the brim, unless you prefer those of fluted chenille, now so fashionable. The elongated shape has made way for a rather squat, square toque, in which I can discover no charm save that of variety! Glacé velvet is still much used for millinery purposes; it is lovely in the gamut of pink, the newest shade being a sort of apricot rose; tomato red, cornflower blue, canary and a serpent blue green are amongst the newest shades. Feathers are universally used, long uncurled plumes drooping over the hair at the back with rather a mournful effect on the large shapes. The white and tan

No. 2.

felts are being trimmed with purple velvet violets in view of the spring; and the stamped leather crowns look smart and uncommon. The Alsatian bonnets are sensible headgears for young matrons; they are mostly built of steel-embroidered velvet, have a wider appearance than the Dutch shape, and are trimmed in front with spikey windmill bows and a few dahlias; bows of ribbon encircle the back, framing the ears and profile in pretty quaint style. Strings have vanished into the limbo of forgotten things, swept away by the current of throatlets and fussy neck arrangements. In these we have an endless variety. Lisse, which is a new name for an improved and less crushable chiffon, is made into short boas, consisting of a series of quillings, ornamented at intervals with bright-hued, leafless flowers of rather large dimensions, or market bunches of violets fasten them on one side. Perhaps the daintiest of all are composed of a number of rows of ruched chiffon sewn together, each row beaded by sparkling spangles, moonlight steel on blue, copper on pink, or emerald on Nile green; sometimes they are further enhanced with a curled feather fringe; the main

point is to provide a becoming frame for the face which should rest like a flower in its diaphanous setting. Even the little seal ties or short boas are bedecked with a jabot of lace, white satin rosettes, or a spray of flowers to modernise them. The large flat fur muffs of 1830 memory are too hideous for words, but the fanciful " Granny " muffs in plush or satin with thin full frills, lined with cream lace, thin vivid silk lining and froufrou of bows, fluttering ribbons, and bunch of fragrant violets are truly charming. The scanty locks and Grecian knobs, so disastrous to women over thirty, have been replaced by a more generous allowance of wavy locks and marteau curls, which lend a softness to faces that time is beginning to wrinkle. Aigrettes, coronets, and flowers or tinsel ornaments are much worn in the hair. Never was colouring carried to greater perfection, and the liberal introduction of mohair into materials lends them a particular metallic sheen. The " Caracul " material is a perfect furore; it is a crocodile mohair surface over a sort of flannel lining, giving an effect of black shot with colour. For evening dresses light materials are much used for young girls; full tulle skirts have seventeen to twenty rows of Bébé satin ribbon round the bottom; for older women there are the blue steel embroidered nets worn over

No. 3.

pale blue or apricot pink ondines. White peaude-soie ball gowns trimmed with colour—dull pink, turquoise blue, or canary—are in high request; many skirts are hemmed with a band of roses or rose petals, surmounted by a design of silver or gold spangles.

Long scarves of wide ribbons, heavily embroidered with bullion or shot spangles, trim ball dresses *en bretelles*, and fall stolewise to the end of the skirt. Once more we have a new skirt which is commendable, for it gives the fullness and flow of drapery without taking one inch from your height. To all appearances, it is an ordinary plain skirt very full, about four yards and a half round the bottom. It has two box pleats at the back, and fastens on the left side ; here the difference is, that the front breadth is quite detached, and has a foundation breadth of some bright silk under it, which shows when the wearer walks or moves. The detached side is trimmed from top to bottom. It would seem that our skirts cannot be made wide enough in Paris. They are quite fabulous, the organ-fold *godets* starting well from the sides. The best way of renovating old skirts now is simply to introduce front and two side breadths of a different material. Jet is much worn, and some of the new trimmings are perfect gems, with their scintillating

diamonds, and instead of the vulgar elastic a flexible gold serpent with emerald eyes keeps the folds close together.

* * *

Shoes are very elaborate, made with appliqué white lace on kid, perforated leather, red

No. 5.

morocco, or gold or silver braid. The perforated cloth for dresses and mantles is now embroidered with silk or chenille in Marguerite, wheel or spider-web patterns, outlined with silk or chenille, and used as panels or entire skirts, or for mantles. The Vitraux or cathedral glass effect is obtained when the perforated cloth is in a Gothic pattern lined with gold or silver cloth, shot in metallic greens or blues. All red tea-gowns and evening dresses are to be found in many of the best houses ; they are a royal feast of colour on dull days. Pelisses derive their styles from the Empire period, as do most of the long opera mantles.

* * *

Fur is worn on every possible occasion, and invariably accompanied by lace, thick or thin ; transparent yokes to dinner-gowns are made of guipure framed with fur. Many ball-dresses are trimmed with sable tails or bands of fur, and for low dress thus trimmed a band of fur fastened with a diamond brooch and small

No. 4.

crescents and squares of finely cut *cabochons*. Much tinsel, spangles, and cut gems are used for trimming, in conjunction with chenille, canetille, etc., etc. Umbrella handles are becoming works of art. They have handles of " Aventurine " stick finished off with crutch handles or knobs of gun-metal, starred or initialled in rose spray of flowers is worn round the neck. Sable is expensive if good, but bands of golden beaver or dark musquash—a lovely fur—are much used. For visiting dresses Caracul is used for waistcoats; revers and even entire bodices of it are seen. Some bodices are in regal ermine. Feathers, fur fringe, and as many strings of pearls and jet as might bedeck a savage, are worn on evening bodices. There is some talk of sleeveless coats and spencers for the coming spring.

No. 6.

DESCRIPTIONS OF FASHION DRAWINGS.

No. 1.—Among the many charming and useful blouses shown at Messrs. Debenham and Freebody's, Wigmore Street, the design illustrated deserves special attention on account of its utility for afternoon home-wear, or by the addition of the dainty fichu it may be converted into a tasteful bodice suitable for a more dressy occasion. The material is a bright green surah silk, and the fichu, which is exceedingly delicate and pretty, is in chiffon, embroidered with silk. Bands of cream satin ribbon are brought round the figure, and arranged in a large bow on the bust, in a veryn ovel and becoming fashion.

No. 2.—Another excellent model, also sketched at the same establishment, is an "at home" dress, made in caracule cloth in a bright shade of dark blue. The bodice is particularly stylish, made in velvet, and edged with Persian lamb and fine black silk passementerie. The waist is encircled by a black satin ribbon, tied in a bow at the left side. A very pleasing novelty is the double collar made in apple green velvet, with a fold of black satin beneath; this being a decided change from the folded bands now so generally worn. The plain skirt is so gored as to allow a large amount of fulness around the feet, and is very elegantly draped at the back.

No. 3.—The practical jacket sketched at Messrs. Swan and Edgar's, Regent Street, will be recognised as an old friend in a modernised form. It is made in a fine brown cloth, with a large pointed collar and edging of musquash fur, and it is smartly frogged across the front, with a braided design on the sleeves to correspond. In appearance this coat is extremely neat and stylish.

No. 4.—Messrs. Swan and Edgar are also showing the very pretty afternoon gown illustrated. The material used is a zibeline cloth, in a chestnut brown shade. The large sleeves and full blouse front are made in a pretty fancy black satin, dotted over with gold and black spots. Both the waist-band and collar are in black satin ribbon; and the revers on the bodice have a beautiful appliqué of jetted passementerie ornamenting them, and are edged with a narrow trimming of jet. The cloth skirt is treated in a similar fashion, with long strips of open bead work relieving the otherwise plain appearance.

No. 5.—A very pretty evening gown from Messrs. Evans, Oxford Street, simply yet very tastefully made in primrose coloured crêpon trimmed with velvet and cream lace. The bodice is cut a little low at the neck, and draped round with a fulness of the material intermingled with black velvet. The large puffed sleeves are also caught across the centre,with a band of velvet, in butterfly fashion. Pointed lace is placed at intervals round the skirt and on the bodice with charming effect; this, combined with smartly-tied bows of black velvet, makes this gown a very suitable and dainty evening dress for a young lady.

No. 6.—This costume, sketched at Mr. B. Marcus', 37, Conduit Street, is a good example of a stylish and practical walking dress. It is made in a bright red face cloth, and very beautifully braided. It has the appearance of being a coat and waistcoat, the latter edged with Persian lamb; but this separate look is in effect only, and is the result of the clever arrangement of the braiding. The bodice is really all in one, with the addition of the double revers; and the upper part of it is braided to form a very neat little vest. The skirt is particularly well cut, and the long lines of braiding with which it is ornamented give an additional appearance of height to the wearer.

A VERY UP-TO-DATE GIRL.

By L. T. Meade.

YPATIA WENTWORTH despised matrimony, and was proud to belong to the emancipated order of womanhood. She was just completing her third year at Girton, and was a very striking, handsome-looking girl. Hypatia from her earliest years had been fond of taking her own way. She intended to mark out an independent career for herself. One of the earliest things she had ever learned was, how to rule. Her father was dead, but her mother, who was extremely fond of her, easily submitted to her sway. Mrs. Wentworth was slightly afraid of her handsome daughter, but she also adored her. Hypatia ruled, but she ruled pleasantly. Mrs. Wentworth was only too glad to consult her child with regard to that child's future. Hypatia managed to make a very good thing out of her life. She was a favourite at Girton, and was now working very hard for her classical tripos. In the Easter recess she had to own, however, to a slight sense of mental fatigue, and suggested to her mother that she should spend her holidays abroad.

Sunset on Lake Geneva, showing Dent du Midi.

"I wish I could go with you, dearest," said Mrs. Wentworth, "but——"

"I prefer going alone, mother," replied Hypatia, in her calm voice. "My friend Lucy Johnson suggests our going to Montreux. I don't care for Montreux myself; but there is a charming little place just above it, called Glion. The air at Glion is superb, and I am told that the principal hotel is well managed. I propose to start to-night for the Victoria Hotel, Glion—the great object of my visit being to climb to the summit of the celebrated *Rochers de Naye*."

Mrs. Wentworth knew nothing whatever about mountain climbing. Her eyes, however, looked full of vague trouble when Hypatia spoke.

" You won't do anything rash, darling ? " she said.

" I won't endanger my life, if you mean that, mother—I am a great deal too fond of it. Now, will you come upstairs with me and help me to pack my trunk ? "

Mrs. Wentworth did not waste her breath over a single word of remonstrance ; she assisted Hypatia with her packing, and saw her off that evening by the night mail to Paris. Hypatia travelled second class, arriving at the Victoria Hotel, Glion, just before dinner on the following evening. She had not telegraphed her arrival in advance, but she judged wisely that the hotel would be scarcely full so early in the season. On inquiring at the bureau, she was told that a small room on the third floor was at her service. It had a full view of the lake. Hypatia ascended to her room in the lift. She was just in time to see the sunset, which at this time of year is one of the most remarkable features of the place. She went and stood on her little balcony, and drew a deep breath of pleasure. The scene on which her eyes rested was magnificent beyond description. All the best part of her rose up with joy to meet the grand spectacle. To her left glowed the Dent du Midi in transparent and palpitating rose tints. The snow-covered peaks reflected the gorgeous colours of the dying day. Each moment the mighty Dent assumed a more spiritual aspect ; in the far west, behind the Jura hills, the sun was setting in a great bed of orange and darkest purple. Every cloud in the sky, the shapes of all the mountains, were reflected in the tranquil, deep blue bosom of the lake. Each cloud at this moment was tipped with softest rose to palest gold. The sunset changed instant by instant from orange to saffron, from saffron to purple, then to blood red, then to the faintest and most exquisite

"I want to introduce a very special friend of mine."

violet. Hypatia's brown eyes grew large and liquid as she gazed. Never before had they looked on so majestic a scene. The dinner gong sounded downstairs, but she took no notice of the circumstance. The sunset on the Lake of Geneva satisfied and filled her whole artistic nature so completely, that she forgot everything else in the world.

When it had quite faded, she turned abruptly and re-entered her little room. She did not take long in arranging her dinner toilet, and went quickly downstairs. Whatever Hypatia was, she was not self-conscious —her mind was too preoccupied for that. She had long ago trained herself to think consecutively, and now her thoughts were completely filled with the wonderful colour picture she had just been permitted to see in the book of nature. When she entered the dining-room, a waiter conducted her to her seat. She gave a quick glance around her. There were three long tables in the room. Two of these, however, were quite empty, and the one at which she seated herself was not more than half full. She began to eat her dinner in an abstracted manner, bestowing no thought upon her neighbours. Presently a voice sounded in her ears.

"Surely I am not making a mistake. I have the pleasure of speaking to my cousin, Hypatia Wentworth?"

Hypatia turned her head quickly. She had very beautiful and intelligent eyes, and some of the pleasure which the sunset had given her was still reflected in them.

"You are Hypatia Wentworth?" repeated the same voice.

"And you are Hugh Trafford," she replied. "What in the world—I mean, why have you come here?"

"Why have you come here?" was the laughing reply.

"Oh, for rest and refreshment," answered Hypatia.

"You have been overworking at Girton, have you not?"

"No—yes—perhaps so—a little—and you?"

"I have also come for rest and refreshment—the fact is, you young ladies have taxed my mental powers rather severely. I don't mind lecturing to the men of my college, but I find that lectures at Girton take a good deal out of me. Why do you girls take everything so dreadfully in earnest?"

"Because we are new and fresh and enterprising," replied Hypatia, with spirit.

"You certainly are enterprising," replied Trafford. "Well, I am glad to see you here. How is your mother? Is she too fatigued to come downstairs?"

Hypatia laughed.

"My mother is in England," she replied. "I have come here alone. I intend to have a capital time. Did you say anything?"

Trafford had not—he had only uttered a faint sigh, and turned his attention once more to his dinner. Hypatia also bent over her plate.

"I wish he were not here," thought the girl. "I have a great mind to leave this hotel to-morrow. This is about the last thing that ought to have happened. Hugh Trafford is my cousin—I have known him since I was a child. I have *never* liked him—I can see by his eyes that he despises the new woman. He is one of those detestable narrow-minded male creatures who look askance at any girl with spirit. I see already that he intends to give himself airs with me. He won't forget for a moment that he is a Cambridge don and that I am an unfortunate girl undergraduate. He will consider it his right to snub me. Well, two can play at that game. On consideration, now that I am

here, I'll stay. I'll show my cousin what a modern English girl can do. It will be rather good fun opening his eyes."

After dinner Trafford came up to Hypatia.

"I want to introduce a very special friend of mine to you," he said.

Miss Wentworth found herself bowing to an elderly lady who was dressed in the height of the fashion, and had a particularly shrewd, humorous, and kindly face.

"I am glad to make your acquaintance, Miss Wentworth," she said. "My name is Weston. I am known here by my red parasol and my white dog. I shall have pleasure in introducing you to my white dog after dinner. She is a pure Pomeranian, and she and her ancestors have belonged to the Weston family for years past counting. Her name is Mona to her familiars; to strangers she is known by her full title, Mona Moumouth Gwyn."

Miss Weston spoke in a very dry voice. Hypatia thought her remarks extremely silly, but there was something in her twinkling eyes which caused the girl to laugh in spite of herself.

"I shall be glad to make Miss Mona's acquaintance," she said, after a pause.

"I daresay you will; she has advanced ideas for a dog. I am not at all certain whether she will like you—if she does, you may consider yourself highly favoured. Did I hear you tell Mr. Trafford that your mother was upstairs?"

"No," answered Hypatia, colouring. "I said that my mother was in England. I told Mr. Trafford what I now repeat to you, that I have come here alone."

"Indeed—*how* advanced. Mona is also a little before her time, but I doubt if she will approve of you; she is intelligent, and looks ahead of her with observant eyes, but she does not care for *too* rapid movement; indeed, the girl who goes abroad alone——"

"Oh, pray don't say any more," said Hypatia, trying to smile, but in reality feeling very angry. "I don't expect to be understood either by a dog of advanced ideas, or by ladies of my mother's day."

Here she stopped, rather ashamed of herself. Miss Weston might not consider herself of her mother's day.

That good lady, however, gave her a serene glance.

"Whatever your views, I hope you will have a good time, my dear," she said, with a nod; "how do you propose to occupy your time?"

"Well, to-morrow I shall probably rest.

The next day I intend to climb to the top of the Rochers de Naye."

"Mr. Trafford, did you hear that?" said Miss Weston.

"Yes," replied Trafford, "I heard."

"Have you nothing to say?"

"Nothing. Miss Wentworth will soon find out for herself that she is attempting the impossible."

"I shall climb to the top of the Rochers de Naye the day after to-morrow," repeated Hypatia, in a calm voice. "I have come out from England for the express purpose. A friend of mine who is now at Montreux will join me. We expect to reach the topmost peak after four or five hours' hard work. We shall start early. I hope to be able to tell you my adventures, Miss Weston, when we meet at dinner."

"Fudge," said Miss Weston. "I am much more likely to hear of your untimely end."

"Oh, pray don't say any more," interrupted Trafford. "I happen to know my cousin Hypatia Wentworth very well. I have often seen her before now attempt the impossible. Why waste words over the matter?"

"I vow and declare that I'll do it," said Hypatia.

"You can't," replied Trafford.

He looked her full in the eyes as he spoke. Her eyes challenged him back with an angry flash. She was about to speak, but making an effort, restrained herself. The conversation turned on indifferent matters, and shortly afterwards the Girton undergraduate went to her room.

The Rochers de Naye are situated between six and seven thousand feet above the level of the sea. As Swiss mountains go, they are not especially high, but the rocks in the springtime are completely covered with snow, and the ascent is full of danger. The railroad, which in the summer carries passengers to the summit, is closed. In short, the Rochers enjoy at this time of year unbroken solitude, anyone who attempts to visit them doing so at the risk of life.

Hypatia sat by her window. She was feeling angry and excited; she disliked Miss Weston, she did not wish to be introduced to the white dog with the ridiculous name, she

could not even think of Trafford with toleration.

"Why is my holiday spoiled in this manner?" thought the angry girl. "Just because I am a woman am I supposed to be incapable of sense, of judgment, and courage? Yes, I am determined now to show Hugh Trafford what a girl can accomplish. I told mother that I would not risk my life, but I am resolved now not to return to England without having accomplished the grand object of my visit abroad."

The next day Hypatia breakfasted early,

"She went down by the Venicular Railway"

and went down to Montreux to visit her friend Lucy Johnson. She went down by the Venicular Railway, and walked quickly to the Hotel National, where her friend was to be found. Lucy was just coming out of the hotel when Hypatia came up. She also was a modern girl, but not of so pronounced a type as Hypatia. Lucy was a copyist, Hypatia was original. By nature Lucy was short and stout; she had a fair, full face, a quantity of light brown hair which was swept tightly back from her full brow, a squat figure which was rendered still more squat by the want of stays, and by indulging in short, full skirts which never descended below the ankles. Lucy would have been pretty if she had taken pains with herself; as it was, she was ugly. She had strong dark blue eyes, but as she invariably wore smoked glasses, no one had an opportunity of judging of their colour. She wished now to pose as a mountaineer, and was dressed from head to foot in Irish frieze.

"This is lucky, Lucy," cried Hypatia. "I was just coming to you. So you arrived safely last night?"

"Of course, my dear. What right had I to suppose that I should be privileged with an adventure?"

Hypatia laughed.

"Of course not," she answered; "adventures only fall to the lot of few. Do you like your hotel?"

"Pretty well—that is, I have not had time to think about it. I have been busy arranging for our climb. Do you think this costume will do?"

"Admirably, Lucy—that is, it is quite correctly ugly."

"Yes," replied Lucy, in an abstracted voice.

Then she gazed full at her friend. Hypatia's slender figure was becomingly draped in gray; she wore a black lace scarf round her neck; her dark eyes were full of brilliant but subdued fire. Her appearance was so striking, her attitude so noble, that several people turned to gaze at her as they passed.

"Hippy, you do not look like a mountaineer," exclaimed Lucy, in some dissatisfaction.

Hypatia laughed.

"I promise to look quite the thing when we begin our climb to-morrow," she exclaimed. "I came down now to ask you, Lucy, if you will be ready to accompany me to-morrow?"

"Certainly," said Lucy. "I am all impatience; but do you know," she added, her voice dropping a little, "that the people at the National think it a great deal too early for the ascent?"

"It may be for men creatures, but not for us," answered Hypatia.

"Capital, Hippy; what it is to belong to the emancipated. You are quite prepared, then, for danger?"

"Quite," said Hypatia; "but for the ele-ment of danger, where would be the fun of going? We must start early. Will you meet me, Lucy, at Glion, not later than seven o'clock to-morrow morning? Bring your alpenstock, a hatchet, a strong clasp-knife, some rope, a small axe, a bottle of brandy, and some sandwiches."

"Have we to cut our way?" cried Lucy.

"We possibly may have to do so. Now then, don't fail to meet me."

The girls talked a little longer. Presently they parted, and Hypatia returned to the Victoria Hotel for *dejeuner*. After lunch she wandered about the lovely grounds. The trees were not yet in leaf, but a few shady glades were to be found, made, it is true, by man's device. Awnings were put up wherever awnings were possible; large umbrellas stood protectingly over little tables. People sat in the shade, and read and worked and wrote. By-and-by, neatly dressed maid-servants appeared, bearing trays of tea, honey, little rolls and fresh butter. Hypatia despised tea and artificial shade; she wandered away to the Chillon woods, which were close by; here she filled her basket with woodland flowers. She saw the far-famed gentians in the most impassable places; she gathered hypatica, wood anemones, violets, primroses, cowslips, and quantities of the lovely purple periwinkle. Having filled her basket, she hurried off to the post-office, to despatch the flowers to her mother. On her way back she met Miss Weston.

"Here's my dog," said that lady, coming up at once to Hypatia. "Come here, Mona; come and be introduced."

The dog, a lovely little snow-white creature, raised two melting eyes to Hypatia's face. The girl felt natural kindness towards all animals. She put down one of her shapely hands, and patted the creature on its small head.

"You are highly honoured, my dog," said Miss Weston. "An emancipated woman condescends to touch you. Now, don't you think you two had better have a formal introduction? Miss Hypatia Wentworth—Miss Mona Moumouth Gwyn."

Hypatia smiled. Mona winked her black eyes solemnly, and began to sniff the points of Hypatia's boots.

"She's going to take to you, Miss Wentworth," said Miss Weston, clapping her hands. "Now, my dear, as that is the case, I hope you will allow me to give you a word of advice—you know that is my privilege."

"Why?" asked Hypatia.

"Because I am an old maid—an old maid

always advises her friends. My name is Adeliza Jane Weston. Did you ever hear of anyone called Adeliza Jane before? Don't you think that I am a character? Don't you feel awfully inclined to laugh at me?"

"No," said Hypatia, suddenly, "I don't— believe me, I don't feel inclined to laugh at any woman. I should like to ask you a question, however—why don't you leave me alone?"

"Because you are a stubborn, wrong-

The proud girl turned away as she spoke. In the whole course of her life before, she had never felt so cross nor so rude.

"What a terrible fight we girls have before us," she murmured, as she walked up the steep little street of Glion. "When will women like Miss Weston and men like Hugh Trafford leave us alone?"

That night Hypatia scarcely slept. The moonlight filled her little chamber. She lay

"People sat in the shade."

headed girl. Mr. Trafford thinks you will not try to climb to the top of the Rochers de Naye to-morrow, but I know you better. I am a woman, and I can read the heart of a girl like you; you are determined to go out of a spirit of bravado. Don't you think you will be dreadfully laughed at when you fail? Don't you think you had better give it up?"

"Never," said Hypatia. "Excuse me, Miss Weston, I do not care to discuss this subject. I may be doing wrong, but I am at least the mistress of my own actions."

in bed and looked out at the mountains; they showed black and portentous against the clear-cut, transparent sky. The moon, now and then, cast broad bars of light across the lake; the water shimmered in the cold beams. In spite of herself, Hypatia felt strangely nervous. Her courage failed her a little at this juncture; she laughed, however, at her fears.

"In the morning I shall be all right," she said to herself. "I intend to do nothing rash. The difficult part of the ascent shall be taken with extreme care—oh yes, I shall succeed—and then for triumph. Triumph and the annihilation of such creatures as Adeliza Jane Weston and Hugh Trafford."

At this juncture in her thoughts she fell asleep. At six o'clock she awoke, sprang out of bed, dressed herself in a short but becoming dark blue dress, took a long warm woollen shawl in her hand. and ran downstairs. She had ordered breakfast the night before ; it was waiting for her. She made a hearty meal, secured a basket of sandwiches, into which she popped a little flask of brandy, and then started on her expedition. She was met just outside the hotel by Lucy, who looked bright and resolute.

The two girls were now in the highest spirits. They walked up the steep village street on their way to Caux, their first resting-place. They had just left the village behind them, when Hypatia, looking back, saw the flutter of a red parasol in the distance below, and also the quick flash of a white object which darted through the grass and disappeared.

"That odious woman has come out to watch me," thought the girl. "I have not the least doubt that Hugh Trafford is with her. Well, let them laugh."

"Hypatia, how your eyes flash !" said Lucy.

"Oh, my dear Lucy," cried Hypatia, "what an awful creature the woman who belongs to the past generation is ! How happy we are to have passed that terrible stage in the development of our race."

"Of course we are," said Lucy, in her matter-of-fact tone, "but don't let us talk too much now, Hippy, for even this part of the ascent takes my breath away."

Hypatia said nothing further, and the girls steadily pursued their walk. The winter had been a very severe one, and even at this early stage in their ascent the young adventuresses were met by great blocks of snow. They reached Caux, however, in safety, and sat down just outside the great hotel to rest for half an hour. Here Hypatia began to lecture her friend on mountain-climbing.

"We must know exactly what to do, and what to avoid," she said. "Our object is success. We must place well before us that we have undertaken a difficult task. The ascent of this mountain at this time of year is full of danger. Were that not the fact, my dear Lucy, we neither of us would have travelled all the way from England for the purpose of climbing it. We are prepared, therefore, for danger and difficulty. Being forewarned is forearmed ; let us remember that. Whatever happens we must keep our heads. I have been examining some statistics on mountain-climbing, and I have found, as a rule, a victim is offered up to the Rochers de Naye most seasons."

"Dear me, you don't say so ; I was not aware of that fact," said Lucy, with a little gasp.

"We have no intention of being the victims," said Hypatia, in her measured tones. "I have long ago learned to do nothing rashly. Now if you are rested, shall we go on ? "

"Yes, I suppose I am rested," said Lucy. "I wish you had not said that, Hypatia, about the victims."

"Nonsense. I want you to learn how important is the task we have set ourselves. I want you to put your whole soul into it ; think that this is a sort of tripos which nature has set us ; feel that we are on our honour, so to speak. Now, are you ready ? "

"Yes, Hypatia, of course."

"Well, then, look up, will you ? "

Lucy raised her eyes.

"Do you see that point just above us ? "

"Yes ; it makes me giddy to stare above me so long."

"At that point, Lucy, the danger begins."

"What do you mean ? " asked Lucy.

"Because the snow covers the peaks from that point. Where the snow lies is the real danger."

"To tell the truth, Hippy—oh, I know you'll scorn me, but I do not feel inclined to offer myself up as a victim to the Rochers de Naye."

"I should think not, you silly child ; that would be scandalous. Lucy, you and I will stand on that summit to-night, just up there where the flagstaff is."

"I can scarcely see it," replied Lucy. "The sunshine on the snow dazzles my eyes so dreadfully. But are we not to return to-day ? "

"We certainly will if we can ; but, after all, that is a small matter. When we have reached the flagstaff, we shall have accomplished our purpose and shown the world what resolute, well-trained Girton girls can do. My dear Lucy, there isn't a man, I assure you, not a single *man* at the Victoria Hotel, who would scale the Rochers at this time of year. Oh, I have no patience with those effeminate creatures who proudly call themselves the male sex. Now, if you are rested, we will get under way. Let ' Excelsior ' be our motto."

The girls continued their climb. The day

happened to be a specially hot one, and the sun beat on them with power. Presently they reached the point where Hypatia declared the true danger began.

"Here are the glaciers," she exclaimed.

axe ready, Lucy? We shall have to cut footsteps for ourselves presently."

"Oh, how hot and tired I am," panted poor Lucy; "my back never ached so dreadfully in all my life before. Suppose the snow

"Do you see that point just above us?"

suddenly loosens. Suppose we return ignominiously to the bottom in the arms of an avalanche."

"Suppose we reach the top and shout for victory," replied Hypatia. "Come on; don't waste your breath talking."

"Where? I don't see them," said Lucy.

"They are covered by the snow, but they exist all over the rocks. Have you got your

They climbed up a little higher. At last they reached a point where Hypatia found it necessary to use her axe. Here

Lucy sat down suddenly on a bed of frozen snow.

"I am too hot to go another step," she said. "The fact is, I can't breathe properly in this high altitude."

Hypatia gave her friend a scathing glance.

"Are you not imagining things?" she said, in a severe voice. "Is not your heart perfectly sound?"

"I suppose so, but perhaps it isn't."

"Fudge — take some brandy if you feel faint."

"I will have a little. How dazzling and clear everything looks. Hypatia, I can't forget what you said about a victim — a victim each season."

Hypatia stood very erect; she drew a deep breath.

"This mountain air is magnificent," she said. "It makes one feel quite splendid. Lucy, you silly child," she continued, "we're not going to be victims. We shall conquer this grand, stubborn old rock. Now then, come on."

"I can't for a few minutes."

"I will wait for you for five," said Hypatia, taking out her watch; "then if you don't come, I shall proceed alone."

"Oh, Hippy, you would never dare."

"Should I not? You will see."

Hypatia stood silent. Lucy ate a sandwich in desperation; then she sipped some brandy and water, then she rubbed her dazzled eyes.

"The five minutes are up. Come on," cried Hypatia.

"I——" said Lucy, not beginning to stir —"oh, Hippy, you are so brave. I feel I am not a bit like you—I never was, you know. Do you greatly mind if I wait for you here?"

"Not a bit, if you are frightened. I shall then have to share the honour with no one."

"Oh, I am so sorry. I hope you don't think me shabby."

"Not a scrap; you can't help your nerves.

I am blessed with nerves of iron, so I intend to go on."

"I will wait for you here until you come back, Hippy; but, oh, do be prudent."

"Of course I will; but don't stay longer than you care to. When I reach the top, I may rest for an hour or two. The hotel is

"She had to lean heavily on her alpenstock."

shut, of course, but I can get some sort of shelter in the porch."

"Of course you will come back to-day?"

"If I can; but if I am not with you in three hours, you had better go back, Lucy. I shall be all right in any case; now good-bye."

"Good-bye," said Lucy, in a faint voice. "Oh, I know you think me shabby."

Hypatia made no reply to this; she continued her ascent.

She soon saw that it was necessary for her to cut many steps for herself on the steep surface of the glistening snow. The work was hard— far harder than she had anticipated; she crept up step by step very carefully. Her back ached, her legs ached, her head felt dizzy; she had a tired, numbed sense in the back of her neck. Her courage, however, never deserted her. She took each upward step with a sense of rejoicing. She knew, however, by certain sensations that she must not venture to look down; there was nothing for it now but to go on—to go on at any cost. The sun beat more and more fiercely upon her head. The snow began to assume the appearance of millions of sparkling diamonds; it seemed to be full of colour; it shone with rose and amethyst tints. The clear air from the mountain kissed Hypatia's hot cheeks, the icy salute was stimulating and refreshing. She struggled and panted; her breath came short and thick. Once or twice she had to lean heavily on her alpenstock, overpowered by a sudden sense of vertigo. She knew, however, that she was gaining ground. There was one more boulder to pass, and then the victory would be hers. Five minutes later she had flung herself down on the summit of the Rochers, faint, sick, and giddy, but victorious. She was all alone on the topmost solitary peak, but she had won the day.

A thousand feet below, Lucy waited for her friend. She waited exactly three hours by her watch. During that time her body became chilled to the bone, and all her courage seemed to ooze out at her feet. Alone, quite alone, Lucy was without much moral stamina. Nothing was further from her wishes than to desert Hypatia, but after shouting in vain several times, she began to regard it in the light of a serious duty to hurry back to Glion as fast as possible. She tottered to her half-frozen legs.

"Another quarter of an hour, and I should be chilled to death," she thought.

She began cautiously and with many terrified qualms to descend the mountain. The dangerous part was quickly got over, and then Lucy began to run.

Meanwhile Hypatia was alone. There was something grand in being alone with nature. A great calm—an infinite and vast silence surrounded her. For the first half-hour she rejoiced at the thought of being all by herself in this vast solitude; she seemed to feel the strong arms of mother nature supporting her. After a time, however, these moments of ecstasy passed; she began to think mother nature's arms a little cold, the solitude a little awful, and her own sensations the reverse of comfortable.

She had left Glion in the morning at a comfortable temperature of a little under sixty; at the top of the Rochers de Naye, however, it was something nearer ten. At ten degrees Fahrenheit one is soon bitten by the icy breath of Cold. Hypatia's teeth chattered, her lips turned blue, her eyes watered, her head was giddy. She staggered to her feet. If she did not intend to spend the night on the peak, she must immediately begin to descend. With resolute steps, she approached the edge of her lofty eminence. The moment she did so, however, she uttered a little cry; she found to her horror that she dared not look down the giddy pass—the mere thought even made her head reel. She was also overpowered by a sensation which puzzled her not a little. The height which she had scaled was between six and seven thousand feet above the sea level. Hypatia did not know that mountain sickness assailed anyone at this altitude; there was no doubt, however, that she felt sick; sick, giddy, wretched, unnerved; she pressed her hands to her ears, they were deaf; she shouted, but could scarcely hear her own voice; there were singing noises in her head, however, which made the solitude no longer solitary; the noises seemed to mock at her, and laugh at her. She felt as if thousands of little sprites had taken possession of her and were turning her and her grand feat into ridicule. Her position was certainly the reverse of comfortable.

Whatever faults Hypatia Wentworth possessed, however, she was certainly not lacking in pluck. She repented now of the thing she had done; she saw that she was in danger of perishing of cold; but she had no idea of parting with her life without a hard struggle. It would not be to the credit of Girton that one of its undergraduates should be found frozen on the top of the Rochers de Naye; it would be very much to the fame of Alma Mater if a child of hers conquered circumstances under such dangerous conditions. Hypatia walked about to keep her blood in circulation. She presently reached the forsaken hotel, and with icy fingers felt some of the lower windows, to see if by any chance she could open them, and so get into shelter. They were all fastened, however—the place was absolutely deserted. The great hotel looked at this moment like a huge tomb. There was a porch, however, and Hypatia crept into it, and sat down. She wrapped the shawl which she had taken with her closely round her, sipped some brandy from her flask, and looked straight ahead of her at the glorious sunset. The sunset was indeed magnificent. She was surrounded by a chain of snow-capped mountains. When the dying sun touched them, they assumed one by one an unearthly and spiritual appearance. Amethyst, gold, rose, violet, blood-red, mingled with their virgin snow; each moment their colours changed; they looked like transparent temples decked with sparkling jewels. Yes, it was worth a great deal to see such a sight, to be so close to the gates of heaven itself; nevertheless poor Hypatia shut her eyes wearily. She had come to a moment in her life when even the beauties of nature ceased to cheer her.

Hugh Trafford was enjoying tea on one of the terraces at the Victoria Hotel, when

' To see if by any chance she could open them.'

Lucy Johnson rushed suddenly into his presence.

"Are you Mr. Trafford?" she asked.

She was panting and eager; her ugly dress was in much disorder; she had taken off her glasses; her face looked wild.

"That is my name," replied Trafford, in a somewhat lazy voice. He was enjoying his

tea, and was not particularly pleased at being interrupted.

"Will you please come up to the top of the Rochers de Naye?" panted Lucy. "Hypatia is there all alone."

"Good heavens, what do you mean?" said Trafford, springing to his feet.

Miss Weston, who was sitting near, also rose to hers. Mona, the white Pomeranian, gave a bark of disapproval. Trafford's face turned white.

"You must be mistaken," he said. "What are you talking about?"

"It is all perfectly true," said Lucy; "we started to make the climb this morning. I had not the courage to go to the top, but Hypatia would go on; she is there now. I don't think she can come back. I shouted to her, and she made no answer; oh, what is the matter?"

"Let me pass," said Trafford, abruptly.

He walked away with quick strides. He was a big, square-built man, with a remarkably resolute appearance. In less than ten minutes' time he was driving up to Caux with a couple of guides. They followed the road as far as they could; they then left the trap behind and began the ascent. The night was falling rapidly; soon it would be dark.

"Hurry; find the shortest way," said Trafford.

He looked like a man of iron. The guides hesitated and remonstrated; they said they dared not go on.

"You must," said Trafford; "you will for gold. I will give you double your usual fees. Come on, come quickly; we must get to the top before dark."

He looked stern and quiet, but his heart was beating fiercely. He was seeing a mental picture of Hypatia all the way; her lovely but defiant eyes were looking into his; their expression seemed to change; she seemed to implore him; he panted and climbed, and went faster and faster.

Hypatia was unconscious when they found her; she was dreaming peacefully as those do who die of cold. She thought that she was back with her mother, that she had won her classical tripos, and that the laurel wreath of renown was round her brow. Trafford and the guides opened the hotel, and soon had a great fire blazing, and after some hours of patient toil, the Girton undergraduate was brought back to life. When she opened her eyes, Trafford was bending over her.

"Where am I?" she asked, in astonishment.

"On the top of the Rochers de Naye," he replied.

"And you?" she asked.

"I came to bring you back," he replied. "Now lie still and sip this hot coffee."

He held it to her lips. She felt womanly and comforted. It did not strike her that the strong arms which supported her were effeminate. When she grew better and was seated by the fire, she suddenly touched Trafford's sleeve.

"I made a mistake this morning," she said. "Will you forgive me?"

"For what?" he asked.

"For my presumption. You nearly lost your life bringing me back to common sense, did you not?"

"Never mind *if* I have done so, Hypatia," he replied.

There was something in his tone which made her blush and look down.

"Hypatia was unconscious when they found her."

LOVE, COURTSHIP, AND MARRIAGE.

By Annie S. Swan.

A WEARY MOTHER is exercised, as so many are, over the problem of how to make the income meet expenditure and leave a margin. She asks a great many questions, one, what I would consider a fair amount to be spent on clothing for herself and two children. Were I in her place I should try to make £20 or £25 cover it. This can easily be done if she buys material and has her own dress made at home. I do not think she would save anything by having the children's things made indoors, unless of course she can do them herself. Ready-made garments for little ones can be purchased so cheaply and are so dainty that it does not pay any one to sit and make them. I should also cut off the expenditure for washing by getting a girl up from the country who would undertake it, except perhaps bed linen, which does not cost much to go out. It is still possible to get country girls who are not afraid of the wash tub. I have many friends who get all washing done at home even in London. Does she buy household stores such as flour, sugar, soap, and dry goods of every description in quantities—a good deal is saved in this way, even on a bag of potatoes sixpence or a shilling can be saved. Economy in cooking also helps. Buy the best quality of food always, nothing else will pay; but if one understands the making of wholesome soups, inexpensive puddings, etc., the daily menu need never be costly. I can scarcely enter on this wide subject here. I sometimes say I shall write a little handbook on household management one day, when other matters press less heavily.

* * *

PARIAH writes with some bitterness about the loneliness of educated and refined girls who like "Another Reader," have absolutely no opportunity of meeting on a friendly and equal platform, men who might either be agreeable acquaintances or something nearer. I had no idea that so much of this isolation existed. Listen to "Pariah's" graphic account of her environment and opportunities.

"I am also that social 'Pariah,' a Dissenter, and belong to a poor dissenting church, the male society of which consists entirely of dockyard labourers, mechanics and petty tradesmen. They are honest, decent, but uneducated men: and their tastes, ideas, and habits are such that anything like social intercourse between us would be only uncomfortable, unequal, and strained. Other opportunities for meeting, on equal terms, men who would be considered to belong to my own class, I have absolutely none. Happily for me I do not consider that marriage is the *raison d'être* of a woman's life, or I should be in a sorry plight. I have my own work to do, and have no desire to marry. I do, however, feel rather sore at times to think that I never have the chance to exchange an idea with men of congenial tastes and ways, simply because I worship God in an unfashionable manner. At any rate, we cannot be said to go to church to look for husbands."

* * *

CONSUELO also writes much in the same strain, though from a wider point of view. She says, "I am a foreigner myself, and though circumstances have obliged me to live in this country for some time, I cannot say I care for the social life here. It is too stiff and formal for any sort of friendliness or intercourse to grow out of a few meetings between men and women. I have often wished for some one to love me, but do not know any young man well enough to marry him. How many are obliged to go through life unloved and unloving!"

"Consuelo" writes a great deal more to the same purpose. I sympathise with her, but beyond printing her letter, I fear I cannot help her in any way.

* * *

I cannot see that A LONELY LASSIE is bound to remain with her aunt. Having given her promise to her lover, I consider her bound to fulfil it, unless some obligations much more binding and sacred than that mentioned in her letter should arise. At the same time, I respect the fine feeling which causes her to hesitate. The majority of people are so extremely selfish that it is a great pleasure to come across one who will give the feelings and claims of others so much consideration. I hope to hear from her again.

* * *

HERZLIEBCHEN seems to be doing pretty well with her limited income. The only suggestion I can make is that she should, if she does not already do so, buy her household stores in quantities, as they are cheaper and often better. Every housewife knows that soap, for instance, bought in quantities and cut up in squares, by becoming hardened, lasts much longer in use. Does she thoroughly understand how to *buy*, which is as important as how to use. A great deal can be saved by judicious choice of what is most nourishing, as well as what will go furthest. The other matter is too purely medical for me to advise upon. I am inclined to think that in her case the money spent on medical advice, though she grudges it now, might save her something in the end.

* * *

"L. L. C." is perplexed, as so many are, over their obligations to kindred. In her case, I think it might be well if they could arrange to give the half of the sum named. He is certainly responsible in part; and though the sum would not be very large the certainty of it would make it valuable. It is a duty which will never be regretted.

* * *

A SALT writes a truly delightful letter, too long, unfortunately, for publication. I give as much of it as I conveniently can. I wish his example could be followed by all the troubled ones who write. "Ours has been a most happy life, begun with much fear and trembling, for I was a Dissenter, the young lady Church of England, and we talked the matter over seriously, and decided that no hard and fast line should be drawn, and soon after we were married the affair resolved itself, for my wife, who had been an earnest seeker after truth, found that peace which she had long sought, and whenever she wished to go to church I accompanied her. She used also to take wine, I did not. I never asked her to abstain, I felt she would, she did. You will guess that she was not an ordinary young lady. I thought so then, I think so still. We have always had one purse, an allowance never occurred to either of us, it has always been in all things, 'Trust me all in all' or not at all,' and I have gone over the boundary line of fifty, my wife is four years younger, and to-day she is 'my sweetheart, my wife,' and she tells me that I am still her king among men. I don't see the force of being in love with one and keeping the knowledge all to myself, do you ? I often think of the question of allowing so much a week for this and that, but we couldn't manage in that way, there are so many calls upon our purse besides the family. I suppose we shall never be rich. I received the other day a letter from my brother, he said, 'If I have to go to the workhouse by-and-by, it seems to me it will be a comfort to feel that I have helped dry tears, fed the hungry, clothed the naked, and when I can t do this, I don't want to live.' So the question of one purse or two doesn't go for much, do you think ?"

* * *

If ESSIE is satisfied that the man's repentance is real, and thinks she will be able to give him the respect she would wish to feel for her husband, let her marry him by all means. But her letter does not fill me with joy, or even with hope ; and were she a friend of mine, I should counsel a year's probation at least. It is not too much when the weal or woe of a life depends on it.

* * *

This hesitation on the part of those who fancy themselves in love is the greatest of all mysteries to me. I should advise EARTHWORM, if it is at all possible, to keep entirely out of the lady's way for several months, and see how he feels. As he has not committed himself by word or by any special attention, this course can be taken in all fairness. He might then be able to come to a decision regarding his own state of mind. I could wish that he were less sure of her, or that another suitor would come on the scene. This would probably open his eyes. I should like to hear from him again.

* * *

WINIFRED is quite right, it is a very great risk indeed to marry a man you have seen only half-a-dozen times. Nothing on earth would induce me to do it. It is possible, of course, that the venture might turn out all right, but will " Winifred " please consider what a very serious step matrimony is for a woman. It practically makes or mars her whole life. That she is sick of her present mode of life, I can very well believe. It does not appear to be very congenial,

but its redeeming feature is that she can leave it any day. Matrimony is rather different, it is not so easy to rush out of it, as it is to get in. Therefore, " Winifred," consider well.

* * *

The letter of MARRIAGE A FAILURE is very sad reading. There appear to be so many faults on all sides, so little of the spirit of forbearance that it seems a hopeless business. No man, having married a wife, ought to put and keep her in the background, while his mother has his first consideration. No woman will stand it, nor is she required to. Further, she is entitled to a house of her own, undoubtedly. I feel very sorry for her, but her letter is so bitter in tone that I fear exaggeration. As she is presently living with her own parents, they, and not I, are the persons to advise. The husband's letter appears to me very reasonable.

* * *

Does " L. W." know what she wants ? Has she laid her reasonable wishes before her husband, in order that a clear understanding may be arrived at ? At present the chaos seems to be appalling, and my heart aches for the little children who are thus tossed about, deprived of their rightful heritage—a home.

* * *

I have always advocated early marriages, but by that I do not mean that boys and girls in their teens are to incur the responsibilities of the dual life. I do not think five-and-twenty is too young for a man if he has some common-sense and a moderate amount of means. The question of means is what is troubling MIGNON. One hundred and fifty pounds a year is certainly not a large income, but it can be made to do, if the wife is not afraid to put her hand to the plough. For the first year at least she might do without a servant, and get occasional help from outside. I have been through it all, and I know that this is the first step towards success in such a venture. In a newly furnished house everything is fresh and easily kept, so that unless " Mignon " be afflicted with the silly but common pride which will not let her answer her own door bell and polish her own kitchen stove, she can do all the work without being unduly oppressed. But she must have a method, a day for everything, as well as a place. But there, this answer is already too long.

* * *

Nine years is a long time, and I don't wonder that GEORGINA feels a little nervous at the prospect of going so far as Western Australia to marry the lover of her youth. I suppose it is impossible for him to come home ? I hope for " Georgina's " sake all will be well, and that her first look into her sweetheart's honest eyes will dispel her natural fears. Far from blaming or marvelling, I sympathise with her very much.

* * *

OPPET'S question is so very odd that I don't know how to answer it. She might try a glass of hot milk last thing at night, and go to bed with the fixed resolve to lie still and quiet. I am glad she is otherwise so happy.

Life and Work at Home.

OVER THE TEACUPS.

By Annie S. Swan.

AS I write this I am still privileged to be enjoying the quiet rest by the sea, though my return to the usual routine of town life is within very measurable distance. A short period of rest, if accompanied by an entire change of scene and environment, is a wonderful quickener of one's energies, a restoration in the best sense of the word. The work which had grown to be something of a burden becomes once more a joy, thus showing that the period of retirement has fulfilled its purpose. I would that such retirement were possible to very many more busy workers. I am amazed that so many, whom experience might have taught, persist in making such toil of the time which ought to be devoted to rest. They tear about from place to place trying to see as many new things as possible, spend half their days in stuffy railway carriages and the other half in rushing about at lightning speed. It is fatiguing even to look at them. Yet they seem to convince themselves of their own enjoyment, though when they get home they do wonder at times why their holiday has done

them so little physical good. My idea and aim in holiday-making is something far different. For those upon whom the stress and strain of life presses so heavily have need to consider how they are to extract the maximum benefit from the few weeks they are spared from the work which no other hand can do so well. To me this little quiet village, which grows more enchanting to us year by year, seems to offer, does offer indeed, all we want in the way of holiday-making. There are enough of people about to redeem it from absolute dulness, but there is no fashion, except what is simple and easily attained; the air is fresh and bracing, and the golden sands—a paradise for the little ones, who are never in any manner of doubt as to what they consider the *beau ideal* of a summer resort. It is a great temptation to me at this present moment to set down some quaint remarks of a certain three-year-old in whom I have a special interest, but I must refrain. But what a fresh and delightful fount of almost living water is the mind of a child. To be able to spend hours in a child's company, provided one has that patience and sympathy and love needful to such communion—what an education it is! What a lesson in simplicity, in honesty, in faith! It makes us, whom the world and the things that are in the world have somewhat disillusioned, obtain a glimpse of a serener clime, where all things are lovely and of good report. Of all the good gifts Heaven so lavishly bestows on men and women both, the child is incomparably the greatest, the most precious. But rich and tempting as is my theme, I must not linger while this mute but eloquent pile of letters lies at my elbow.

* * *

I can't think of any suggestion which would be of practical value to " J. S." She wishes to augment her income without leaving home, or taking paying guests, or doing anything that would make an appreciable difference to her present mode of life. The things she suggests, such as doing plain or fancy work, are no good so far as money-making is concerned. There are thousands in the field. The "paying guest" indeed seems to me to be the only way out of the difficulty, especially as she lives in such a healthy and desirable place.

* * *

A WOMAN ABROAD writes a very pleasant letter from the south, where she is an English governess. She says :

" How I often wish that every one in a similar position were as happy as I am. Until I came here I had never left my happy home except for a term or two at school. Naturally I felt nervous, but my fears were soon dispersed. Everybody is so kind, I could not but be happy. The heat is very great here, even in the hills where we go in summer."

I hope she will forgive me making this extract. I was tempted, because it is so rare to hear of a being perfectly contented with her lot. Her other question must be directed to the health department, which is not mine.

* * *

" A. D." writes from Birmingham on the subject of " lady servants."

" If ladies would only take up domestic work as a means of livelihood, it would be a very natural employment, as most women have to be their own servants on occasion, and often regularly when money is scarce. Lady helps are often in little better positions than servants, except for the name ; and a lady servant could still be called so—or better still bring the name of servant into honour again, as nurses have. There was a time when a lady would not have become a hospital nurse, and though the same now applies to servants, why should the experiment not be tried ? In point of fact a hospital nurse has far more objectionable and dirtier work than any domestic. Of course there are details of dress, references, accommodation, etc., to be considered, but a lady would remember that she is employing a lady and treat her accordingly. The lady engaged, being thus con-

sidered, would study the necessity for simple dress in return. The hospital nurse's dress is very becoming, something of the same kind would answer admirably."

The theory is excellent, and, if it could be carried successfully into practice, would bring about the reform for which there appears to be such great need. I have not suffered much misery through servants myself, having, with some slight exceptions, been favoured by having sensible, kind and willing women in my house, but the universal outcry being for some such reform, the need is evidently great. It is undoubtedly the case that if gentlewomen in reduced circumstances could be induced to take such situations, and to fill them conscientiously—which means shirking no part of the duty involved, the domestic sky would be largely cleared of its clouds. But how many of us would always remember that we have a lady in our employment. I myself think that the ordinary servant, though she may be humbly born, is quite as much entitled to consideration as the lady help. Her feelings are as keen, sometimes more so. It is this lack of consideration on both sides, a false idea of relative positions, in fact, coupled with a good deal of incompetence also on both sides, which is at the bottom of the evil that undoubtedly exists. I think the lady servant might be successful in small households where only one is required ; in larger establishments I fear the complications likely to arise would add one more to the housekeeper's goodly pack of worries. What do my readers think ?

* * *

VIOLET sympathises with " K. E." in being an only child, but she writes very sensibly. " I have a dear mother and happy home, a few relatives and many friends, still our real home circle seems so small compared with some families ! My great comfort is, I do not think any one could fill my place or do my work, or God would not have placed me here. I think if we all thought of that more it would make us feel proud and thankful that God saw we were able to fill worthily the little corner wherein He has placed us. I think that by making others happy around us our own lives will be enriched, and even as ' only children ' our lives will not be lonely."

* * *

LITTLE DOT, in the same position, is not quite so happy and contented. " It is dreadfully lonely sometimes, as my friends are married and gone away, and I have always been brought up with grown people. I do not think I make friends easily. I have my work, for I teach music, piano, violin, and 'cello, and when I am busy have no time to be lonely, but the holidays are dreadful. My dear mother is wrapped up in me, all her thoughts are for me, and if I am with her she does not want any one else ; but of course one does want a companion who can enter into one's thoughts, read the same books, and enjoy the same recreations. This lovely summer weather one would like to be out of doors a great deal, but I do not go because I have no one to go with."

Shall I tell "Little Dot" that though my cup is full of blessing she has one possession which I envy her, and which perhaps one day, when bereft, she may envy another. She can still say "mother"—sure of a response. The word is only a memory to me, graven deep on my heart, until the day when, please God, this great yearning will be satisfied "within the veil."

* * *

BRITOMART has a difficult part to fill, and so far as I can judge she is filling it well. It is always a serious and trying thing to witness family quarrels and steer clear of them. There appear to be faults on all sides. The extreme selfishness and pigheadedness of the elder members of the family appear to suggest some deplorable error in their upbringing. Such absolute lack of self-control can only be the outcome of indulgence. Go on as you are doing. It is the quiet life that speaks, the silent influence which is felt most.

* * *

I know of a little place on the Pembroke coast that would suit you. It is called Little Haven, and is distant a few miles from Haverfordwest. I was once there in the long ago, and have sweet memories of it. Absolute freedom and rest you could be sure of. It is primitive, old-world, and undisturbed. Try it.

* * *

I agree with TIRED-OUT that in many cases the summer outing is not a rest to the house-mother, but the reverse. She finds herself crowded with a big family into limited space, robbed of many of her home resources, and far from the facilities which give ease to city housekeeping. Consequently the strain upon her is even greater than usual. We have had a good many revolting daughters lately; suppose we have a few revolting mothers for a change, rebelling justifiably against the present mode of things, which ordains that she shall not rest this side of the grave. I have always held and tried to advocate in holiday time, the idea that the house-mother should resign the seals of her office for the time being. Let take them who will, she ought to be relieved. But nobody seems to think it is of any consequence, and so we keep on having mothers and wives who are over-tired always, why? because their work is never done. This applies equally to those who work with their own hands, and those who only guide the work of others. The strain and pressure of thought is the same. Who will start an association for the relief of tired mothers? Are they of less importance than birds and horses and dogs, who have all societies for their special protection and aid?"

* * *

I have no patience with invertebrate persons like JOE. Whatever my faults, I always know my own mind—what I want to do—and I do it. It is a great help in the battle of life. "Joe" can't make up his mind whether he ought to remain in his present employment, where his prospects appear to be fairly good. He has got himself into a grumbling state of mind, but I would remind him that in these days of keen competition it is easier to give up one situation than to obtain another one. I think, were I in his place, I should suffer present ills, which are more or less imaginary, than fly to others that he knows not of.

* * *

Yes, LITHOS, it is a great mystery why so many good men have shiftless and ne'er-do-well sons. Those who study heredity and kindred subjects will tell you that it is a wild strain in the blood of some fiery ancestor which has to come out. It really seems the only feasible explanation. Much can be done by up-bringing, of course, still it would appear to be sometimes insufficient to keep that objectionable strain in check. Parentage is indeed at times but a fearful and precarious joy.

* * *

The Caledonian Christian Club appears to be what you require. Before you send your boy away to London, write to the Secretary, 46, Tavistock Square, W.C., and you will get all the information you want. It is a link between this great city and the country villages of Scotland. I speak with some personal knowledge of its good work.

* * *

Youth appears to me to be the most precious of all gifts. Its peculiar preciousness is embodied in the fact that it can only be once possessed, never again, though often sighed for. Therefore it fills me with a little sad amusement, if I may use such a paradoxical expression, when I hear anyone bemoaning extreme youth. GERALDINE says everyone puts upon her because she is young. Never mind, you have the consolation that very soon, perhaps sooner than you will like, you can, from your superior height, put upon other people because *they* are young. Every dog has its day—meanwhile yours is passing, I should say, though you may think it is to come.

* * *

The nursing profession is so sadly overcrowded like most others, that it is extremely difficult to obtain admission to any hospital. Private nursing is very profitable, though many women dislike it because it is quiet and monotonous. There is a great deal of "go" in hospital life, and a certain excitement which is fascinating. But of course it is very wearing. Most occupations however, if heartily engaged in, take a good deal out of the worker. It is the earnest and the absorbed who succeed.

* * *

I am sorry to be obliged to repeat here that I cannot undertake to read the MS. of my readers and give advice thereon. Some day, if the editor will allow me, I should like to write a little paper on "How best to succeed in the literary life." Till then I hope my readers will forgive me if I decline to add this serious burden to an already over-crowded life.

54

"G. W." has returned from a visit to Palestine. She says: "We have visited the City of the Great King; our feet have stood within the gates of Jerusalem. The Church of the Holy Sepulchre was interesting, but as we believe Jesus was buried without the walls, the spot was not sacred to us. The Jews' wailing place was very solemn and touching. Part of the wall is built from the temple of Solomon. Beside this high wall men and women stand sobbing and wringing their hands for the desolation of their beloved land. With sacred awe we visited the Garden of Gethsemane; the old olive trees there had a sweet charm for us, and we could have wished to linger and meditate on the great love of a suffering Redeemer."

* * *

If choice were mine, I should live in the country, not in a rural suburb or a country town, but in the green heart of the hills or by the sea, where life must of necessity be a simpler, purer, and holier thing. But since choice is not always left to us, it behoves us to try and make the most of such things as we have, if we would live usefully, and bless others as well as ourselves. So I think COUNTRY MOUSE should cease her moaning over what cannot at present be hers, and try and find in her town life some grains of compensation. And we who have known both find many.

* * *

If any of my kind readers in the country have the power and the heart to send a few flowers occasionally to brighten the homes of working women and girls in London, they will be gratefully received and acknowledged by an earnest worker among them at 35, High Street, Battersea, London.

DRESS AND FASHION.

The great Worth was responsible for the quick fluctuations of fashions—past and present. To meet the demands of perpetual novelty, the manufacturers have been compelled to flood the market with cheap materials, and the good old silks and satins that "stood alone" will soon become things of the past.

* * *

Our dressmakers' bills have increased tenfold, because whereas the best black silk gown did duty for at least a year at functions of importance, we must now have quite a variety of costumes. The wardrobe of the average woman calls for a tailor-made dress or two. A cycling garb, what with dresses for the seaside, tennis, small dances, theatres, dinners, and balls, added to innumerable blouses, shirts, and theatre jackets and "fronts," constitutes a wardrobe the magnitude of which is very expensive.

* * *

Many girls sensibly learn the dressmaker's art themselves. The cheapness of materials, and the impossibility of finding good dressmakers who are willing to make at moderate prices, has made this an imperative necessity. Under those circumstances the yearly allowance can be regulated with proper economy. A good tailor-made dress (a genuine one) once a year, an evening dress from a competent dressmaker, and a model blouse are all that really require a great outlay. The rest can be made at home. A bicycling dress could be purchased one year in lieu of the tailor costume, as it will also serve as a travelling dress. Where there are sisters or a mother and daughter, the fitting becomes an easy matter, for unless one has a block made on one's own measurements, it is not always easy to fit oneself. Proficiency even in this matter is attainable, however, and the fingers soon acquire a knowledge similar to that of the eyes, for they become sensitive to every crease and wrinkle by the sense of touch.

We are now in possession of a new skirt more graceful and far more practical than those we have been wearing hitherto. It fits tightly over the hips, and all the fulness is at the back; it no longer "flares" in unequal "godets" at the front and sides. The sleeves are still on the diminishing scale; but here I must place a word of warning for thin women with sharp elbows. It is quite obvious that the fulness at the shoulder, either in a full puff or in two or three flounces, gives a length of scraggy arm which should be covered by a rucked or gathered sleeve, and in no case, save that of a very plump arm, can the plain, tight sleeve be adopted.

* * *

The high Empire belts of draped silk or ribbon are still very fashionable and much worn with Zouaves, but this style is for slender and long figures. Plump, short-waisted women can still make the Eton or Zouave becoming if worn sufficiently long and with pointed fronts. The back is often made to fit tight with a full basque.

* * *

We never seem to be able to get our sacque coats to reach the French stage of perfection. I have seen some ideal ones with the trimming forming seams, which outline or indicate the figure in the most becoming way imaginable. They were made of the new putty-coloured cloth, embroidered by hand with a lovely pattern of tiny cut jet beads. For smart winter dresses, the greatest novelty will be the Zouave fronts or entire bodices of fur, beautified with "incrustations" of lace medallions or beaded passementerie. A quantity of fur will be used, all more or less mixed with guipure, ochre lace ribbons, or beaded passementerie. The fur capes have enormous Medici collars, or others equally large, cut in square battlements. An effort is being made to dethrone the useful *beastie* that was wont to curl its tail, paws, and head round our neck, but like the blouse, they are likely to

The jam-pot hat crowns are more worn than ever; they are not, however, universally becoming. Ribbons are much used, and new bows have arisen on the horizon of fashion. The Japanese bow is very large, and sprawls across a bodice, almost covering the bust. Others are of more reasonable proportions, and affect the butterfly shape. Ribbons appear again in the pointed and dressy belts, sashes with long ends, and all the ruching that is so widely used.

* * *

Boléros are made entirely of the new ochre or saffron-tinted guipure, and very dainty they look worn over blouses of accordion or crinkled mousseline de soie. Russian belts are in white kid, set with turquoise and other precious stones, or in flexible gold ribbons with clasps of burnished silver or platinum. Japanese patterns are seen on velveteen or Pyrenean flannels destined for tea-gowns. Chenille embroidery on tulle mixed with tinsel or spangles is to be worn on our winter dresses.

* * *

The newest contrasts of colour are geranium pink on saffron, pale green

No. 1.

die hard if ever they lose their hold on popular favour. Riding hats and the eternal boat-shaped things are still to be seen, but they will gradually disappear in favour of some new models that I am pledged not to reveal until next month.

* * *

The latest ruinous fad is lace with appliqué flowers made out of humming-birds' feathers. We are despoiling the poor birds for our imaginary needs to such an extent that one wonders where all the plumage comes from. Wings bristle on all the hats, and a broom of paradise plumes springing from a jewelled ornament like the Shah's aigrette is considered the smartest possible trimming for a hat. Black and white mixtures are deservedly liked, and the prettiest of Paris model gowns was a Pekin silk with rather deep black satin stripes on a white ground, made with a new sleeve tucked lengthwise and finishing in a small puff close to the shoulder. The blouse worn with this was composed of narrow white ribbon and ochre lace insertion, over which was a Zouave of dead white Peau de Soie caught in the centre by fancy buttons held by tiny gold chains. The Zouave had revers of black velvet, edged with ochre lace on a bias fold of white silk. The belt of black ribbon velvet fastened in a large bow which reached half way up the chemisette. The accompanying hat was of white felt, trimmed with black velvet and black and white plumes.

No. 2.

No. 3.

of guipure made to mould the hips, and from this an accordion-pleated skirt of mousseline de soie. A great deal of crêpe de chine will be seen for evening wear, as it is admirable for draping on skirts, and, indeed, for all draped effects. Appliqué or incrustations of lace, with the material cut away at the back, are also a very dainty if expensive ornament for smart evening dresses. Skirts will no longer be lined, but they will have separate under-skirts of silk, which is a point worthy of note. Ruches of ribbon edged with bébé ribbon velvet, lace, feathers, or frayed silk and lace, are worn as collarettes. Some are made into flower-like points, edged with spangles; they are warmer in reality than the late lamented *beastie*, which never looked well unless of the very best fur. The long ends of ribbon or silk worn on sash ends should not be cut out or frayed, but they can be edged with fringe, or with a small bias fold of silk and a tiny kilting of mousseline de soie,

on blue and white, red (a fashionable colour) on white or black, rose pink on grey, turquoise or gold on putty colour. Three tints are often blended, such as mauve, violet, and pink ; pale pink, rose pink, and pale blue.

* * *

A detail I must not omit to mention is the short sleevelet or flounce which forms part of boléros and zouaves.

* * *

One of the prettiest fashions of the season is the useful guimpe or chemisette, which fills a square at the neck like a yoke made of velvet, lace, or chiffon, according to the different purposes it is intended for. All of these could be made for a black silk dress, and they would give quite a variety of transformations if chosen in different colours. Now that the skirts are deprived of steels, and have a minimum of stiffening, great attention must be directed to the petticoats. The newest have a piece of whalebone sewn lengthwise down the back breadth, and are fastened at the sides. Others have three lengthwise bands of horsehair. Many skirts are trimmed from the waist with sharp V's of lace or coloured silk, the narrow point being downward and the wider portion at the waist. Much of the trimmings are put on in this way.

* * *

The evening dresses have an entire upper part

No. 4.

or narrow Valenciennes. If glacé silk is used, the ends can be entirely pinked all round; these long ends are quite permissible at the back when a high-draped belt is worn; they are graceful, and give length to the figure. Ribbon should be used for young girls, silk for matrons. Flounces and ruches of ribbon are certain as trimmings for the winter skirts.

* * *

In tailor-made costumes we note an absolute flatness in the coat sleeve, and the best houses are making the back guiltless of flutes. Velvet collars and polished steel buttons will be used. Seams are sewn with double rows of stitching, and pencilled stripe cloths with very faint lines are very smart. Skirts are not worn quite so short, and even when unlined still show a *frou-frou* of coloured silk at the foot.

* * *

Green seems to be the favourite colour with claret and mulberry. In the light shades petunia, a blending of pink and mauve, and the old "celestial" or silver blue. Black silk gauze and cream Valenciennes still make black dresses delightful, and are also used on coloured silks. Bébé velvet ribbons, rows of small buttons and tiny cord, and narrow tinsel ribbons mixed with green or red, are amongst the new colouring.

* * *

There is a change in hair-dressing, fringes

No. 6.

No. 5.

and curls being rather tabooed. The hair is now dressed in broad waves and lightly raised over the forehead; in fact, there is talk of plaits coming in for the chignon; the 1830 coiffure shows a very wide and elaborate plait at the summit of the head. Stocks as collars are the latest eccentricity; they can be worn headed by a narrow band of linen or a ruching of lace. Velvet fuchsias, nasturtiums, and geraniums are the flowers of the moment.

* * *

DESCRIPTIONS OF FASHION DRAWINGS.

No. 1.—A becoming mantle for a matron, or elderly lady, is here shown. The under cape which is circular in shape, is made in black satin, with long straps of jet widening out from neck to hem. The upper cape in black velvet, is pointed both at the back and front, and a thick ruche of satin or lace is placed round its edge. The collar is cut all in one with the small shoulder cape in Medicis form, and fastens beneath a large bow of spotted net with long lace-edged ends.

No. 2.—Promenade or visiting dress in black wool canvas over green silk. A fitting bodice, with a short full basque, rather cut away from the front; with graduated revers of green and white silk, fastened back with tabs of green satin. These have bright buttons arranged in threes on them. Full godet skirt with ruffle at edge, lined with green silk.

No. 3.—This charming bodice for evening wear, somewhat in Zouave shape, is made in satin and covered with fine point lace. The sleeves are quite new in design, looped up on to the shoulder, and showing a pretty soft flounce of chiffon confined to the arm by a band of lace edged with jet, like the edging shown on the bodice. The vest is also in chiffon, with a deep corselet band around the waist in satin.

No. 4.—A very neat and yet stylish coat and skirt is next illustrated. It is fashioned in a bright, warm, brown-faced cloth. The coat is of moderate length, and can either be worn closed or open, as shown in the sketch. The vest and large bow are made in soft pink silk, the latter edged with lace. The walking skirt is rather short, with the fulness kept mainly to the back.

No. 5.—A pretty blouse for visiting, or for home wear, in green silk, with jet bretelles edged with narrow cream lace. Black satin waist band with silver buckle.

No. 6.—For a schoolgirl's dress the accompanying design will be found very useful and suitable. It is plainly made in dark green cloth, and trimmed with bands of red cloth, edged with black braid, and machine stitching. Both bodice and skirt fasten at the left side in a simple and easy fashion, and the sleeves are of the comfortable shirt shape, which are the best both for outdoor exercise and for study.

The " Woman at Home " Paper Pattern Department.

Paper patterns for all the drawings published this month can be obtained from

THE WOMAN AT HOME *Paper Pattern Department,*

27, Paternoster Row, London, E.C.

PRICE LIST.—Flat Paper Patterns in any stock size, 6½d. ; Cut to Measure Patterns, 2s. 1d. Skirt and bodice count as separate patterns.

For the convenience of new readers we repeat this month the Measurement Order Form, and the measurements of stock sizes :

MEASUREMENT ORDER FORM.

Description.	Measure-ments.	Description.	Measure-ments.
1. Size round neck		8. Under arm seam, from sleeve to waist line	
2. Size round waist		9. Length of sleeve, inside of outstretched arm	
3. Size round bust, under arms ...		10. Length of sleeve, outside of bent arm ...	
4. Back width from sleeve to sleeve ...		11. Length of skirt in front	
5. Chest		12. Length of skirt at back	
6 Back length from base of collar to waist		13. Size round hips	
7. Front length from base of collar to waist			

A narrow piece of tape should be tied round the waist, and measurements made from it. All measurements should be as accurate as possible.

Stock patterns are made in three sizes according to the following table :—

No. 1 size	...	Bust.	40 in.	· ...	Waist	28 in.
,, 2 ,,	...	,,	36 ,,	...	,,	24 ,,
,, 3 ,,	...	,,	34 ,,	...	,,	22 ,,

HEALTH AND PERSONAL APPEARANCE.

ESSIE.—Treat yourself for indigestion and a sluggish liver and the pains and palpitations will probably disappear ; as the doctor assures you, your heart is not affected. The rules are very simple—never go long without food ; never eat in a hurry, or work immediately after eating, and be sure you have plenty of good air in your bedroom at night. Avoid sugar, potatoes, or any root vegetable except onions ; beer, tea which has stood too long on the leaves ; new white bread and pastry. Eat underdone meat, all green vegetables except cabbage ; brown bread, toast, butter and cream ; fruit, stewed or raw, especially figs, prunes, and raisins, and plenty of fish and underdone meat. Do not eat meat that has been cooked twice if you can avoid it, and use cayenne rather than ordinary pepper. A large glass of hot water sipped slowly after a meal, will relieve both the pain under the shoulder and the palpitation.

ORCHID.—It is a pleasure to answer such a tidy, concise, and practical letter ; you give us no trouble at all. For your questions. 1. Soap frequently causes pimples, especially the cheap, much-advertised kinds ; Cleaver's are good, so is Dr. Mackenzie's arsenical soap. 2. A scar from a hot curling-iron will probably disappear of itself, if it does not there is no remedy except a difficult, tedious and expensive operation. 3. Straps are not of much use to a person who stoops ; after the first few days they adapt themselves to the figure. Have your frocks made loose on the chest, and never wear tight shoes. In the morning, when you rise, swing your arms round and round in the sockets, rising on tip-toe as you throw them back, and so filling the lungs with air. This exercise will strengthen your chest and then you will not want to stoop. 4. Stoutness is generally the result of indigestion ; follow the advice given to "Essie," walk as far as you can without tiring yourself, remembering to raise your feet well and hold your head up ; drink as little as you can, but as much as you really feel to need at meal time, remembering the glass of hot water you will have afterwards.

MURIEL.—Peroxide of hydrogen will lighten the hairs on your face, and certainly will not cause them to grow. It will be much more likely to slowly destroy them, as anyone who has used it to lighten the hair of the head could tell you.

SATANITA.—Take one of Fraser's sulphur tablets every night for a fortnight, during which time your face will appear to grow much worse, because the spots will come to the surface, wash night and morning in hot water, with a little of Juno's Health Bath Salt dissolved in it ; after washing in the morning apply the following lotion : calcined magnesia, ¼oz., elderflower water, 4oz., alcohol, ½oz., tincture of benzoin, ¼oz. ; at night, simply rub in a little lanolin. As acne nearly always indicates some form of indigestion, read the answers to "Essie" and "Orchid."

T. J. P.—You can tone down the extreme colour if you will take a little trouble. Mix calcined magnesia into a stiff paste with water or milk, let it dry on—this will take about a minute and a half—then wash it off with hot water, do this every night. Avoid beer or much strong tea. A cold bath every morning, and plenty of exercise will lessen the tendency to blush. You too should read the answer to "Orchid," as you appear to suffer from slow circulation of the blood.

ADMIRER W. A. H.—Indigestion causes your trouble also. Read the hints given to "Essie" as to diet, though you need not follow them strictly, eat a charcoal biscuit after each meal and use Dr. Calvert's Carbolic Tooth Powder twice a week.

BRIAN.—You can tell a doctor anything, you are not a young lady to him, but a case, and you had certainly better consult one. Possibly your father is right when he says if you would eat more you would have better health, that is if you eat the right things, not "tea and cookies," but the diet recommended to "Essie." Consult the July number as to your hair.

SWEET WOODBINE.—Dry your hands thoroughly every time you wash them, and then dust them over with fuller's earth. Use cold water rather than hot, and rub on glycerine at night in winter.

MAIMSI M., HELENA and others.—Take the exercise recommended to "Orchid," and follow it immediately by a Russian bath, that is, wash the entire body in very hot water and then sponge in cold. You might put a little of Juno's Health Bath Salt in the hot water. Perspiration is a natural and healthy function when the skin is in a proper state. It is only unpleasant when repressed by a clogged skin, it breaks out locally. Powder the places which give you trouble with fuller's earth.

PRIMROSE.—Since you have so few grey hairs there is no harm in pulling them out. An excellent lotion for the hair is : Precipitated sulphur, ½ oz., almond oil, 1 oz., tincture of iron, ½ oz., rectified paraffin, 10 oz. Rectified paraffin has no smell. Read the article on the hair in the July magazine.

LIVERPOOL.—You had better consult another doctor.

MAY.—For acne, or blackheads, follow the advice given to "Satanita," but only take the sulphur tablets every other night, as your case is not so severe. Use a Turkish loofah, rather than a sponge for washing, and dry the face well, rubbing firmly but not roughly. The snoring is a more difficult matter. Snuff up hot salt and water into your nostrils to thoroughly clear them before you go to bed, and never lie on your back.

GERTRUDE.—You must consult a doctor at once.

MAVIS.—Rub round the nose and nostrils gently with cocoa-nut oil, and then powder with fuller's earth. Be sure always to dry carefully after washing.

DUTCH DOLL.—Read the above answer ; but you must carefully wipe off every vestige of the oil before applying the fuller's earth.

COOKERY.

FRENCH MENU FOR A SEASONABLE DINNER.

Menu.

Potage à la purée de Concombre.
Filets de Truite à la Tomate.
Salmis de Perdreaux à la Chasseur.
Côtelettes de Mouton à l'Avignonnaise·
La Hanche de Venaison rôtie.
Choufleurs à la Française
Charlotte de Melons.
Gelée de Pêches
Soufflée au Fromage glacé.

CUCUMBER SOUP.

Peel 6 cucumbers and cut them into small pieces, taking out the seeds, boil the pieces for five minutes in salted water, drain them, and then cook them in 2 ozs. of butter in a stewpan for twenty minutes, keeping them at a very gentle heat. Season them with pepper and salt and a little white sugar. Melt 4 ozs. of butter in another stewpan, and stir in 4 ozs. of flour till smooth, add the pieces of cucumber and 2 qts. of veal or chicken stock. Let the stock come to the boil, then skim it well, add 2 pts. of boiling milk, and cook gently for half an hour, at the end of that time pass all the soup through a fine sieve. Separate the yolks of 4 eggs from the whites, beat up the former, and add them to the soup, let the eggs just thicken, then pour the soup into a hot tureen and serve with fried croutons. Cost—3s.

FILLETS OF TROUT.

Scald a large trout in boiling water for two or three minutes, then skin it, beginning at the gills and using a sharp knife. Make a slit down the back, take out the bone and divide the fillets, wash and dry them well, then dip in egg and breadcrumbs, and fry in hot fat. Drain the fillets, and serve with tomato sauce handed separately. Cost – 2s.

STEWED PARTRIDGES, HUNTER'S STYLE.

After singeing and drawing two young partridges, cut them into twelve pieces and brown them well in a sauté pan with 1 oz. of butter, cooking each side. When a nice colour, add a little salt and pepper, a finely chopped shallot, ½ pint sauce espagnole, and 12 whole mushrooms. Let the partridges cook in the sauce for half an hour, not allowing them to boil, then serve on a dish and garnish with croutons. The chopped rind of a lemon is an improvement to the sauce. Cost—3s. 6d.

MUTTON CUTLETS WITH AVIGNONNAISE SAUCE.

Trim away the fat from 5 or 7 cutlets, and boil them in flavoured stock till just done. Drain them, dish them in a circle on a dish, and pour the following sauce over : Take ½ pint of good Bechamel sauce, and after coating the cutlets with it sprinkle 1 oz. of grated Parmesan cheese and a few fresh breadcrumbs on the top. Put the dish in the oven, and bake the cutlets till the cheese is melted and the crumbs slightly coloured. Cost—3s.

HAUNCH OF VENISON.

Roast this about four hours, according to the size, keeping it well basted with mutton fat and covered with a greased paper. Serve with red currant jelly and good gravy. Cost—9s.

CAULIFLOWER IN THE FRENCH WAY.

Trim the cauliflower, cut it into quarters, boil it in salted water till almost cooked, then drain, and finish stewing it in white sauce, seasoning with salt, pepper, and a little nutmeg. Cost—10d.

CHARLOTTE OF MELONS.

Line a glass bowl with sponge fingers placing them close together, and fitting them on the bottom of the bowl as evenly as possible. Peel a nice ripe melon, cut it into very thin slices, and place the latter on the sponge fingers, sprinkling plenty of sugar between the slices and squeezing the juice of two lemons over. Let the bowl stand in a cool place for some hours, then pile whipped cream on the top. Cost—1s. 6d.

PEACH JELLY.

Peel 12 peaches, and after halving and stoning them, cook them gently for four or five minutes in a little thin syrup. Crack the stones, and skin the kernels, and add them, and after leaving them for an hour drain the peaches carefully on a sieve. Put the strained juice of 6 lemons to the peach syrup and pass it through a jelly bag till clear. Dissolve some gelatine, allowing 1 oz to a pint of juice, and when well mixed with the liquid pour some of the latter into a wet mould. When this layer is set, put the peaches in very carefully and the blanched kernels, and pour in some more jelly, repeating till the mould is full. Set the jelly on ice till wanted, then turn out very carefully. Cost—2s. 6d.

COLD CHEESE SOUFFLEE.

Grate 1½ oz. of Gruyère and 1½ oz. of Parmesan cheese, and stir it into ½ pint of whipped double cream. Season to taste with salt, cayenne, and a little made mustard, and add 1 gill of aspic jelly also whipped. Put bands of paper round the top of some small ramaquin cases, put in the mixture, place a little grated cheese on the top, and cover with a thin layer of aspic jelly ornamented with truffles and sprays of chervil. The band round the ramaquins will prevent the jelly from running off, so they can be filled quite full, and when set the band can be carefully removed and they will look much better than if only half filled. Ice is necessary to set them, and in whipping the aspic jelly it should be allowed to get quite cool before commencing ; it will then set white and frothy. Cost—1s. 6d.

COST OF THE DINNER.

			£	s.	d.	
Soup	...	...	... 0	3	0	
Fish	...	...	... 0	2	0	
Entrées	...	...	... 0	6	6	
Roast	...	...	... 0	9	0	(about)
Vegetables	...	...	... 0	0	10	
Sweets	...	...	... 0	4	0	
Savoury	...	...	... 0	1	6	

£1 6 10

THE GLASS OF FASHION.

By Lady Mary.

The Simple Tastes of our Royal Family.

The simplicity of taste and feeling which distinguishes the members of our Royal family has always struck me as their most charming characteristic. "There is no woman in this world as artless as the Queen," once declared a friend who had had every opportunity of studying Her Majesty's character. Simple joys and simple pleasures are what most appeal to them, whilst the earnestness and warmth of the affection shown to one another by the brothers and sisters and cousins and aunts of the Guelph family, show their real unworldliness in a very charming light. One of the most homely and lovable members is the Princess Christian of Schleswig Holstein, as the following little anecdote will serve to show. Princess Christian, "Lenchen" they call her in the royal circle, takes a deep interest, as we all know, in charitable doings ; nay, she spends half her life in helping to clothe the poor, and feed the sick and hungry. Not so very long ago she persuaded a friend to adopt some poor little waif and stray. Soon the friend came to Her Royal Highness with complaints. "This child," she told, "for whom I have done so much—can it be believed?—is dainty about her food. She actually objects to cold mutton !"

And what do you think Princess Christian replied ? That paupers ought to have no tastes, no likes, or dislikes ? Oh ! no. The Princess is too sweet and human for that. She merely laughed, and said with a delightful simplicity of accent, "Well, cold mutton is not so *very* nice, after all, is it ? I am not fond of it myself, and as to mamma, though she rather likes cold beef, the one thing she cannot and will not stand is cold mutton !"

Even the Prince of Wales, man of the world though he be, retains a vast deal of simplicity. He and the Duke of York are like boys together, sometimes, rather than father and son, and will chaff one another, and laugh together as heartily as two young undergraduates. I remember how when the Duke of York presided over his first big charity dinner at the Great Ormond Street Hospital for Children, and a larger sum was subscribed after his speech than had ever been the case when the Prince of Wales himself was at the head of the table, how the Duke drove off to Marlborough House in triumph immediately afterwards, to "crow," as he put it, over his sire. Whether the Prince or Duke was most delighted it would be difficult to say. The life the royalties lead, guarded, as it were, from so many outside influences, and kept from absolute contact with the world, exempt from the petty cares which harass the majority of their subjects, conduces to keep them young and simple-hearted. As for a practical joke there is nothing they enjoy so much. The Princess of Wales herself is a great hand at making apple-pie beds, and is up to no end of fun, as those who stay at Sandringham will vouch. The Queen, although never given to practical joking now, as in her youth, is quick to see the point in a funny story, and loves above all things to hear an amusing recitation, aye, and enjoys a display of mimicry, if the mimicry be not ill-natured. We know that she even insisted that one of her equerries (a very clever amateur actor) should give an imitation of herself. No joke causes her the least amusement that is not perfectly refined.

A year or two ago a large party of youthful Princes and Princesses were laughing very heartily together in the drawing-room at Osborne, when Her Majesty entered with Princess Beatrice. She asked to be told the joke, and after a good deal of hesitation a young Princess gave it as it stood. The joke was rather, shall I say, an advanced one. The Queen did not smile, and her rebuke, gentle as it was, made itself felt. "We are not amused," she replied, answering for Princess Beatrice and herself.

The Queen's Gloves.

The present fashion of wearing white gloves with all costumes and at all times of the day has made the glove bills of daintily dressed ladies an unusually large item in their personal expenditure. It leads one to reflect upon Her Majesty's economy in matters of gloves. She will wear nothing but black ; generally they are of kid, but sometimes she wears Suède gloves which have been dyed black. I believe that she does not use more than two dozen pairs of gloves in a year, and each pair costs eight-and-sixpence, so that Her Majesty's glove bill only comes to about ten pounds per year ; a very small item compared with that of ladies of fashion. The Queen's size in gloves is seven-and-a-half, but it is necessary to slightly modify it to suit her fingers which are very short in proportion to the width of her hand. She has never favoured the modern fashion of long gloves for out-door wear, and is disposed to think the one button, which sufficed as a fastening in her young days, is the most comfortable arrangement, and certainly the least trouble. The Queen is one of those old ladies who have settled down into her own style of things, and takes no heed of the varying winds of fashion.

Amongst her hobbies in matters of ornament is a great fondness for pearls. In her young days she wore these chaste and lovely jewels amongst the braids of her fair hair, and to-day she still continues to collect them. West-end jewellers are fully aware of this, and reserve their choicest· specimens for her inspection, occasionally indeed they are obliged even to break faith with a customer. Not long ago a lady ordered a handsome pearl necklace, the price had been agreed upon and the bargain virtually completed, but when she called at the jeweller's to carry off her treasure she found to her vexation that the pearls had in the meantime been seen by the Queen, or probably by Princess Beatrice, who carries out most of her mother's shopping, and the salesman said that it was as much as his business was worth to refuse the jewels to the Queen. I scarcely think, however, that Her Majesty would have pressed the matter had she known of the lady's prior claim, and one fancies that the jeweller was more responsible for the lady's disappointment than the Queen, who would never take an undue advantage over another, even when pearls were in the question.

The Prince of Wales and the Queen's Indian Shawls.

The long-established custom of the Queen to bestow Indian shawls upon ladies whose services she wishes to recognise affords the Prince of Wales a little amusement at times, and although His Royal Highness is ever the essence of filial devotion to his august mother, he does now and again crack a joke over her shawl-giving propensity. I heard only the other day of a little incident which happened

at one of the Henley regattas. There was a merry company · of theatrical ladies and gentlemen, among whom was Miss Ellen Terry, enjoying themselves on a steam launch. Suddenly, without the usual announcement, the Prince of Wales came on board. The company were engaged in scrutinising the other craft on the river, and their attention was specially drawn to a boat containing a pleasure party, one member of which was an elderly lady bearing a remarkable likeness to the Queen, and she seemed bent upon doing all in her power to heighten the resemblance. One of the actors on board the launch approached the Prince, and ventured to draw his attention to the lady in question, jocularly suggesting that it was the Queen viewing the regatta, *incog*. Just as his Royal Highness was levelling his field-glass upon her, she rose, and taking the shawl on which she had been sitting threw it around the shoulders of a young girl who was with her. "It is undoubtedly the Queen," replied the Prince quietly, "she has discovered herself; I see that she has just presented one of her Indian shawls."

Princess Charles of Denmark and her Wedding Presents.

The simplicity which marks the tastes and feelings of our royal folks is also apparent in their manner. Although naturally very sedate and dignified when before the public gaze, in private life they are as hearty and genuine as possible, ashamed neither of expressing their joy and sorrow, as quick to laughter as to tears. Princess Maud of Wales, I can assure my readers, was as delighted with every wedding gift which reached her as any school-girl. Those which pleased her most of all were, as she put it herself, "the amusing ones." I will only mention one which tickled her fancy, and which, as she assured her friends, she would use every day. Thirty friends of the name of "Maud" subscribed together, and bought for her four miniature silver toast racks, the pretty design being executed by one of the Mauds. They were just in the shape of the letter "M," and at the top of each toast rack, wherewith to hand it about, rested a little silver crown. The gift was presented "From thirty Mauds." Why not from "Mauds of thirty ?" exclaimed one of these sprightly ladies. The royalties are very fond indeed of present-giving, and like to prepare little surprises for one another. The dear Queen's gifts are valued most of all, and those which her grandchildren prepare for her cost them time and trouble as well as pocket-money. Pieces of embroidery and sketches in water-colours abound in her sitting-rooms, the work of loving and busy fingers. Of all her possessions the Queen, I think, values most a curb bracelet of thick gold, to which are attached row upon row of tiny hearts, containing each the likeness of her great grandchildren—such an array of sweet baby faces, as you may imagine. Prince Albert once said of the Crown Princess, his daughter, that she had the head of a man with the heart of a child. He might as aptly have described his wife in the same fashion. For the Queen still preserves her childlike heart, and has taught the beauty of modesty and simplicity to the children and children's children born to live after her.

Princess Maud's Danish Home.

Much as Princess Charles of Denmark loves her Norfolk home, where her honeymoon was spent and where she and her husband will reside for several months during the year, her principal home will be in Denmark. Prince Charles as an officer in the Danish navy is in a measure obliged to be near the scene of his duties, and a handsome suite of rooms has been prepared for him and his bride in the King of Greece's Palace, a town house not very palatial in aspect standing in Bredgarde, one of the chief streets in Copenhagen, which runs down to the Langelinie, the public promenade by the sea. King George of Greece rarely spends much time in his native Copenhagen, so that his palace can readily be spared for the use of Prince and Princess Charles. There they will be within sight of the royal palaces occupied by the King and Queen and the Crown Prince and Princess, and only a very short distance from the Gûle Palais where the Princess of Wales was born, which to the young bride will make her foreign residence very homelike.

The Empress of Russia and her Dairy.

The ex-Empress of Russia has quite a weakness for dairies. At Pavlovsk, where she established her first, she invited the St. Petersburgers to come and enjoy free luncheons—those St. Petersburgers who were anxious to start dairies themselves—be it told. "Only please, visitors," she wrote, "do not walk on the grass, for that would hurt me as much as if you walked on *me*." Here she established a farm to instruct the neighbouring peasants in approved methods of

work, and how to improve what stock they possessed. To the successful workers she still bestows presents of calves. I need hardly add that Pavlovsk is a very favourite resort. Here, too, there are performing bears, tame pigeons, and peacocks. A museum of the Empress's china and dairy utensils is kept in a building at the farm, under the charge of the familiar "Old Soldier" ever ready to tell you anecdotes of every member of the Russian royal family.

The Engagement of the Duc d'Orleans.

The engagement of the Duc d'Orleans to the Hungarian Archduchess Dorothea is one which gives undisguised satisfaction to the members of both families concerned. When first I saw the Duc it was, I remember, at a jeweller's shop in Bond Street. We were both choosing Christmas presents, and the Duc, after he had made his selection, hurried out, speaking as he went to the shopman who had served him, and raising his hat politely at the door to the various employés. A pretty act of foreign courtesy, I thought. Well, the Duc lived long enough among us for us to learn to like him well, notwithstanding his youthful bombast. A thoroughly cheery manly fellow everybody declared him. It was thought that the young French Pretender had left us for good with his mother, the Comtesse de Paris, and his beautiful sister, the Duchesse d'Aosta. "Regardez moi ça," he said to a friend, pointing out of the window to the fog, which enveloped London on the morning of his departure. "Quel climat! Mais le pays est un pays généreux—le peuple est généreux aussi,—je ne les oublierai jamais!" So it would seem. For the Duke is coming back in all probability to live with us again ; this time at Wood Norton, the seat of the Duc d'Aumale, with his bride, the Hungarian Archduchess Dorothea. A singularly accomplished Princess she is, we learn, able to talk with fluency in many languages, fond of music and of painting, and in both proficient. Then, we feel kindly towards her when we are told that she is extremely fond of England, and had at one time quite made up her mind to become a hospital nurse in this country, just like the Duchess of Teck when she was a girl. Only when she imparted her secret longing to her cousin Princess Victoria, that decided young lady (who many, many years ago did not approve of ladies taking to hospital nursing) quite over-ruled her. "I wept bucketfuls of tears," tells the good

Duchess, " but you see it was all for the best that I took the Queen's advice." Since that day the Queen has quite altered her opinion on the subject of hospital nursing. Nay, I believe she owns to quite a *penchant* for lady nurses. But if, instead of marrying and living happy for ever after, the Duchess had become a nurse, where would be our beloved Princess May? and little Prince Edward of York, our future king, whom, by the way, I saw only this morning driving with his nurse in a landau. The bonniest little fellow, looking about him so wisely, and saluting as he went. Now I have wandered far from my original subject. Only this goes to prove that there are many good women who should become hospital nurses, and that we can't spare our Princesses for the purpose. May the Archduchess Dorothea prove a charming wife to the Duc D'Orleans, and may they both live long and happily in Old England.

Lady Battersea, of Overstrand.

Lady Battersea has shone for several years as one of the most familiar lights in London society, and now as hostess-in-chief of the Eighty Club, her star rises ever in the ascendant. For to be at the head of the Eighty Club, and to acquit oneself gracefully under the circumstances, means much. Do you know Lord Battersea's charming house, opposite the Marble Arch? That crimson and white drawing-room, illuminated by countless wax candles, overlooking Hyde Park, has been the scene of many distinguished gatherings. "A landscape without water is like a drawing-room without a mirror. That is why I like Surrey House." I don't think I need add that these lines are Lord Beaconsfield's. One can hear his very voice in their cadence. Lady Battersea as a member of the house of Rothschild is the natural inheritor of wit, kindliness, and a "feeling" for the Arts. Only to mention a few of her most cherished friends will be to give an idea of the catholicity of her tastes and sympathy. First and foremost come Mr. and Mrs. Gladstone, Lady Dorothy Nevill, Lady Breadalbane, and Edmund Gurney; whilst in earlier days Mr. Matthew Arnold and Mr. Frederick Sandys were among the most welcome habitués of the house. In the country, whether at Overstrand or Brecon (Lord Battersea has a charming home in that lovely neighbourhood where Adelina Patti has elected to pitch her tent), the hostess of the Eighty Club is seen to as great advantage as in London, and dispenses hospitality with a tact and kindliness which have won her quite a host of real friends. In the autumn Lord and Lady Battersea are wont to disport themselves upon the shores of the Italian lakes, and return home laden with furniture, jewels, and curios of all kinds wherewith to beautify and enrich their English homes.

The Fashions of the last London Season.

Two good fashions were introduced—or rather two bad fashions went out—during the last London season. Let us hope that these fashions will keep in during the years that are to come. And what were they, you will ask? The first was that smart ladies were visible about here, there, and everywhere with their little children, instead of leaving them altogether to their nurses and governesses. Even in the Park it was most usual to see as many as three or four mites with their mother in a landau! And mothers who had hitherto neglected their children learnt to love them through this new companionship. What was first a fashion became a pleasure. Then the second new mode? Women of the upper classes did not wholly discard those white and pink roses on their cheeks which are bought in the perfumers' shops. But they let them bloom more sparingly than they have done for years past. It was quite refreshing to see so many natural-looking faces. The Queen and her daughters have a positive objection to paint and powder, and no one about the Court can hope for favour who resorts to them. The fashion of painting and enamelling, indeed, cannot be too highly deplored. Englishwomen, fortunately, do not practise the art so universally as Frenchwomen, but when they do paint and powder, they apply their pigments with less art. An olive complexion is replaced by a pink one, which invariably quarrels with the hair intended by Nature for the olive skin. Many women paint under the impression that they rejuvenate themselves by so doing. Prettier they *may* look, I admit, but never younger. For bright colour tends ever to harden the face. Nothing beautifies a face so much as exquisitely and becomingly arranged hair. Perfection of *coiffure*, too, is the cachet of smartness. "By their heads ye shall know them," is the proverb of a certain distinguished woman. Let us, then, try to make ourselves legitimately pleasant-looking by the acme of daintiness and neatness. Not by the painting of our faces, and the pencilling of our eyebrows.

INCOMES·FOR·LADIES

BY WILHELMINA WIMBLE.

A HUNDRED years ago the ways of the gentlewoman were different from those of the gentlewoman of to-day. Do we not all possess tokens of our great-grandmothers' accomplishments?—quaint little water-colour drawings, on vellum and velvet, of rose-buds, forget-me-nots, or other blossoms stiff in arrangement, sentimental in meaning; their marvellous samplers proclaim an industrious girlhood; about the china vases that have come down to us hang ghostly wafts of the perfume of *pot-pourris* manufactured by fair hands long fallen to dust; rare and voluminous letters, not always correctly spelt, speak of a leisurely if busy and perhaps narrow life; their housewifery —who can doubt it, with these volumes of receipts handed down from mother to daughter?

It is always the picture of a life of which marriage is the central fact; for which girlhood was a preparation; and from which radiated all the after life's activities and pre-occupations.

THE gentlewomen of to-day are the daughters of an alert and self-reliant age, in which marriage is no longer the simple solution of every girl's life; in which strikes and speculations wreck fortunes every day—portionless, or next to portionless, unmarried women, of gentle birth and breeding, find themselves face to face with the necessity of making money; some in order to keep the wolf from their doors, others towards supplementing a meagre income. These ladies, actuated by the modern spirit of independence, have yet nothing in common with the "New Woman"—if, which we doubt, this feminine Frankenstein be indeed among us, waiting to fall upon us to our undoing. It is to meet the wants of women who wish to turn their accomplishments, the advantages of their social tact and position, to account, that this department of THE LADY'S REALM will devote itself.

THERE are two kinds of work in which women can show their capacity: that for which the highest training is required, and the lesser work, which, while demanding certain aptitudes, and punctuality and precision in its execution, is not yet dependent for its success upon any special training. It would lead only to heart-breaks and disillusions if we were to admit the possibility of women succeeding in art, literature, tuition, or other professions, without being able to bring into the terrible mart of competition, work than can hold its own with that of the highly trained.

To deft-fingered women of taste the various branches of decorative art offer many chances of remuneration. Take lamp-shades for instance: the days are over when an artless petti-coat—usually pink—was considered all that was necessary for tempering the glare of our lamps. We, who have passed the days when our complexions were a compound of milk and roses, shrink from "*la brutalité du grand jour*," and the thoughtful hostess keeps her drawing-room delicately dim. Lamp-shades will there-fore be always a necessary article of feminine furniture. A lady who realises this demand for lamp-shades has organised a depôt for these dainty trifles. She provides lamp-shades of every style—Tudor, Empire, Louis Quinze, Louis Seize, etc.—to suit the prevailing character of the rooms they are destined to adorn. A friend of mine is among those who work for her. She is paid from sixteen to eighteen shillings for each lamp-shade; but these are elaborate and beautiful—quite little works of art. She is a woman of charming taste, clever at adapting the figures and ornamental devices from old prints, for her designs; and the result is always graceful and suitable. She also paints fans, and on china. She went to Paris and mastered the art of *Vernis Martin* painting. She ornaments boxes, caskets, miniature Sedan-chairs for holding china. Hers is the history of many women of good social position. She was left when her first youth was passed with but little money; she had had no training as an artist, but she was clever with her pencil and brushes as an amateur. She now applied herself to gain further mastery over her implements and to cultivate versatility. She brought to bear upon her art her social tact and knowledge, keeping herself in touch with the currents of taste—for taste has its moods, as well as its more definite periods of fashion. Once a year she has an exhibition of her work—much as artists have their " Show Sunday," before the Academy opens. Her work is gaining a certain celebrity, and is much in vogue for wedding presents.

LATER we will speak of book-binding for women, and of the charming metal and leather *repoussé* work that is used for the ornamentation of books and panels. At Bushey, in the colony of art-students growing round Herkomer's school, there is some very fine metal work done by the ladies.

ART-needlework has many developments. This branch of " The Working Ladies' Guild " is under the superintendence of Lady Eden. It has executed some restoration of old tapestries that are a marvel to see. We will treat exhaustively of what money can be earned by the needle. The works of Mrs. Sparling, the daughter of William Morris, might take rank with that of great artists with the brush.

ADAPTABILITY to the new developments of fashion and customs; inventiveness in devising means of meeting the claims of these new developments;—will ensure many a prize. The bicycle is one of the momentous facts of the day. Its appearance has done much to re-volutionise the habits, and the costume, of women. With the bicycle has come the need of the chaperone. There is a demand for ladies, vigilant and of a lively spirit, to accompany young girls on their flight through crowded thoroughfares and lonely country lanes. The chaperone must be aware of routes, and be versed in the laws of the road; she must know what to do in cases of emergency, should the faithful bicycle come to grief and be in need of repair. The literature of the bicycle she should have at her fingers' ends, for it contains all needful hints and suggestions. Sometimes the chaperone takes her party of girls for a tour of some days, through the country or even on the Continent; she knows the best inns on the way. The bicyclist chaperone, whether for the half-hour ride or a ride extending over days, is a valuable member of the community, and is hailed as a friend by mothers, unable to be their daughters' companion on the wheel.

TABLE DECORATION gives openings of employment to women of taste. An American lady formed for herself in New York quite a connection and a reputation as a table-decorator. She was an artist in the arrangement of foliage, flowers, china, glass, and silver, working in these materials as a painter might with his pigments. Her method was simple and practical. Having ascertained the resources of the plate, china, glass, and napery to be put at her disposal, also of how much or how little she could expend upon flowers, she sketched a scheme of colour and line. On a hot summer afternoon, one of her luncheon-tables, a symphony in green and white, with hints of roses, was a refreshment to the eye. She had an original and charming manner of mingling fruit with flowers—lilac china-asters with purple plums, roses with peaches and apricots; a glance at her sketches would show how all had been thought out to the most delicate detail, alike in an elaborate or simple arrangement. She went into partnership with a friend, who possessed some fine plate and china; these were turned to excellent account by hiring out, and often formed an integral part of some of her most original designs. The hiring out of plate and china is, I know, occasionally done during the London season, by the lucky possessors of these treasures

À PROPOS of the table, the art of cookery is providing openings of careers for women. It is not only the manner of the cooking of a meal, but of its ordering, that the young housekeeper should learn. A fine and cunning arrangement of flavours gives distinction to the plainest repast. One of the wittiest women I have ever met, heiress to a fortune that had got involved in a lawsuit, pluckily went to work while lawyers were disentangling the web of her fortunes. She knew she was a born cook, and she organised courses of lessons in cookery in her own home and in private houses. She even went out to cook dinners. She also imparted to her pupils the art of mingling flavours. To listen to her was to understand how, to the civilised man, eating may be raised to the level of an art and a science

INDEXING, in an age when time is valuable, is the rising profession that promises to give much employment to women. It is a sedentary occupation, requiring method and a knack of choosing comprehensive headings under which to range the various subjects and allusions found in the work. To a lady has been entrusted the indexing of Hansard's parliamentary debates ; and this lady takes pupils and gives out work. A well-known editor employs women to index his journal. We hope to enter later more largely upon this field of activity, to which many women may look for employment. Meanwhile, we would suggest the indexing that women of Society might do better than any other—the cataloguing of the pictures, the china, the books and MSS., in country houses—the sorting and arranging of old family letters and archives lying in hopeless confusion in muniment chests. It would be easy to select and adopt a simple plan of cataloguing.

A lady I know earns £400 a year by indexing the autograph letters of a millionaire collector. Her plan is to summarise the contents of the letter ; to give a short account of the writer ; of the circumstances attending the writing of the letter ; and explanations of the allusions therein. This involves much study at the British Museum, as the collection she is indexing is unique.

A MODE of earning money is by type-writing ; but that means close work and poor pay. To add to type-writing a knowledge of shorthand, more than trebles the value of the applicant for employment. To be an amanuensis or secretary, proficiency in both accomplishments is absolutely

necessary. The orphan daughter of a retired officer in the army prepared herself for the battle of life by mastering these two qualifications, adding thereto a knowledge of proof-correcting ; and before very long she had as much work as she could do. On the other hand, the daughter of a clergyman in the country, one of a large family of girls, came up to London to make her way. She learnt type-writing, and found employment in a house of business in the City. Her earnings ranged from fourteen shillings to a pound a week. To be able to translate business letters, especially from the French and German—Spanish running these languages close in importance—is a great recommendation in the labour-market. A literary knowledge of foreign languages does not always include familiarity with business terms, and it is well to master these and their exact equivalents in English.

THERE are manifold modest ways of making small sums. I know a lady clever at millinery, who turns her deft fingers to good account. She will make you the prettiest bonnet, if you furnish the materials, and she charges half-a-crown. Looking after servants and the carrying out of the orders by tradespeople and workmen, left by the absent mistress during the holidays, is another way of earning. Shopping for others has its dangers ; but a woman of taste, who goes into Society, does, I know, undertake such commissions, to her own advantage and to that of the friends for whom she caters. Looking after the pet animals of a household is a source of pleasure to the lovers of dumb animals. I have heard of ladies who take dogs out for walks and generally tend them at the rate of eighteenpence and two shillings per hour.

THERE is a delightful character to be found in *The Spectator*—my namesake Will Wimble, a friend, if I remember rightly, of dear Sir Roger de Coverley. Will is not young, he is not rich, he is not witty, but he is welcome everywhere, for he can turn his hand to everything ; he is ready to help to fill a gap, when there is a gap to be filled. If you are not a trained worker, be a Will Wimble, and there will be many a corner for you to fill profitably in the great social scheme.

From a photograph by Lafayette.

A STUDY OF TWO HEADS.

DRESS AND. FASHION.

Skirts never remain long stationary; their latest transformation is to forswear horsehair for a simple lining of silk; they are wider than ever, and the trimmed or corded seams give them a certain stiffness. Embroidery of jet and steel, tinsel, or plain braiding will characterise them for some time to come.

* * *

Flounces are to be fashionable once more, and very pretty they will look on the gossamer material used for evening wear. For this purpose Paris is sending over an immense quantity of shot gauzes of more than double width. Ideal silk crépons have cross lines of black or colour

and showers of tiny little floral sprays. Glacé silks have the same cross lines and flowers showered lavishly over them.

* * *

Amongst the styles we can copy from are the Stuart, the Pompadour, and the Renaissance. The Stuart wired ruffle and the turreted collar are equally popular.

* * *

Large collars or capelets glittering with tinsel and spangles will be worn, edged with fur for outdoor toilettes.

* * *

Jewelled clasps, buttons, and paste buckles, old-fashioned silver filigree ornaments are to be used

No. 1.

for dresses, and the amount of crude colourings blended together is appalling. Gold, copper, with an attendant train of coloured metals, relieve dark dresses with a glittering line of light. The skirts, we hear, will have square tabs or rounded scallops at the foot.

* * *

Cloth strapped and oversewn seams are the newest form of ornamentation—the small straps of cloth of a contrasting colour, held in place by a single metal button, particularly if the coat is an "habit Garde Française." With suéde or glacé kid waistcoats and bows of bright ribbons fastened with jewelled buckles, the cloth tailor suits will have become anything but austerely simple.

* * *

Coats and skirts are too useful ever to be discarded. The coats vary from the reefer jacket to the scalloped, strapped, and altogether more elaborate coat.

* * *

Winter alpacas, and quite a series of thick, luminous crépons, afford a slight element of variety, as do the tiny check woollens and mixed suiting. In reseda, blue, grey, or lavender, the former look very well. If it be true that we have to part with the blouse, we shall have cause to regret it. In point of usefulness the blouse is unsurpassable, and one fails to see how it can be replaced or why any sensible woman should relinquish it.

* * *

There is very little alteration in bodices—they continue to be fussily trimmed—blue or fawn cloth, costumes have the corsage elaborately

ornamented with straps of white cloth outlined with tiny gold braid and tiny gold buttons. For alpacas in golden browns, blue plum or ruby, wide collars cut in petal points are made of light or contrasting shades of satin. These are braided or spangled with gold or steel, and trimmed with fur. The new mantles are striped lengthwise with bands or tails of fur. Chinchilla is much worn, so are sable and fox. Very rich mantles are being made at the best modistes' in Lyons, velvet, red plum, sapphire, emerald, or mouse-grey. These will be trimmed with one, sometimes two sorts of furs.

* * *

Long driving double-breasted coats will also be much worn. Short smart collarettes will replace the eternal "beastie" one has become so tired of. These collarettes are also made of ostrich feathers or of the new "plumes lisses" now so much used in millinery. Short boas run on the same lines. The incrustation of *medallions* of rich fur in jet or "mat" passementerie will be quite an innovation in fur trimming.

* * *

Linings are superb, gold brocades being much used, or the most delicate Trianon satins for younger styles. Dresses will also show panels and "incrustations" of fur, inlaid in tinsel embroidery.

* * *

There is a tendency to adopt red for winter mantles, but at present it has not gone further than popularising vivid shades of claret and Burgundy. Sleeves seem to show little alteration, but there is a marked tendency to lower

No. 2.

them from the shoulder. They are much draped in a sort of butterfly's wing fashion and in thin materials. They are mostly gathered from elbow to wrist. There is also the piped sleeve, the "melon" sleeve, both used largely for cloth or heavy materials. This is in accordance with the front breadth of skirts and coat backs, which are treated precisely in the same way.

* * *

Coat basques are a little longer than of yore, and their fulness less exaggerated. Some are made like an Eton in front with double revers, and a full basque at the back only. A double-breasted waistcoat with lozenge buttons is worn underneath. It is cut in an open square filled in with white silk, which is covered with cream lace.

* * *

Tea gowns promise to be both costly and elaborate, mostly in the Renaissance or Tudor styles.

* * *

Cloth cut out in lozenges and embroidered will be worn over bright satins and plush, and we can recommend this mixture in brown cloth and ruby velvet, or fawn cloth and green velvet—the effect is really beautiful. Hand embroidery as an industry will be again revived, and velvet visites and mantles will be richly hand-embroidered with silk and beads. Matrons will rejoice in that dressy and convenient form of outdoor garment, the visite, which outlines the back of the figure, giving grace and elegance to the whole appearance.

No. 4.

In millinery we are bristling with birds' wings, notwithstanding all that has been done to reduce cruelty to a minimum. Plumes of lisse are the standing novelty in rosettes, borders, tufts, etc. The Marie Stuart bonnet will be a boon to some faces. Worn with the collarette of the same period, it is really charming. A great quantity of chenille will be used both in dress and millinery. The prettiest hat shapes are made of chenille and cut felt woven like straw. Borders of chenille are most becoming to the face. Many of the loveliest flowers are composed of feathers, the plumes of lisse being largely used. There will be a dash of white, pure flour white, in all our winter dresses and hats. In Paris the magpie craze goes so far as to bestow white kid heels on our black shoes. White gloves will be worn, to which rumour whispers we are to add white stockings and white starched petticoats. Belts, purses, and card cases are made of white leather; and white felt hats are now selling in the best Paris houses.

* * *

White cloth blouses, with lozenge-shaped jewelled buttons, are the garment of the hour. I have seen some ideal ones made out of Råmpoor Chuddah shawls. Evening bodices are all made off the shoulder and framed in ruches of poppy or rose petals. Opera mantles, when worn short, will be lined with ermine or swansdown. Long mantles will be of darker hues, lined with white or light satins, and will be very elaborately trimmed.

SUGGESTIONS FOR NOVEMBER PURCHASES.

Towards the beginning of November cold winds and chilly evenings suggest to our minds

No. 3.

No. 5.

ing chills and rheumatism, it enables autumn and winter dresses to double their lease of life. In olden times a waterproof was a hideous and unwholesome article of dress, but great improvements have been lately made in the manufacture of rainproof materials, and very smart cloaks can now be purchased at a moderate cost. The "Distingué" waterproof can be worn by any gentlewoman with satisfaction, also cloaks made of "cravenette" in black and other shades, which can be had in various shapes, and these are very light and comfortable.

Many tweeds are practically waterproof, without any suspicion of mackintosh in them, and some people like a dress or costume of such material for walking or cycling, which does not need protection from bad weather. A golf cape to match such a gown can be worn either with or without it, and will be found very useful by those who object to waterproofs pure and simple. For doubtful weather with occasional showers a circular cravenette cloak is very suitable, as it can be carried easily on the arm during intervals of fine weather. These cloaks in any shape can be bought from one guinea upwards.

The prices of such furs and rainproof garments depend, of course, a great deal on the quality selected, and it is not advisable to attempt to make such things at home. Sealskin and Persian lamb capes can be had new from about

that it is time to bring out all our furs for the winter, or to invest in new ones, if those which did duty last year are too much worn to be worth remodelling. Full fluted capes are both fashionable and becoming, and anyone who has the means will find it difficult to resist the temptation of a seal cape lined with rich satin brocade.

The latest novelty is an ingenious combination of sealskin and Persian lamb in alternate strips, which go off to a point at the neck, where a fluted collar of the two furs finishes off the cape. Another fashionable combination is sealskin and chinchilla, but in this case the light fur is only used as a collar and facings for the cape. Sable probably looks better with sealskin than any other fur, but it is, alas! too expensive to be within the reach of everyone.

Very comfortable and less expensive capes can be made of cloth lined with an inexpensive fur, such as is usually put into fur cloaks. Squirrel back is very nice, and even less expensive is the white part of the squirrel skin. A collar of richer fur can be added to such a cape. Sable muffs will be as much in favour as ever, and Persian lamb will be very much worn. It is an excellent fur for wearing in smoky cities, and it is always ladylike if it is of good quality. Another recommendation is that the moth does not like it.

Another very useful article of dress for winter wear is a good waterproof, for, besides prevent-

No. 6.

14 gs., but if any old-fashioned seal coats and Persian lamb trimmings are at hand a great deal of them can probably be remodelled into a cape such as that described above, and in this case the cost would be much reduced. In any case it is false economy to buy cheap furs, so the best possible price should be given for them.

Simple dresses for evening wear are much in demand in November, and such pretty light crépons, muslins, and veilings can now be bought, that it is not difficult to make a stylish dress at a very moderate cost. Pale-coloured nun's veilings with tiny silk spots or sprigs upon them are very suitable for young people, and these can be bought from 1s. 6d. per yard upwards. They look best gathered slightly on a separate foundation, and if an old silk dress is available for an underskirt, so much the better; full sleeves and a baby bodice, prettily trimmed with satin or chiné ribbons, will complete a charming toilette.

Crépons look well made in a similar style, and quite eight yards of these soft, semi-transparent materials should be allowed, as they look very bad if they are at all scanty, and the cheap makes are generally only forty inches wide. A charming variety will be found in any of these materials, which will make a pretty frock for 21s. to 25s., and if the simple style suggested is adopted, it can be quite well and satisfactorily made at home. Old silk bodices and skirts, if cleaned, make excellent foundations and save much trouble, as the new material has only to be draped on.

DESCRIPTION OF FASHION DRAWINGS.

No. 1.—Is a most original blouse composed of shaded silk with velvet revers and elbow cuffs, edged with bullion braid and finished with gold buttons. It is low necked and filled with a white chiffon chemisette. From John Barker's, Kensington.

No. 2.—Is a blouse of two colours of silk, one of plain surface, the other of figured design on light. Black velvet bands and rosettes are arranged in a new form, which outlines the figure in a becoming manner. Also from John Barker's, Kensington.

No. 3.—Is a cape of the universally worn circular shape, with stitched strappings. A sailor-shaped collar of fine beaver finishes this charming cape. This garment is contributed by Alfred Goodson, Boar Lane, Leeds.

No. 4.—This jacket has the new sleeve, with seam down outside of arm. The collar also is of original shape, and can be partly or wholly turned up with good effect. From Alfred Goodson's establishment, Boar Lane, Leeds.

No. 5.—This walking costume is composed of bright brown cloth, having the neck and under sleeves of a darker shade of velvet edged with fur. On the skirt are also two panels of velvet. Carved gold buttons finish this most charming arrangement, and a hat of brown velvet with gold and brown ribbons and yellow roses is well worn with it. Also from a design for Alfred Goodson, Boar Lane, Leeds.

No. 6.—This is a walking costume of heliotrope cloth, made with deep square collar and braid frogs, the neck front and collar being edged with dark brown fur. The sleeves are very full to the elbow and tight to the wrist. From Mr. Alfred Goodson, of Boar Lane, Leeds.

WRINKLES.

How to Preserve your Gloves.—When putting gloves on always begin by buttoning the second button; then, when buttoned to the top, you can easily fasten the first button without tearing the kid. Never remove the gloves by pulling the fingers, but by drawing the part covering the wrist over the hand, and leave them thus wrong side out for some time before turning them to their proper shape. Always lay gloves lengthwise; never roll them.

* * *

The Care of Lamps.—The chimney of a lamp should never be touched with water. A few drops of alcohol will remove the dim, smoky effect, and make the chimney bright as possible when it is polished with a chamois leather or soft flannel. Every part of the outside of a lamp should be rubbed dry every time it is filled. Old burners may be boiled in soda and water to cleanse them, but this sometimes removes the lacquer put on most brass. Do not cut the wick after it has been evenly trimmed once, but each day brush off the charred portion. The wick will last longer and the light be kept even and clear if this rule is strictly adhered to.

* * *

Remedy for Ingrowing Nails.—Take a piece of strong muslin about an inch wide and long enough to make two loops, by sewing, one large enough to fit over the large toe, the other to slip over the third toe, and bring them close together, letting the second toe rest over the bandage. The second toe in this position permits precisely the required pressure to crowd the soft parts away from the nail, and at the same time remove the pressure that causes the disease. Another remedy is to cut the nail to a curve in the centre, and scrape it quite thin in the same spot with a piece of glass or a sharp knife. The nail will then grow from the sides to fill up the curve made in the centre.

* * *

How to Clean and Curl Feathers.—Wash the feathers in warm soap-suds and rinse them in warm water, then dry them in the wind. If they are white, add a little blueing to the water. To curl, place a hot flat iron so that the feather can be held over it. Take a bone or silver knife and draw the fibres of the feather between the thumb and the dull edge of the knife, being careful not to take more than three fibres at once. Begin at the point of the feather, curling the two halves of the fibres in opposite directions. A hot iron makes the feathers stay in curl longer than a cool one does. A little practice will enable one to make them look almost like new. When the feathers have been worn while the dew was falling, hold the hat over a hot stove, and the curl will be temporarily restored to them. Be careful not to hold them too near, as they will scorch readily.

Harmless Cosmetic.—Half a cup of oatmeal and two cups and a half of water; let it stand all night, and in the morning turn the water off and the coarser part of the meal; strain the rest, and add enough bay rum to make it the thickness of cream. Apply to the face, hands, and neck every night and frequently during the day; it will make them very soft and fair.

* * *

To Dry Autumn Leaves.—Hang them with the cut stalks uppermost, and after two days take them down and dip them in a solution of size and water; then hang them up again to get perfectly dry. Bramble and beech leaves make a beautiful winter decoration for table and flower vases. All grasses and rushes should be dried with the heads downwards, as this sends the sap into the leaves and flowers.

* * *

To Dye Straw, Grasses, etc.—Various aniline dyes dissolved in alcohol can be got at the chemist's, and thus prepared you can obtain any colour on grasses, etc. Pour some boiling water into a basin, and add as much of the dye as will colour the water to the tint you wish. Allow the water to cool a little, and then plunge in the grasses and keep them there until coloured to your taste. For violet, use one part aniline violet and one part aniline blue de liau; for red, aniline fuchsin; for scarlet, one part aniline fuchsin and one part aniline violet. For grasses and moss, if required a dark green, in two ounces of boiling water mix one ounce powdered alum and half an ounce dissolved indigo carmine. Add more water according to the shade of green desired. Dry in an airy shady place out of the sun.

* * *

Cover for a Plant Pot.—Procure a small bundle of straws of an equal size, cut them the length required, according to the height of the pot; use sharp scissors, and handle the straws delicately, for if they are broken or split they will be useless. Cardboard must form the bottom and top of the cover; the bottom must be whole, and the top cut out in a circle about half an inch wide near the edges. Holes must be made for the straws to pass through. The cardboard for the bottom of the pot cover must be a little larger than the bottom of the plant pot. The top piece of cardboard must be a little larger round than the top of the plant pot. The number of holes must be even, and close together. Fill the holes with the straws, one in each hole, allowing them to protrude evenly for about half an inch at the top. Ribbon may be threaded through at intervals, interlacing the straw, passing over and under the straws alternately, always observing that the straw passed "under" in the first row must be passed "over" in the second row, and so on.

MASTER WALLER, DIPLOMATIST.

By W. Pett Ridge.

HE proudest sometimes unbend, and the Botanical Gardens were, for one afternoon, throwing off their usual reserve. Ordinary folk had only to come across Regent's Park from Chester Gate and present a card at the entrance to the gardens, and the bowler-hatted old gentleman at the gate welcomed them as though they were most important members. Miss Llewellyn and Master Kenneth Waller, her friend, walked on the grass in the direction of music.

"Anybody you know here, Miss Llewellyn?"

"I don't suppose so, Kenneth."

"You don't know many people, do you, Miss Llewellyn?"

"Very few!"

"Wonder at that," said the small boy, "because you're not bad-looking, you know. Did you use to come here when you were well off? Do they sell lemonade here?"

"Seems possible. You think that everybody ought to have plenty of friends?"

"Plenty of friends," said Kenneth, wisely, "but one in particular. Wonder how old you are?"

"That," said the young woman, good-temperedly, "that is the only question, Kenneth, that you must never put to a lady."

"I should guess," he said, critically, as they sat down in the low chairs near the refreshment tent and watched the people, "that you were about twenty-six." Miss Llewellyn gave a quaint gesture of horror. "Well, twenty-five then. Fancy!" The small boy whistled amazedly. "Twenty-five and not married yet."

"Young man," said Miss Llewellyn, flushing and affecting a tone of great severity, "I find your conversation much too personal. You would like lemonade, I think, and two pieces of cake."

The scarlet-coated band perched on seats near the glass house, with a crowd of smartly dressed folk in front of them, started a cheerful selection from a comic opera. Miss Llewellyn, a composed young woman in an ordinary way, as young women are who work for their living, found herself in quite a delighted mood. Music can do much when it tries.

"Of course," said her candid guest, with cake at his mouth, "I don't mean to say that you mightn't get married even now. I had an aunt once who was close upon thirty before she could get anyone to look at her."

"The instance is encouraging, Kenneth. Don't eat too fast, mind."

"Still," said the youth, wisely, "if I were a girl I should be jolly careful not to miss a good opportunity. Are those orchids they're carrying there? Hasn't that chap got a brown face who's telling the men where to take them? Seem to have seen him somewhere before. Shouldn't like to be an orchid, should you, Miss Llewellyn? Why, you'd have to grow out in South America, and people would have fearful trouble to find you, and risk their lives—— Hullo! Brown-faced chap's coming this way."

Miss Llewellyn looked up, and then looked down again quickly, and for a moment her face went rather white. Her hand trembled as she held it out.

"Mr. Bradley," she said. "How do you do? I did not expect to see you here."

"I did not expect to see you again anywhere," he said.

There was the pause that comes after the banalities of greeting. Master Waller, not having spoken for quite half a minute, felt that he was in some danger of being overlooked, and coughed.

"This is my little friend Kenneth Waller," she said. "Kenneth, this is Mr. Bradley."

"What's the matter with your face?" asked the small boy. "Have you been abroad?"

Mr. Bradley placed a broad fist on the round iron table, and leaned down towards Master Waller good-naturedly. He seemed as confused at the meeting as Miss Llewellyn, and as unprepared with conversation.

"I have been abroad, young man. I've been hunting orchids."

"Are you home for good now?" asked Kenneth.

Miss Llewellyn gripped the parasol that rested in her lap with both hands.

"I can't do any good at home," said Mr. Bradley. "I am off again to South America in a day or two."

"Why don't you stay in London?"

"Nobody asks me to stay."

"Should have thought," said Master Waller, "that you could have got somebody to do that. Have you got any foreign postage stamps about you?"

Friendship between the two gentlemen was cemented and made permanent by the production of several foreign stamps and an envelope to place them in. People were coming up to the

Master Waller. "I'm awfully good at that. And tell us some of your adventures."

"They wouldn't interest Miss Llewellyn."

"Girls don't count," said Master Waller. "Tell me. Make it," said Master Waller, appealingly, "one where you nearly lost your life."

So ten or fifteen minutes were thus occupied, the small boy seated on Bradley's knee, and staring at him with open-mouthed astonishment. Miss Llewellyn, her head bowed, studied the band programme in apparently a laborious search for the mis-

"Brown-faced man's coming this way."

refreshment tent now, the band having decided to rest for half an hour and recover breath, and Master Waller invited Mr. Bradley to take his chair.

"You don't mind?" asked Bradley of Miss Llewellyn.

"Not at all," she said, politely.

"May I smoke?"

"Let me strike the match," interposed

prints that a musical programme always offers. Bradley told the story very well, without obtruding his own share in the adventure, and when he had finished, punched the small boy humorously to bring him back from South America to Regent's Park.

"And is that story true?" asked the small boy, respectfully.

"It has that drawback, youngster."

"Well," said Master Waller, "I'm a man that's awfully fond of adventure, but I shouldn't care for that. What did you think of when that fierce animal was waiting to spring upon you?"

"Guess."

"Can't," said Master Waller. "Can you, Miss Llewellyn?"

She shook her head, and again became interested in the band programme. Bradley looked at her and waited for her to speak, but she made no sign. Now silence may at times be tolerable for grown-up folk, but for impatient young men like Master Waller it brings nothing but weariness.

"Is there any chance of seeing these orchids, Mr. Bradley?" asked the youth. "It'll be something to brag about to my people if I could just get a sight of them."

"We'll all go over to the marquee and have a look. Miss Llewellyn, will you come, or shall we leave you here? There's rather a crush."

"Let's leave her," suggested Master Waller. "Miss Llewellyn likes being alone."

"I think I will stay here," she said.

"We shall be back in ten minutes," said Bradley.

Master Waller had to trot to keep up with the long strides of his new friend, but he did not mind this, because he felt a kind of reflected glory in being accompanied by the man who had brought home some of the rarest of the amazing specimens in the crowded tent.

"Girls are a nuisance, aren't they?" said Master Waller, looking up confidentially.

"Sometimes," said Bradley.

'Here, I say, don't grip a man's shoulder."

"She isn't so tiresome though as some."

"I think I agree with you there."

"Works awfully hard. Too hard, my mamma says."

"No necessity for that, surely," said Bradley, rather sharply.

"But Miss Llewellyn has to live," urged the small boy. "My mamma says that she was well off for a year or two before her father died, but since that——"

"Her father dead?"

"Here, I say," said Master Waller. "Don't grip a man's shoulder like that."

"Sorry!"

"They came into money, so my mamma says, a few years ago——"

"I remember that."

"And then Miss Llewellyn's governor put it all into something, and it never came out again. That's why she has to manage the calisthenic school that I go to. And I say! Can you touch your toes with the tips of your fingers without——"

"Where does she live now?" Mr. Bradley seemed excited.

"In rooms," replied Master Waller, volubly. "I've been there to tea along with my sisters. (That's a fine orchid there. You can't see it now; a girl's hat's in the way.) And Miss Llewellyn's got awfully nice furniture and photographs, and ——" Master Waller slapped his knee suddenly. "I remember now where I've seen your face before, Mr. Bradley. Only without the short beard."

"Come outside," said Bradley, "and tell me."

They made their way through the crowd and reached the exit. Bradley held his breath, and bent to hear the small boy's reply.

"On her dressing-table," whispered Master Waller, confidentially, "in the beautifullest frame you ever saw, and—— Where are you going?"

"Back to Miss Llewellyn," cried Bradley.

"Well, but," said Master Waller, protestingly, "wait for me."

Bradley did not obey the young man. He strode across the lawn, past the band, which was playing a quick march that was not quick enough to keep pace with him. Before Master Waller found the two, there had been a swift exchange of low sentences that altered their views of the world, and made them both think of it as a place where happiness is to be found.

"And why did you refuse me before, dear?"

"Because all my people pressed me to accept you," said Miss Llewellyn.

"The excuse of a very obstinate young woman."

"Why did you—why did you not ask me again?" she demanded.

"Because," said Bradley, "it was just then that your father came into that money."

"The excuse of a very independent man," said Miss Llewellyn, touching with pretty affection the big hand that rested on the

round table. "When—when is it that you leave for South America?"

"Not until you tell me to go, dear," he said, promptly.

"Here, I say," cried Master Waller, arriving after some difficulty. "You two! Don't lose

" Why did you refuse me before, dear?"

sight of me, mind. Miss Llewellyn, have I been a good boy?"

"I've a great mind to kiss you, Kenneth," she said.

"Rather have some more lemonade."

"As Kenneth declines your suggestion," said Bradley, signalling to a waiter, "may I venture to submit myself——"

"Hush!" said Miss Llewellyn.

Life and Work at Home.

OVER THE TEACUPS.

By ANNIE S. SWAN.

I AM glad to be able to tell my readers that the new series of

Annie S. Swan's Penny Stories

has from the first met with a most gratifying reception. As I write, the sixth story,

"A RUNAWAY DAUGHTER,"

By ANNIE S. SWAN,

has just appeared, and there has been no falling off in sale, nor any decline of interest. The series has indeed been a striking success from the beginning, and I am deeply grateful for the kind sympathy and the practical aid of my readers in THE WOMAN AT HOME. Many letters have been received from parents, and among them I may quote the following from "A Mother":—

"I cannot thank you sufficiently for the bright and wholesome stories you are giving us. My daughter, aged seventeen, will read hardly anything but fiction, and I am grateful for the new series, which supplies exactly what I like her to read. I rejoice specially in the earnest religious teaching which the stories provide in a simple and unobtrusive form. I earnestly pray that you may have strength to carry on this work."

The Press has also been generously appreciative of the new venture. The *North British Daily Mail* says of "The Secret of Dunstan Mere":—

"This is the first of an intended weekly issue of penny stories, which will be designed to supply healthy and improving fiction for general consumption—qualities in which the average penny tale is not conspicuously rich. As regards get-up—printing, binding, and illustration—there is not the least question as to the superiority of this series over all its rivals, the illustrations especially being of an artistic excellence that almost warrants us in bestowing on the publishers the title of philanthropists, so impossible does it seem to provide such pictures at such a cost. We wish the series all success in its effort to combat the mass of cheap, pernicious literature from which too many of our youth of both sexes derive their sole literary nutriment."

ONE feels reluctant to break in on holiday time, and work generally pleasant and congenial becomes a trifle irksome when the tired mind is bent on play. I will therefore ask my readers' indulgence if I have little or nothing to say to them this month. I am thinking as I write here at my sunny turret window, with the whole glorious expanse of the sea before me, that by the time this meets the reader's eye the holiday will be over, and all, or nearly all, will have set themselves to the winter's work. But what of those who have no holiday—who toil, year in and year out, without change or relaxation of any kind? There are many such. But there must be compensation. I think a great deal in my quiet moments, when the problems of life press, about this law of compensation. Its working is visible everywhere, and there is comfort in it to all upon whom the sorrows of others lie heavily. Some day, when space offers, I should like to return to this thought, and consider it in relation to the daily happenings that are the lot of all. Meanwhile, I will to the letters, which have crossed the border after me and lie at my elbow, mutely demanding answer.

* * *

How can I thank E. M. M. (Brighton) for her words of cheer? I do thank her from my heart, and I shall try more and more to reach the high ideal of which she so sweetly writes. Sometimes when many cares press the heights seem very far off, but it is always helpful to look up.

* * *

I am very much amused at the letter signed THREE SCOTCH GIRLS. It refers to a recent story of mine published elsewhere, in which two of the characters were not satisfactorily disposed of at the end. "Three Scotch Girls" naively enquire "whether I would mind saying what I have done with them." I was so glad to get my heroine extricated from a desperate situation that I did not give the minor personages of the story the consideration they deserved. But there is not the slightest doubt in my mind that they married and lived happily ever after.

* * *

The letter of ANNIE has puzzled me a good deal. I fear there is some hitch in the domestic arrangements. It could not be very pleasant for anybody to spend a holiday in a house where one of the inmates took her meals in a separate room in consequence of disagreement with her sister. Yet the letter has interested me, and if "Annie" cares to give me any further particulars, I shall be pleased to hear from her.

* * *

I thank AN OLD FRIEND AND CONSTANT READER for her kind letter and all its good wishes. I assure you they are treasured and remembered. I am full of sympathy for her in her bereavement, but I think she is able to look on the brighter side of things; and after all, her dearest is only within the veil, her without, for a little while.

* * *

I am sorry that I do not presently know of any child likely to suit J. M., who wishes to adopt a little girl. The difficulty is to get one for whom board would be paid. I thank her for her kind letter.

* * *

Can any one tell A. V. O. whether there are agencies for houeskeepers similar to those for governesses? I rather think not, and that house-keepers' situations are obtained through any ordinary employment bureau or by advertisement. Perhaps some kind reader would advise. Experience is more valuable than any diploma always, in the practical affairs of life.

* * *

I regret that the exigencies of magazine publication cause unavoidable delay in replying to letters. I fear that this will appear too late to be of the slightest use to LAUNDRY; nevertheless, I think it wise to insert it. This correspondent, along with another lady, has started a laundry near Birkenhead, and is troubled about getting suitable people to do the work. She makes rather a novel suggestion. "Do you think any of your readers would be likely to know of ladies, or perhaps themselves feel inclined to do the work, as, with the exception of the wash-house, I see no reason why the work should not be entirely done by ladies? They could always find accommodation in the village. They need not do the actual washing, but the plain and fine ironing, and perhaps shirts and collars. The latter is hard work, requiring long practice to do well, but if any of your readers care to entertain the idea, they might write to me direct: Miss Darbyshire, Beechbank Farm, Manor Road, Liscard, Cheshire."

* * *

S. W. is too late in writing. By the time this meets the eyes of my readers, the holiday season will be entirely over. She wished to ask whether any kind, benevolent person would offer a holiday home to her young daughter presently at school, S. W. herself being in a situation and unable to receive her daughter for the holidays. Perhaps, however, this appeal may be fruitful of good results for another season.

* * *

WANDERER is a wise woman. Like the prodigal of old, she has tasted the husks of life and found them bitter. Let her emulate the prodigal in the later and wiser portion of his wasted life. Let her "arise and go to her father."

* * *

So long as WEXFORD continues in such a frame of mind there is little likelihood of the old friendly relations being established between the two families. "Whispering tongues can poison truth," and how obvious it is that out of the veriest trifles great misunderstanding and often great tragedies arise. If "Wexford" really desires a reconciliation—and in the interests of the younger members of the families it seems most desirable—let him hold out the olive branch. A little pride, not unnatural in the circumstances, prevents him, but even though his advances should not be cordially met, he will have the approval of his own conscience. Also, he should not forget that he was very greatly to blame in the first instance. Please write again.

* * *

Reduce expenditure at once. There is no

other way, if Doreen really wishes to help her husband and get rid of the many harassing complications in their domestic life. No ; I should not feel the slightest shame. I have no pride of that kind. As to what the neighbours will say, read the story of the old man and his ass. It is one of the parables that never grow old. I don't think myself advice is much use to anybody. People seldom act on it, unless they go to a lawyer and pay for it ; then they are bound to act on it, to refund themselves for the outlay. It is a solemn truth that

most people value highly what costs them dear.

*   *   *

No, I don't think the world is worse than it was, Langley, but, if anything, rather better on the whole. Don't forget that we live in a glare of publicity, and that our deeds, good and evil, are proclaimed from the housetops, as they never were in the good old days. But light is a good thing. Don't you remember what Scripture says of those who love the darkness—that "their deeds are evil"? So there is compensation in all things.

DRESS AND FASHION.

There is no striking change in the world of fashion as yet, but we may chronicle the new skirt, and almost predict with safety the advent of the train. Not only are we to wear trains for home, dinner, and evening wear, but our

No. 1.

walking dresses are actually made to sweep the microbe off the streets !

*   *   *

We must, I suppose, bow our necks to the yoke of Madame La Mode, but it is not without a pang that I can relinquish those smart walking skirts which relieved us from the painful necessity of holding up a portion of our raiment, giving us the freedom of motion so necessary to a graceful method of walking. French women who make a study of detail will probably be able to gather the overplus drapery in one hand, raising it gracefully a few inches to the required height as they wend their way over the muddy streets. One consolation is to be derived from the new state of things, and that is the little weight we shall have to carry. The over or "skirt proper" will be unlined and made over a silk foundation, which will no doubt assume the rôle of petticoat as well. We shall have to be more than ever fastidious about our boots and hosiery, as the uncertain limits attained by the lifting of a skirt often shows more ankle than was at first intended. In fact, under the new régime we find many details which we shall have to point out and attend to, and which were never mentioned in the history of the short skirt.

*   *   *

There are several varieties of new skirts. The first is plain in shape, but rather fuller at the back than those worn of yore. Trimming of some kind is always adopted, whether it be put on over the hem or over the hips. For tailor-made gowns barrel-hoop rows of silk braid are put on from the waist-band to a little below the hips in graduated lines. Perhaps the same rows in three, five, or seven will appear at the bottom of the skirt or the front breadth alone in longitudinal lines of three on either side. This is a style eminently adapted to short,

No. 2.

set with large square stones, turquoise, coral, etc. The coat or blouse fastens on the left side in a straight line from the neck under a band of embroidery, fur or braided material.

* * *

Oxidised silver is often introduced into the handsomest broiderie, but its beauty must perforce be transient in a climate like ours. In some cases the moujik blouse is of velvet of the same colour as the skirt. A golden brown cloth will have a coat blouse of a deeper hue in plain or ribbed velvet. I am happy to note the return of the rich golden browns which we had thrown into the limbo of forgotten things. With a touch of lemon, turquoise, or almond green, brown assumes a smartness that one would hardly credit such a quiet colour with ! Manderine which is redder than its wont blends admirably with dark or navy blue, as does a vivid ruby, coral, or "canary," a curious opaque yellow.

* * *

Blue and brown will be a very favourite contrast of colours for the autumn, though personally I prefer brown and green, as it is a true autumn colouring. The russet tints are always seen at this season of the year ; when they deepen into raspberry reds or rosy coral, they are most becoming to those they suit.

stout women, as it adds to the height ; it is more adopted for matrons than maids, however. Designs of different kinds, key border pattern, V's, etc., are formed with inch-wide silk braid on many of the winter skirts, and later on we shall have fur generally worn on almost all the dresses. In fact, fur will be, with Russian and other embroideries, the most fashionable of trimming. The embroideries are all in different and mixed colouring on cloth, velvet, net, etc., cut in long bands, panels, vests, etc. In lighter guise the Louis Seize embroideries on fine muslin or chiffon will supply a resourceful trimming for ball dresses. A little, very little glitter will be introduced into some of these in the guise of spangle or jewels, but the duller gems will be used, such as lapis, turquoise, black pearls, and pink coral.

* * *

Russian schemes of colouring and methods of dress will be thought out by the leading modistes. Green, "Vert Russe" will be a leading shade, trimmed with black silk braid and flashes of red, orange, white, or tartan. There is a marked tendency to pouch the bodices of whatever shape they may be. The Russian blouse bids fair to be much worn in the winter, as it is smart, easy to make, and comfortable to wear. It is a sort of blouse with a basque belted in to the waist by a fancy belt of Russian oxidised silver

No. 3.

The blouse is flickering; it has assumed warmer tints. The tartan silk ones show under kiltings of red silk in the collar and trimming. I cannot as yet foresee the final end of blouses, but they are destined to play a very secondary part in the history of winter dress.

* * *

Very light coloured cloths trimmed with fur will make elegant visiting gowns; but the acmé of elegance is to be the velvet dress trimmed with fur. Millinery will participate in the same style, that is to say, that very many of the hats will either be trimmed with or made entirely of fur; in fact, there is a sort of Eastern and barbaric splendour in some of the new fur "toquets," or "bonnets," with their sweeping aigrettes, heron's or eagle's plumes, fastened by superbly jewelled clasps or buckles. The hats are worn boldly on one side, without any ornament or trimming under the brim, unless it be a roll of velvet of some bright hue which gives a turban-like appearance to the headgear. The new felts have a lovely gloss, and are as supple as velvet; they are called "feutre velours." They are as easily draped as a piece of material, and will be sold "en plateaux," or in flat round pieces when required, so that the milliner or amateur can drape them according to her own fancy. We have the usual "boom" about the coal-scuttle bonnet-hat, but as we have the same thing every year, one grows rather sceptical.

* * *

Lovely hat crowns are being made of the ibis and humming-bird feathers; these are made with brims of white or pale green felt. The shades of the new felts are endless in the variety of colouring — lavender, blues, rose-leaf pink, pale "buff," all kinds of dove and pearl greys, lilacs, etc. Flyaway bows of twisted velvet, ruffles of lace stiffened with gold wire, and feathers *ad lib*. The Rubens hat is most picturesque. The brims of black velvet hats will be lined with white or coloured velvets. If we are to be sober in our dress, we will make up for it in our headgear, which appears destined to the greatest eccentricity. Gold, silver, and jewels will be profusely used. Some closely-fitting baby bonnets are embroidered like Alsatian caps. The tendency for hats to be trimmed high at the back and low in front is a relic of the

Mildred Harris

No. 4.

Louis Quinze and Seize periods. Some of the hat crowns are made in this way.

* * *

We do not know how women with large hips will accommodate themselves to the fashion of full-gathered or pleated skirts. Some double skirts, slightly draped, are showing in the shop windows. As yet I have not seen them worn. Grey as a colour is no longer considered smart; it had a brief but successful reign. Very pretty dresses for girls of fourteen to sixteen are made thus: The skirt would be of green serge, with blouse bodice of fancy or tartan silk, over which is worn a very deep sailor collar, almost a capelet, of the green serge, trimmed with bias folds of itself; a green sailor tie is worn with this. Sashes are popular for young girls' dresses.

* * *

Wedding dresses are simplicity itself. In Duchesse satin or the new stone moiré, the train-skirt alone is hemmed with trails of orange-buds on a billowy puffing of chiffon. The high-draped belt confining a pouched bodice of chiffon is fastened by a knot of blossoms, and a smaller bunch fastens the neck.

* * *

Feather boas are still very fashionable; they must never meet under the chin, as they shorten the neck; they should be invisibly fastened on each side to frame the face and protect the back of the neck and ears, which is really all that is needed. Neck ruffles are popular also in three shades of rose or lavender chiffon, silk, muslin, or ribbons, edged with velvet or gold braid. These ruched collarettes are prettier for very young girls than the feather boas.

* * *

Very pretty seaside wraps or travelling cloaks are of thick Moleton or Pyreneen flannel; they are very long and ample, and provided with a cape and very large hood, which can be turned over the hat. Two slits admit of the hands being at liberty to carry parcels, and deep inner pockets are placed in the inside. A wide black mohair or tartan fancy galoon trims these mantles effectively. Reefer-like jackets are only buttoned on one side by three buttons, and are much braided. The new Princess gowns are

fastened on the left side, and often scalloped in rounded festoons from neck to ankle. Accordion pleatings are again seen in three flounces to form skirts made of light woollen materials. The blouse is accordion-kilted, and the bolero vest

No. 5.

is of palm or shawl pattern velvet with double revers, the inner revers being of white moiré. This makes a really elegant and uncommon toilette. White in square or round chemisettes is much worn near the face. The hair is being worn much lower, as the very high chignon suits so few people. Tucks and flounces are still much worn as trimming.

* * *

DESCRIPTION OF FASHION DRAWINGS.

No. 1.—This charming evening dress for a girl is made in pink and white checked silk, with white chiffon ruches on bodice and skirt, and small vest and sleeves of the same. The bodice is crossed with bands of lace lined with pink satin, finished on either side with chiffon rosettes. A pretty satin sash encircles the waist, and is tied at the left side. Three little silk frills edge the skirt. The original from which this sketch was taken was made by one of the leading dressmakers in the West-end.

No. 2.—This very charming evening bodice is made in pink silk, with a pretty drapery in pink silk muslin, caught together on the bust. This is edged with a soft frill of the muslin, while frills of the same fabric form the sleeves, which are fastened to straps of jewelled passementerie crossing the shoulders.

No. 3.—This lovely little evening cape was shown at the same establishment as No. 1. Its foundation was in white satin, beautifully embroidered with white and gold cord and studded with turquoises. The neck had a ruche of chiffon delicately edged with a tiny band of lace, and the deep full frill of lace at the lower part of the cape was again headed by another little ruching of the chiffon.

No. 4.—A stylish gown in blue mohair or faced cloth trimmed with narrow black satin ribbon. The bodice fastens a little on the left side, and slightly overhangs the waistband; it is made with a short basque piped with satin ribbon. The smart shoulder collar is covered with guipure lace, and edged with a frill of lisse or satin. The sleeves are tightly fitting, with small puffs gathered in three divisions at the shoulders; these and the skirt are trimmed in the same manner with narrow satin ribbon and frills.

No. 5.—The next illustration shows a very useful and ornamental coat and skirt for autumn wear. It is fashioned in brown Melton cloth, with collar and cuffs in watered silk (or in biscuit-coloured cloth, if preferred). Black and gold cord makes a pretty trimming on both coat and skirt.

By Annie S. Swan.

ALIAS is in a pretty fix. He has engaged himself to a girl under an assumed name, and she has found him out. Well, I can't express sympathy when I don't feel it, and I am not sorry for "Alias." He richly deserves all he has got. His motive in behaving so dishonourably is not clear. He began to amuse himself with the girl, and to safeguard himself, paid her attentions under an assumed name. Now he cares for her in earnest, and would like to redeem himself in her eyes. This, I fear, is hardly possible. She has behaved like a woman of spirit and proper womanly feeling, and there is but little chance that she will ever respect him again. There is nothing he can do but retire as gracefully as the circumstances permit, and let the sharp lesson he has received help him to act like an honourable man in the future.

* * *

BILLINGSGATE is quite right, and his language is so temperate that I don't know why he has chosen the above pseudonym. The young woman is an incorrigible flirt, rejoicing, like the Indian brave, in the number of scalps at her belt. Let her severely alone. Her day of reckoning will come.

* * *

There is no use in expressing any opinion on second marriages, MAUD. It is one of the most vexed of social questions. The expediency or wisdom of such a step depends entirely on the individuals most concerned, and on the circumstances in which they are placed. The case she presents would certainly seem to justify an early marriage. It is really the only course open to the man. As to her own action in the matter, that she must herself decide. It is too great a responsibility for me to advise.

BETHIA HARDACRE, I think, stands on a perilous brink. How often have I advised girls in these columns to shun a man who wants to make love secretly, and who dreads anyone, especially his sweetheart's parents, suspecting his existence. There is something wrong. Refuse to meet him. If he really cares for you, and is a man worth troubling your head about, he will seek you in your father's house, as he ought.

* * *

Poor little WINTHROP asks rather a pathetic question: "Do you think God takes any interest in my poor little love affair?" I certainly think He does. Has "Winthrop" forgotten the words of Scripture concerning the sparrow which cannot fall to the ground without His knowledge? I should like to see "Winthrop" trying to cultivate a little more backbone. I fear that may be an obscure sentence to her, so I will elucidate it. She is too meek and yielding, and humble. A man soon tires of that. If "Winthrop" keeps on as she is doing, and marries the man, she will develop him into a petty domestic tyrant. This is inevitable. I hope she will take warning in time.

* * *

WAITING ONE asks for my advice, but I rather think, reading between the lines of her letter, that her mind is already made up. And I am glad that it is so, for there is no reason why she should not be happy with him. One sentence is a little obscure. She says: "I am very strong against marrying a man who takes drink." Am I to infer from these words that that is the real lion in the path, and not the disparity in years? That is a more serious matter. I hope she will write to me more explicitly again. But I repeat that the age need be no barrier. Love can easily bridge it.

I hope that VIOLA will not allow any of the silly and prejudiced remarks of other people to bias her in her decision at this crisis in her life. The disparity in years is nothing. It is so slight that in a few years it would not be noticeable. A woman ages sooner than a man. I feel sure that if all she writes about her lover is true, she will be very happy with him. I am glad she takes such a sensible view of the estate of matrimony. It is incomparably the happiest state of existence, provided there is love and unity of purpose to cement the bond. A house divided against itself cannot stand.

* * *

I am much interested in the letter of ROTHESAY. Although I am no match-maker, I think something might be done. Could not "Rothesay" and her sister let their house for a time and travel, living preferably at hydropathics, or in hotels where there are other boarders, not mere birds of passage? Impostors are not likely to come forward unless some fortune is suspected. "Rothesay" and her sister would take care to say nothing about means. I quite understand all she has written and all she feels for her sister. A little change is certainly imperative for both. Please write again.

* * *

Many girls are placed in the position of STRAWBERRY, and it is a hard case. A young man pays a certain amount of attention, succeeds in interesting, and finally in winning a girl's affections, and stops short of actual declaration, leaving the girl in a cruel state of uncertainty. I have carefully read "Strawberry's" letter, and I am inclined to think the lover in this case is all right. There is nothing she can do but wait. To wait is the woman's heritage. It is hard, harder than any work. But let "Strawberry" not lose heart altogether. God looks on, and they also serve who only stand and wait. Whatever she does, I hope she will preserve her dignity and womanly pride.

* * *

D. is very hard on M. B., who asked the question, "Should a girl who is a Christian marry a man who is not?" She reminds M. B. that the teaching of Scripture is authoritative. "Be ye not equally yoked with unbelievers." She says: "I know there are many young men who are the embodiment of everything that is true and noble, and who would make ideal husbands, but if they lack the 'one thing needful,' are they not regarded by God as His enemies, and classed by Him with the vilest sinners on earth?" I cannot help saying, God forbid, to that last sentence. I should like to hear the opinion of my readers on this subject.

* * *

AUSTRAL's letter is very long, twelve closely written sheets. It is impossible to take up all the points it deals with. The writer is very sound on most subjects evidently, and takes a wide and tolerant view of the troubles of married life. There is nothing very original, however; we all know that where confidence and love exist no matrimonial troubles arise. He does not approve of the matrimonial bureau, but thinks the good old way the best. I am delighted to hear of all his good fortune. I feel sure he deserves it. If only he carries all his written precepts into his daily life, his wife will be a happy woman. I should much like to have a contribution to the marriage question from him twelve months hence. I sincerely thank him for his kind words about the aims of this magazine.

* * *

I am sorry all is not smooth sailing for M. J. over her approaching marriage. But as she only states the fact, it is not for me to offer comment or advice. It would be correct for her to buy a small wedding cake to offer to guests who may call afterwards. It would also be correct to offer such a cup of tea.

* * *

WILLOUGHBY is right about the child. It would make all the difference. I earnestly pray that she may be granted her heart's desire.

SIMPLE HOMES AND HOW TO MAKE THEM.

By Mrs. J. E. Panton,

AUTHOR OF "FROM KITCHEN TO GARRET."

I.—THE SMALL HOUSE OF THE FUTURE.

T is undoubtedly a puzzle to many young people starting in life, first where to find a house which they can develop into a home at their leisure ; and secondly how best to obtain the necessary surroundings which can make that home a thing of beauty ; which if it cannot, in these migratory days of ours, be a joy for ever, can at least be a pleasure to them and to their friends for as long as they may choose to inhabit it.

I have noted with real and sincere sorrow that whatever the "glorious sixty years" have done for us—and I am not backward for one moment in acknowledging to the full how very much this is—they have not developed and fostered that passionate attachment to the house as home, that used to be part and parcel of one's life in the middle and later middle half of the present century.

Then the mere word home was enough to cause one's heart-strings to thrill as one recollected the dear old house, which still possessed the very same carpets we had crawled over as a baby, the tables we had knocked our heads against, and the chairs we had fallen off, and which all seemed, and indeed were, part and parcel of the good days of one's youth. Then one's father and mother succeeded to the very surroundings where the old folks had brought up one's father, and we too some day knew that in the course of nature we or ours should go on in the same place—where every stone had its story to tell us, and where we were as small gods, because those by whom we were surrounded had in their turn known us and looked up to us for generations, and had shared our joys and sorrows as we too had shared theirs, in the way nothing can be shared save by those who have known, loved, aye, and hated each other, all the length of their mutual lives.

I am not alluding to the lords of the soil either, though even in these days they change as often as the rest of us, and where once

flourished a "good old family" the newly-made millionaire glitters, or the tremendously successful tradesman keeps up his luxurious and startling household. But I am thinking of the many excellent "family houses" I have known in good old country towns, of the smaller domains in villages, and one or two fair-sized houses in London. Still these, I am free to confess, are few and far between : which have passed from father to son, where father and son have carried on and developed businesses that have been as the apple of their eye, and which, in my humble opinion, are but ill-replaced by the tremendous "companies" where the individual is swamped by the "board," and where the delightful servants who were once our joy and pride, as we were theirs, are replaced by the "hands" or by the employé, a more detestable development still, who is neither fish, flesh, fowl, nor good red-herring. In fact, the whole tendency of the age is to break down the barriers that fenced in the home, and which were once considered sacred, and few indeed are the young wives who do not dislike and dread the troubles of housekeeping. While they regard their houses as mere shells to hold them when they are tired or ill, and out of which they may escape as soon as they possibly can, for the fascinating, all-absorbing bicycle ride, or for the many enjoyments that are as inevitable now as they were impossible in the days that are no more, and that were no doubt as dull as they were decorous and desirable. But this is not a question I wish to debate at the present moment. I am not at all sure which days were the best ; I remember the one, and am an amused spectator of the other, and while I naturally believe the days of my girlhood cannot be improved on, while I am quite sure that no one can now love their first home of their "very own" as I loved—aye, and still love—the one I first called mine, I can quite well remember grey expanses of time when I had nothing to do but read, walk, or make feeble calls on people I did not want to see in the least, and when I should have been thankful for one or two at least of the many delightful digressions that are now a matter of course in the lives of the very humblest of us all. At the same time, I want to plead very strongly for the keeping up among us of the real English home that has been so much to us for so many generations. There is a very great deal, very much more than we really understand, in what we mean when we say that almost all we are, or may become, springs from those things by which we were surrounded when we first began to notice life, and to realise that we too were part and parcel of that great mystery. No one can possibly forget, for example, how in one moment certain scents bring back infallibly certain events or pictures to our remembrance as vividly as if they had only just occurred, as if they had only just been seen. For example, does not gardenia bring back to us at once a perfect recollection of our first real dance ; the odour of white pinks, a certain " long border " in a country garden from whence many a bouquet, many a wreath for the beloved dead were gathered ; while scented verbena and lavender recall other pictures to us, which without their kindly help might die altogether and leave us poorer by the loss of many good and kindly recollections of the blessed days when we were young.

Yet perhaps my readers will say, a trifle impatiently, and what has all this to do with the making of a home, let alone a simple one ? Well, and if they do, I can but reply, surely almost every single thing ; for without the aids of romance, of memory, and of dreaming, it is impossible to lay even the foundation stone of a moderate and modern house that shall be in any degree of the least satisfaction to the owner thereof.

The Jerry Builder.

Ah ! would that I could place my foe, the suburban jerry builder of the period, in an hypnotic trance, and so influence him for the future in his desecration of " eligible building sites " that he will no longer put one plank between the dining-room floor of his " residences " and the bare earth ; that he will no longer consider electric bells, slow combustion stoves, and an artistic appearance —all good things in their way—as substitutes for responsible building, good drainage, and some idea of the way a house should face. Then perhaps when he buys some beautiful old house and park, once the home of a real old family, he will not at once proceed to tear down the house piecemeal, to cut down the trees and clear out all that once made it a lovely possession, but he will endeavour to preserve the special old-world charm of the place, and to arrange and distribute his new houses, so that the inhabitants shall not at once become bitter enemies by reason of their nearness to each other, and the utter inability they possess to get out of each other's way, in the direction of smoke, smells, domestic jars, pianos, and the thousand and one items that mar one's existence in a suburb or in a country town even more than they can in the smaller and narrower London streets.

If the jerry builder would furthermore depart from his one idea of a suburban residence, which at present consists of getting as much discomfort as he possibly can into a certain space, and caring for nothing save that he can advertise the orthodox and horrible three "reception-rooms," four bed-rooms, bath, dressing-rooms and usual offices, and would realise that another style of house would be far more useful and much more likely to be lived in, than the hundreds of empty houses which abound wherever his trail is over the earth ; we should then have more hope than we have at present that our ideal should be realised, and that the home would be once more a feature in the land.

But at present no one seems to understand that if we live simply and honestly we can be much happier than we are at present ; if they did, they would certainly begin at the beginning, and take care that the house should be built with common sense and with an eye to lasting, and, moreover, in such a manner that it could be enlarged should one desire to have a bigger place without the expense, discomfort, and misery of a move. Besides, once be certain that a move is inevitable, that sooner or later it must come the "temporary" feeling seizes one ; that draught which has caused so many colds is left alone, the paint and paper are allowed to remain in a hideous and shabby state. What does it all matter ? another year will find us elsewhere ; and so it goes on, until we get into the habit of not caring, and insensibly we lose affection for home-life, because we have never put in our roots and become, as it were, part and parcel of the soil.

On Avoiding Hurry.

Therefore, before we can make our home, it is absolutely necessary that we should find a house and a congenial place to live in, and never let us be driven in a hurry to make such an important choice. Hurry is always a fatal mistake. There is never any good done when one has not the necessary time to weigh, consider, and think over what we are going to do, to be, or to have, let it be the small matter merely of a hat or coat, or the great and everlasting business of choosing a mate, and afterwards the place in which one's future life will grow, and become either a good or evil thing as one chooses to let circumstance and fate make of it. Indeed, the real drawback to happiness now-a-days is the desperate haste in which we set to work to get it. "They complain of that material fading," said one good friend of mine, with whom I often have a chat on the ever-absorbing subject of furniture and decoration, "but they have no one to blame but themselves in the matter. Constantly I have to send material to the dyers on Monday, and they won't give me a day longer than Thursday before they must have it, and what is the consequence? out goes the colour, and then they come and scold me. Formerly dyers used to mix their colours and allow them to stand for at least a fortnight before they were applied to the fabric, which in its turn took some time to stain; now it's as much as they can do to colour the material at all. Fade! of course it must fade, but then folks can only blame themselves for that and for the machine-made rubbish of furniture that floods the market and that cannot possibly be anything save most unsatisfactory." First of all, then, we have to consider the fact that the really simple small house of the future is well-nigh impossible at the present; and secondly we have to recollect that to have a house that will give us pleasure, we must spend a certain amount of money on good, plain, substantial furniture that shall have a reasonable chance of lasting at least some good portion of our lifetime. Here let me say most emphatically that as a rule the furniture is most undoubtedly to be procured, is far more easily obtained, than is the house, if we go slowly and are not influenced by what I may call the "penny-three-farthing" style of thing. By this I mean we must not allow ourselves to be induced to buy some particular chair or table because it is just a few pence cheaper than a similar article we have seen in another shop; for be well assured if those few pence are taken off, there is some deep and subtle reason for it, and that we cannot possibly have the same thing at a less price unless we are prepared to support the "cutting system" in the trade that is doing such an immense amount of harm to honest work, or unless we are prepared also to find

the "same thing" glued together, instead of being properly fastened in such a way, that nothing save bad usage will render it the wreck the glued article will become the moment it is exposed to an extra warm fire, or even to the rays of our seldom seen and much-prized English sun. Another undoubted curse of the present day is the tremendous rage for advertisement. Someone must pay for these advertisements, and though by their aid we are undoubtedly able to obtain excellent literature at a twentieth part of the price we should have had to pay before advertisements appeared even in the field and on the sides of our beautiful river, I question much whether we had not better merely rely on our own judgment, or better still on the recommendation of someone we can emphatically trust, than on the many and varied temptations spread before us in the pages of almost every paper and periodical we take up.

The Choice of Furniture.

Another almost fatal thing to do in furnishing is to pin one's faith on one special firm, and go to that firm, and that only, for every single thing. This I should do, were I beginning life once more, as regards the less ornamental and more solid parts of the plenishing, but I should never get every stick and stone at one place, any more than I should buy my pictures, ornaments, glass and china where I buy my beds, and I am always sorry when I see the "stores" or "amalgamation" system of the present day invading any of the excellent shops I have known ever since I knew anything at all. I can at this moment put my hand, as it were, on the best armchair and sofa in the world, but the glass and china procurable at that same place are not to be desired in the least. I know where to get real old furniture, but then the new at that same establishment is not as good as it is in some less well-known place. Eastern carpets are to be procured at one place, English ones at another. There is only one shop in London for lamps, gas-fittings, and similar odds and ends; and in the same way I maintain that each establishment one knows, as I know those I have carefully frequented for something like fifteen years, for my own benefit first and then for the many hundreds of "correspondents" I have helped in the way they should go, has its one speciality, and that careful and good house furnishing can only be done by those who know what they want: this above all: who know where to get that special thing, who are not influenced by the shopman in the least. While they consider first of all what they have to spend and what their house requires ; and who are content to begin life with just the bare necessaries, for it is only until we have lived in a house that we understand it and it understands us, and we can then become mutually attached and comfortable. Of course it is very difficult for young people to be able to wait, or to be able to believe that they do not know a great deal more on the subject of home-making than anyone else, and I have often had to talk to young folk who only want a gorgeous and " up-to-date " (odious expression !) place in which to sleep, be ill, and receive their friends : the only three things some people require a house for, for even their meals are often enough taken out. Or else to those others who appear most anxious to learn, whose foot one puts finally in the right path, and yet who fall away the moment one's eye is off them. For are they not talked into buying the ancient gray-brown or muddled wall-paper as the " next thing " by the enterprising builder, instead of the beautiful real coloured one we have carefully selected for them ? Or do they not possess some great-aunt who dreads a draught and can't come to tea unless the carpets fit the rooms ? Then their uncle by marriage has a " friend in the trade " who has a beautiful " suite " he can let them have at cost price : a suite, by the way, the friend would really have gladly paid someone to make away with ; and finally, they have such a weak-eyed set of acquaintance that they persist in stuffing up their windows with a hideous blind and two sets of curtains, no matter what their size or shape, adding some great chair or sofa there which entirely prevents the windows being approached, while the flood of beautiful clear air and bright sunshine which alone can keep us in health is excluded because someone can't " stand the glare," which I have never yet found exist in any appreciable quantity in our own country. Glare, indeed ! why, what can come up to the real glare of some of the places one constantly goes to abroad ; yet where do we find the insensate manner of treating the windows we invariably discover in Britain ? Abroad I have never yet seen a single blind, save in the proper place, *e.g.*, outside the window, where it fulfils its purpose of preventing the sun striking on the glass, while in dismal, sunless side-streets in English towns one sees long processions of fearsome " half-blinds," toilet tables well in the

centre of the glass, and then festooned curtains as well, becoming perfect dust-traps, and an absolute disgrace to the house, in less time than it takes to tell of it.

I have not the least intention of mentioning in these articles the name or address of one single tradesman, lest my readers should imagine I am anxious that they should only go to special shops with which I have mysterious and undefined links. At the same time I shall not mention anything that cannot be procured ; save the ideal house ; on which I shall dwell in my next paper, and should any individual be anxious to obtain that article, the address can always be forwarded in a stamped envelope, should one be sent me for the purpose. For I am most anxious, really anxious, to persuade my readers to really study their homes, and to fully understand that I want them to do so because every beautiful home is always a joy, and because every single thing in the shape of a home, if it be but a cottage, can be made beautiful if it be treated with common-sense and a loving hand. It is not so very long ago that I was suddenly confronted with a real cottage that fell into our possession sooner than we expected, and about the ultimate destination of which we were at first a little dubious. It happened that at the special moment it became vacant I was unable to go and see it myself, and my emissary returned from the first inspection with a very sorry face. " It can't be inhabited by anyone much. I don't think even you can make anything of it," were among some of the opinions I elicited, but at last I went myself, and I must confess my spirit quailed ; the dirt, the absolute grime, were so appalling that I almost gave in. But common-sense reasserted itself. Cleaning began and continued some days, and I paid another visit, to find four good square rooms—and a valuable and good thing, too, is a square room—an excellent kitchen, and another square room at the back, and at once I saw what could be made of the unfortunate place. It was a cottage ; well, it should be treated like one. Simple decorative enamel paint replaced the grimed graining of the late tenant ; none of the wall-papers, save one, cost more than $9\frac{1}{2}$d. a piece, and the whole of the furniture for the six rooms, including kitchen, came to just over £100, and at the same time is good, plain, and pretty and has been of comfort and joy to many more people than I ever thought it would be. The dearer paper was in the hall, or I should say passage and staircase, and this cost 2s. 3d., but then it is a very thick, washable paper, and has to stand the sundry bangs and bumps that it cannot help getting when boxes are taken up and down stairs, or when small people wend their way up and down. The carpets in the four best bedrooms are all square Dunelm carpets; in the kitchen we have Napier matting, and on the stairs there is also a Dunelm carpet, while in the servant's room there is a square Dutch carpet of unimpeachable wearing qualities, warranted to withstand the evil doings of the genus page or young footman, who as a rule occupies that superior chamber. I cannot help contrasting my dear cottage, where the bedroom "suites" cost £10 apiece and are a joy for ever, with the more gorgeous surroundings of a young couple in a humble walk of life, in whom I take great interest, and with whom I went to tea to "see their house" just after their wedding, and whose three or four rooms had cost nearly double what my cottage had, and yet which had every fault that decorative surroundings could possess. There were the stuffy fitted carpet in hideous patterned Brussels, the stuffed tapestried chairs, and a "suite" in the bedroom, so tortured, patterned, and inlaid that I could only think of it afterwards as an embodied nightmare, and so appropriate, perhaps, for a bedchamber! Well, I could only sigh internally and outwardly praise anything I honestly could, and the outlook from the windows dimly seen through a festooned mass of Nottingham lace was one of the things I should have loved to have had constantly before me. The money was spent, there was nothing else to be done, yet I came away mentally vowing that as soon as I could I would leave for awhile the "unlimited" style of decoration I have been writing about for so long, and try my best to induce young folk commencing life with a small house and little money to try my plan of elegant simplicity, and to avoid anything like elaboration, and to content themselves with plain good furniture, devoid of ornament, save the truest ornament of all, that given by good workmanship and excellent "lines," and by surroundings which in colour and design at least shall be all that they ought to be, whether in a cottage or in a palace.

QUEEN OF ITALY.

BY MRS. HAWEIS.

THE Quirinal Palace stretches its noble length upon the summit of the Monte Cavallo, and its old Papal associations have made the Queen, it is said, who is a good Catholic, yield with pain and reluctance to the stress of national polity which made the Quirinal the Palazzo Reale. Within the stately Renascence entrance arch a great courtyard extends. If you want to reach the grand suite of the King's apartments, which are shown to the public, *Casa di S. M. il Re*, you mount a vast staircase at the right-hand extremity. If you are going to the private apartments of the Queen, which have never been photographed, you are set down at the Grand Entrance *en face*, from which a short cut—one of those wondrous circling stairways, of extreme breadth and shallowness, which old Roman architectural skill makes it a pleasure to climb—leads to the great private corridor.

To me, half the beauty of cinquecento architecture lies in the ceilings and friezes, which unite roof and wall so ingeniously, and bring gold and painting, *alto-relievo* and flat surfaces, richly carved marbles, freschi, and dainty needlework, into a bewildering but perfectly harmonious whole. The Quirinal gives the art-student superb examples of perfect colour, design, and, what is still

more rare and subtle, *proportion :* the Sala degli Svizzeri being one. This is one of the King's suite of rooms, chiefly used for official purposes. You pass through it on the way to the throne-room and to the ball-room— the former is Raphaelesque ; the latter, with its vast mirrors and dome, is Louis Quinze— through numerous magnificent saloons hung with heavy silks in vivid and contrasting colours—green, purple, opaline, streaked, ringstraked—one a rather painful blue; but it contains a good picture by Giulio Romano —one yellow, where there is a very libellous portrait of the Queen by De Cricheto. One is veneered in plain red marble. The throne-room is crimson. There is a good deal of cinquecento gilding and carving, even the cornices containing life-size *amorini* and all the strange monsters of Raphael's fertile fancy ; whilst the chairs and sofas, as in most Royal palaces, ring the changes on Louis XIV., XV., and XVI., with carpets woven to corres- yond with the delicate Gobelin tapestries on the walls.

A city set upon an hill cannot be hid— and when years (*eheu fugaces !*) ago it was announced that Humbert, then Heir Apparent to the Throne of Italy and eldest son of King Victor Emmanuel, was to marry his charming cousin Marguerite of Savoy, that kind of sympathetic thrill of rejoicing ran throughout Italy which salutes a *mariage d'amour* (too seldom, alas!) in Royal circles. Even then Italy had been for some time familiar with the beautiful face of the Princess Marguerite, and from the time of her honeymoon she emerged freely and came amongst the people on all occasions; and wherever she went her gracious presence, her exquisite charm of manner, her entire absence of affectation, and, above all, her quick and gentle sympathies, won all hearts and excited the enthusiasm of a nation which in the space of her own girlhood had become one.

Not the generic goodness of queenhood, but the particular goodness and beneficence (especially to her own sex) of the Queen of Italy, has long held my heart, as it holds many women's hearts in England, in a sort of *culte*. In 1895, being in Rome about Easter, I greatly desired to see this celebrated Queen; but she had left Rome, and no chance remained that year. This year, at the same season, I again found myself in the Eternal City, where, because it is eternal I suppose, time makes but little impression, least of all on the Queen and the worship of her. Therefore when, the very next day, I received an intimation through the most courteous and kindly of British Ambassadors, Sir Clare Ford, that the Queen would be graciously pleased to receive my husband and myself at the Quirinal on the morrow, I felt the dawn of a "red-letter day."

For years the women of Italy have owed to the Queen their improving position, education, and trade. Under her, literature has arisen, and women have come forward to help themselves, and to help others, by words and works, because she has helped them. It is Her Majesty who has found new avenues for women's labour and women's safety throughout that *benedetta terra*; who has revived the lost and lovely art of lace-making—the point and pillow stitches of faëry skill—restored the embroidery-trade in all its delicate branches; founded asylums for poor little waifs and strays; rescued and housed thousands of ill-treated babes and old women; discouraged the inveterate begging. She personally visits the innumerable *crèches* and hospitals in which she is interested,

helps the nurses, washes and binds up with her own Royal hands, saying, " I WISH TO DO IT." She heads the splendid " Scuola Professionale Margherita di Savoia " (which I had just visited by the courtesy of the able and accomplished Direttrice, Madame Amalia Prandi Ribighini), where eight hundred girls, increased from eight only, are taught every womanly handicraft under the sun, and given a livelihood which is both a protection and a *dot*. Her sympathy has borne fruit in the activities of such indefatigable and charming philanthropists as the Contessa Pasolini, who has herself founded a large school of lace-makers on her own estate—a school, by the bye, where orders for exquisite lace and also for all sorts of antique stitchery will be gladly executed, and, it appears to me, at very reasonable rates. Yes, the " Ideal Queen " is an example and a pattern, not only to the noble women of her own land, but to all women in all lands. Endless are the stories of her love of children. A small middle-class baby lately smiled and held out its arms to her: she stopped her carriage, embraced and did not forget the little thing, and, frequently passing it, always kissed her hand. There is an amusing story of the beautiful five-year-old son of a well-known physician, playing the part of a page in the " Sleeping Beauty " theatricals got up at one of the palazzi. Unprompted, and engrossed by his part, the child, when he passed the Queen, knelt on one knee, and raised his wee fist for the Queen to lay her hand on it, for him to kiss. The Queen, accustomed to the ceremony, automatically *did* extend her Royal hand— then, realising the absurdity of treating a baby as if he were a real courtier in a State function, she laughed out, caught him up in her arms, and kissed him repeatedly. All the great ladies wanted to follow suit, but, with the quaint tact and wisdom sometimes revealed unto babes, this little creature would permit no kisses after the Queen's.

On the auspicious morrow we present ourselves, and are ushered up wide spirals and through rich ante-rooms. The gorgeous State lackeys, with their fine Piedmont figures and scarlet liveries, doffing their feathered hats to the ground, remind us a

THE THRONE-ROOM.

THE SALA DEGLI SVIZZERI.

little of the glories of our Governor at Ceylon, who affects, as is customary in our Indian dependencies, an Oriental splendour The Royal private apartments are extremely beautiful, and decorated much like the more public ones, in the old French style chiefly, hung with silk and furnished with Buhl, *marqueterie*, and golden carvings. The primrose-coloured Sala degli Specchi, or that called degli Arazzi (sometimes used for small diplomatic dinners), gives a good general idea of them, if we import more furniture and daintier curiosities. The first ante-room opening from the corridor was all sky-blue satin and Louis Seize *bergères*, with a domed and painted ceiling, and portraits of former Marguerites of Savoy — one very fine, perhaps a Velasquez, in which the lady

THE QUEEN OF ITALY.

carried a quaint long gun or carabine in quite a modern and sportive fashion, red ribbons in her hair A great golden frame of historic miniatures curled about in a corner. The next room opened in amber tint, the panels formed of striped and waved brocade, with Louis Quinze furniture. Both were full of flowers: both gave upon a beautiful garden of ilex and palm-groves. Presently the Marchese Guiccioli presents us to Her

Majesty's present lady-in-waiting, the Duchesse Massimo Rignano, a very handsome, fair-haired woman, who possesses some English blood, and certainly speaks English with a perfect accent. On the previous day had been made the attempt to stab King Humbert whilst driving on the Pincian—an attempt which the bogey-men say was astrologically foretold last March, and also in 1896. All Rome was aroused by the miscreant crime, and a perfect passion of loyalty centred around the Royal Family.

"It was," said the Duchesse to me, "such a shameful, such an ungrateful outrage. The Queen is so good, no one knows what she is—how warm-hearted, how generous; the King is so devoted to his people, and works so hard for and with them!" Certainly no one can forget what he did in the cholera time, toiling in the hospitals, his garments so soiled that he had to change them five times in the day— no one does that without loving the work.

"But the man was surely mad!" I said.

"Not mad at all—I do not believe it: he was just one of those fanatics who want to upset the monarchy. These wretches are mad to get other people's property, and they think that a revolution of any kind must

96

bring luck to the proletariat. But the thing is senseless; for were all the rich people robbed to-morrow, who would be better off in a year?" I had heard of the calculation having been made for England with a handsome residue of fourpence-halfpenny per head, and I said so, with an allusion to "killing the goose which lays golden eggs" as the image of the capitalist, without whom not a single economic experiment could be made in the cause of progress. I asked the Duchesse why she thought this assassin was backed by others.

"I do, because," said the Duchesse, "the moment the man was seized he exclaimed that he had no accomplices. To my mind his very eagerness proves he is a member of a secret society, pledged not to betray their fellows. I had just been driving with the Queen, and curiously enough her quick eye had caught sight of a creature with a villainous face of hate. 'What an awful countenance has that man!' exclaimed Her Majesty, with a shudder: 'I am sure he must be a malefactor.' This was indeed the assassin. The Queen did not see the attempt. She knew nothing of it till the King himself told her of it, saying coolly, 'This is the most nearly fatal of all the attempts made upon my life.'"

The Queen's private rooms in the Quirinal mirror the tastes of a refined and home-loving woman. Whilst we waited Her Majesty's leisure we admired the soft curves, the delicate old bureaux, the dainty flowers—the Duchesse drew our attention to one mighty tree-azalea standing between the windows, on which grew blossoms of three colours, pink, white, and streaked—a floral sport Presently the Queen was ready to receive us, and the Duchesse went to the door of the inmost apartment with a curtsy to announce us, and left us alone with the beautiful woman, not one of whose photographs do her any sort of justice. She was sitting on a little sofa of pale satin, beside which stood a comfortable *escritoire*, and more flowers, and a screen of diamond-graven glass of the old time, sparkling like dew, but softening the glare of Roman sunshine. She was quite a picture, sitting in her pale grey satin *toilette*, with the vest of pink cut-velvet and the inevitable rows of huge and perfect pearls as big as nuts, hanging from her neck to her waist. They originated the pretty play upon her name which Romans love, and make her doubly Margherita and doubly "Queen of Pearls." Her photographs make her look dark, but

THE PRINCE OF NAPLES.

she is a delicate blonde, with a fresh, natural complexion, high, delicately cut features, a most beautiful nose and mouth, cut like a cameo, and a bearing which for its grace and dignity is of course a proverb—no one could more quickly set her visitors at their ease.

One soon ceased to observe details in the charm and simplicity of manner—which is quite indefinable and indescribable ; but you are happy when you have got it. All we were aware of was the presence of one of the most beautiful and intellectual women we had ever met. She has a little, quick way of speaking, whether English or Italian, which evidences a mind brimming over with ideas, and with the most graceful readiness of expression ; and it is said of Her Majesty that there is not a subject started on which she is not sure to contribute some bright and vivid thought. She is certainly widely read, and to her the best thinkers and talkers find that they have to talk their best.

Seated beside her on the sofa to which she motioned me (my husband in an arm-chair on her right), I forgot that Royalty is omniscient and infallible ; that information must never be volunteered ; that no sort of correction is permissible—forgot all the instructions common in England : how one must wait till one is spoken to, and answer in the fewest and most colourless words ; never tell an unpalatable truth, even in the best cause ; correct no error, and never attempt to lead talk. All such useful rules are well calculated to reduce intercourse with Royalty to something portentously insipid for both sides, if adhered to. But they do not seem to apply to the fascinating Italian Sovereign ; and although the Italian Court is said to be extremely punctilious, the Queen, in her personal intercourse with those whom she chooses to see, is quite free from anything which can check the pleasure of a real interchange of ideas. She seems eager for all knowledge, great as is her own, and her speech and replies are extremely ready, and show the rapidity of her thoughts.

The Queen spoke of books, and music, and of the English Church and its formularies, more than once deferring, with a gracious

" I ask, because you must know these things so much better than I."

" You English are so serious. Your work is so solid and so careful," she said of a work of mine, " Chaucer for Children"—Chaucer, who loved the daisy—(and I was later told that she admires the English " seriousness " of character). " I know the book very well," she said of one by my husband. " I have it in my library, and although I have not read it I shall look forward now to doing so with new pleasure."

Comparing popular with scholastic music, which Her Majesty presently did with a good deal of real intuition, she compared various composers whom she had heard and not heard. She had never, oddly enough, heard Liszt play, though he lived so long close by in Rome, and at the Villa d'Este ; and she asked us somewhat of his style and manner. Her saying it reminded us of Liszt's once telling us that he had never heard Bottesini. " I have heard Rubinstein and Paderewski, and I prefer Paderewski. Rubenstein made such a noise, and always seemed to be breaking the hammers and strings."

" But," I said, " all the modern school of pianists do that at times, even Paderewski."

" Well," said the Queen, " I daresay Paderewski does it too, but he does not seem to do it, and it is not so painful. He has " (this will delight the charming player) " *a touch of velvet.*" Her Majesty's remark struck me as felicitous. It exactly hit the distinction between force and extravagance (which many distinguished artistes now confound), and I surmised wherefore her musical Majesty had " never heard Liszt." She said a few kind words of Sgambati, the eminent composer who arranges, week by week, the Queen's private concerts, and the rest of the conversation turned rather upon matters antiquarian and artistic until, whilst the Queen made no direct sign for the termination of our interview, the first faint pause warned me to rise and curtsy low.

Then the Queen gave us each a jewelled hand of pressure, which we stooped and kissed, and with a sweet smile she returned the orthodox obeisances with which we retired—retired actually with a sense of enjoyment, pleased with a conversation full

THE SALA DEGLI SPECCHI.

THE SALA DEGLI ARAZZI.

of cordial kindness, and bright sayings, and real thoughts. That pleasure and honour had been ours for nearly half an hour, absolutely alone with this Royal and gifted lady, to whom kindness and sympathy come so naturally that they are as the air she breathes. Her Majesty's last graceful speech and gesture to us (a mark of special consideration and kindness which I do not repeat, just because it was so sweet and touching) made me understand the rapture with which her name is always received.

That Queen Margherita, with all her sweetness is a brave and percipient ruler of the Court every one " in the know " knows well. Persons, however elevated, whom she does not wish to see, cannot be thrust upon her. If any one, however privileged, oversteps the right and correct bounds—and a recent occurrence will be remembered—the Queen's quiet " I do not appear "—be it ball or concert—is socially as fatal as Alice in Wonderland's " Off with their heads ! " The Court circle is therefore indubitably the

Queen's own circle, and its purifying influence is as strong as under our own beloved Victoria's gentle sway.

A pretty story was told us of the pearls of the Queen of Pearls. The King has given her, on every birthday since the Prince of Naples was born, a new string of wondrous pearls, and the jewels of the Queen of Italy are second only to the Czar's in beauty.

A year or two ago, at Monza, the Queen said to her Consort, as many a beautiful wife with a grown-up son might say, " I am becoming too old now to wear white any longer " (in summer Her Majesty is always arrayed like a white daisy), and King Humbert looked at her and said, " We will hold a State council on the question." Quietly he sent to the sartorial authority who possesses the Royal measures, and in a few days six of the richest white costumes that could be made arrived for the Queen, by King Humbert's special command.

That was his reply : and a wife's best jewels are such courtesy and such love.

THE ANTICA CAPELLA PAOLINA.

AN · INCIDENTAL MAN

BY MRS. AUBREY RICHARDSON.

"WIVELTON, NORFOLK.

"*January 27th*, 189-.

"MY DEAREST DI,—
I am flying up to town for a fortnight; rushing away from self and from a *person*. His name *you* will guess. Can you put me up? I want *you* even more than I want town, though I am trusting to the efficacy of the shops and the theatres—the park doesn't count at this season. I leave here on the 9.50 to-morrow morning. If you can, come to St. Pancras to meet me. If you can't, I shall go to the 'Midland' and look out for you later in the afternoon.

"As ever, dear,

"Yours,

"SUE."

Diana Boulter raised her eyebrows as she read this note, but she was not exactly astonished. The friendship of the two women had gone too deep for surprises. She was only a little puzzled to unravel the threads of circumstance which had led to the writing of Sue Arlington's remarkable letter.

That a steady-going little woman of the right sort, like Sue, a woman who seemed to get all her amusement out of the duties of life, should have been worked up into a state of reckless excitement in the fourth year of her widowhood, by the forming of an acquaintance with an ex-military man, seemed an irony of circumstance which, to say the least of it, Diana had not anticipated.

Standing before her easel, putting in certain touches which her latest portrait (that of Lady Griggs, Mayoress of Elcaster) seemed to be crying out for, Diana had ample time for reflection. The Mayoress was not possessed of an elusive personality. Such as it was, it asserted itself quite frankly. So Diana pondered the situation all the morning. She was pondering it still on her way to St. Pancras in the afternoon.

"She must be in love with Captain Eaton," was the reluctant termination of her musings. And yet—Sue Arlington's devotion to the husband of her youth had seemed complete; the wifehood, attained to with him, final!

The friends met on the platform, as they had met many times before in the ins and outs of their lives' journeys. Old school-fellows, they had never faltered in their interest in one another, though Sue, at twenty-two, had married a hard-working junior partner in a London banking firm, and Di had studied at half the art-schools of Europe and travelled the wide world over, upon various artistic pretences, before settling down to portrait-painting in London.

Sue, in her dark, tailor-made travelling suit, and Di, in her embroidered velvet shoulder-cape and smart gown, had neither of them the look of women whose heart-experiences must needs lie behind them. "Middle-aged" they were not. Yet Di had years ago dismissed a lover who had proved himself unworthy of a woman—though, with feminine inconsequence, she loved him still; and Sue could count ten years of married life behind her four years of widowhood.

No confidences were exchanged until, seated in a hansom, the friends were being driven towards Chelsea.

THE FRIENDS MET ON THE PLATFORM.

"I had to come," said Sue simply. "There are things doing I should have stayed for. Theatricals for our cottage-hospital, and two village concerts I was organising. But I have let them go by the board. They would not have saved me. Nothing can, but dissipation."

"Good Heavens!"

Sue laughed in spite of herself, but replied quite earnestly,—

"Say rather, 'Good Lord deliver us!' He'll rescue me, Sue, but not by conventional methods."

"Penances have failed then?"

"Oh, yes. The country is well enough when the way is clear before one. But for a hand-to-hand fight with destiny one must be where tides are strong."

She gave a sweeping glance that took in the carts, cabs, and omnibuses, the foot-passengers and shop-fronts, of the Tottenham Court Road.

"Ah!" Sue drank in the scene, as if it were a draught of strength. "The stream runs high," she said.

Di did not ask for detailed explanations. Sue's tone and look explained so much.

"If it's destiny," she commented, "that's serious."

"Very serious."

"But Sue, perhaps after all——"

"No, no." Sue shook her head vehemently.

"There would be no wrong in it," urged Di.

Sue gave a bitter laugh.

"Wrong! I daresay not. It's Nature, I suppose, and all that kind of thing. But I won't be bossed by Nature. I'll have my own way or die for it!"

Her lips set tightly.

"You've been *living*, Sue," cried Diana sympathetically.

"Living? Yes. Suffering, agonising! But it has been pleasant, too. A relief from the stagnation that went before. But do you think I am going to let a chance pleasure, a passing acquaintance, an incidental man"—her accent was very scornful—"spoil all my plan of life, destroy the ideal of love, rob me of Leigh?"

She tightened the grasp of one hand on the fingers of her friend, and of the other on the edge of the cab door.

"You can't forget then?" queried Di softly.

"I don't want to forget."

Her brave and vehement manner changed. As she turned to Di the expression of her mouth softened, and her eyes brimmed with tears.

"Oh, it is no question of memory," she went on piteously. "He is my husband. I love him. More than ever I love him."

A hand-squeeze demonstrated Di's true sympathy.

"You knew him," went on Sue; "and were fond of him. The worst thing about Wivelton is that they don't know him there. It helped me at first—the freedom from old associations, the complete severance from all that had gone before. It is hindering me now. I want to remember. I want to be reminded. Of course, Captain Eaton and I became chums. He is the only intelligent mortal there is to speak to in Wivelton. He knows his world, and I—well, Leigh and I knew ours. We knocked about, we read, we kept our eyes open. The inhabi-

tants of Wivelton don't do any of these things. And then, Tom Eaton is an awfully nice fellow. The sort you can say things to without being misunderstood. The kind you can't help being friendly with. And it would have been all right in Leigh's lifetime. I could have had my little flirt and then told Leigh about it, and Tom and he would have smoked the pipe of peace together, and everything gone on in a pleasant, casual sort of way until Captain Eaton became engaged, when I should have been grandmotherly and nice to his *fiancée*. But as it is there is no Leigh for him to smoke with, and he has taken to pitying me. You see he has got hold of the general idea in Wivelton that it is a shame for a young widow like myself to be a widow long. But if it had not been for public opinion, I don't believe the thought would have entered his head. Of course, it has been very refreshing meeting some one at their stupid old dinner-parties who could talk without being vapid or prosy. And at a Primrose Meeting, or any parochial gathering, he always sees the little humorous things that keep on happening just when I do, and no one else sees them at all. And, as I said, it would not matter a bit if Leigh were here. But as it is, Tom Eaton has a false idea of me, and through him I get a false idea of myself. And that's the worst worry of all. But I want to feel like my old self. I am Mrs. Leigh Arlington, Leigh Arlington's widow—his relict. Oh, I'd rather be called Leigh's *relict* than the wife of any other man in the universe. He made me what I am. He helped me to be something better, something more solid and sensible than the hysterical, lop-sided sort of a creature the ordinary woman is."

"Thank you!" interpolated Di.

"I said *ordinary* woman. You are *extra*-ordinary. I'm not. And you see, Di, this other man thinks a lot more of me, in some ways, than Leigh did. But he does not know me. Leigh had no need to think things; he——"

"Oh, stop Sue!" broke in Diana. "You have come up to town to get away from it all. Be firm, and do the thing thoroughly. Let us put everything and everybody—even Leigh—away from us that has belonged to

DI STOOD AGHAST.

ADOLF THIEDE
·97·

flat was on the fifth, beneath the skylights) with snatches of melody of a *timbre* they were but little accustomed to hear proceeding from Diana Boulter's rooms.

Yet in the small hours of the morning, Sue, tossing on her pillow, muttered fiercely, "I hate comic-operas. Low, unsatisfying things!"

Ten days later, Sue, coming in from what Di had taken to be a shopping expedition, was greeted by the words:

"I have had a visitor."

"Yes?"

"It was Captain Eaton."

Sue looked a little troubled.

"How did he find out?" she asked.

"He had been three days looking for you, and happened to meet your Uncle Henry, who suggested I might be able to give some information."

"That's rather calm."

"He was full of apologies, but his excuse is, he is off to Egypt to-morrow. Has had an appointment suddenly thrust upon him. I did not inquire what. But he leaves Charing Cross at six."

Sue glanced at the clock. It was twenty minutes past five. She breathed freely.

"He wanted to see you, to shake hands he said, and to ask you to forgive him if he had been impertinent."

"Impertinent! He could not be it if he tried."

"He talked very freely. I let him see I knew."

"Di"—Sue rose and grasped her friend's arm—"you don't think he cares?"

"I think he might have done. But he is not hard hit."

"Oh, I'm so glad, so glad. He is too good a fellow to hurt; and it might have hurt."

"I can't understand it all, Sue."

"Let me explain. The mistake was burying myself in the country. It was too much of a pose. I meant it in the right

the last fifteen years of life. Be as if we had just left school. Get down to the original bed-rock of our women's personalities."

"That's the nail I want to hit, Di. Help me strike it square on the head, and I'll bless you for ever."

Tea, daintily set out beneath a shaded lamp, was served in the studio, soon after the friends reached Diana's Chelsea flat.

For all the table looked so tempting, Sue refused a second cup.

"It is not sufficiently soothing," she said. "We'll dine at a restaurant—they give you such meagre rations at your club—and go to see *The Great Big Gou-Gou*. That's the biggest rage just now I think."

"I believe so. You know I don't waste time over comic-operas."

"It's the sort of thing men go to when they are worried. It's better than intro-spection."

So they dined heavily at a restaurant, and went to see *The Great Big Gou-Gou*. And on their return to the flat Sue astonished the fourth-floor occupants (Di's way at the time, and never doubted I was strong enough to go through with it. But when a woman"—her voice faltered for a moment as the passion of a past regretted mastered her—" when a woman is left alone as I was—in the midst of life, death making sport of her, she must not dare to nurse her sorrow. To run away from the world is to court pursuit. Here is hum and stir!" She stepped impulsively to the window. Her gesture carried Di's glance and hers across the roofs and chimneys of hydra-headed London. " Here life's music sounds : Let her take a part in the great *Chorale*."

" But work is everywhere," interpolated Di.

" Not for the city-bred. London people are my people and Leigh's people. The din and bustle, the theatre gossip and the art-jargon—the movement of life—are my natural stimulants. Even the slang of the pavements is a trumpet-call. With these to rouse me I can live and work—aye, and, by God's grace, do good work—tread down the base and exalt the holy."

" All places are alike to me," said Di.

" Because you are an artist. Your world is within you. In me the social instincts, the human sympathies, swamp all the rest. Having lost the best—the dearest—I must open my arms to all mankind. It is swim with the mass or sink altogether for me. I shall not go back to Wivelton."

" Captain Eaton will be no longer there."

" Oh, don't you understand? If it had not been he, it would have been another. I have been planning all these days I have spent in town, and only this afternoon I looked up an old acquaintance—a parson—who has put me on the track of work. Those fiddle-faddling village benefactions don't take hold of one body and soul. London enterprises make sterner demands. I shall be the better for responding to them. I had such a nice talk with the clergyman. He understands things."

" What, another?" Di stood aghast, in an attitude of melodrama.

" Another, if you will. He is going to be married next week, and sang me many praises of his future wife. But yes, he is another—an incidental man. In London they are soon lost sight of in the crowd. They don't block out the horizon here as they do at Wivelton."

From a photograph by Walery.

Jemima D. Richardson

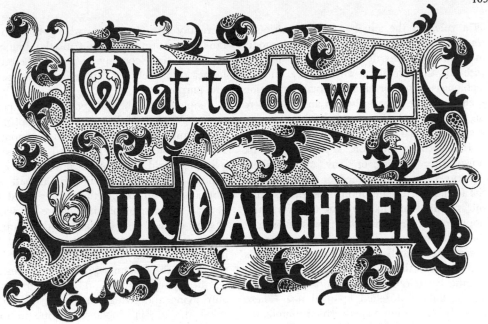

What to do with Our Daughters.

I. BY THE HON. MRS. HENRY CHETWYND.

IT may occur to some people that this question is an idle one, since many daughters of the present day, who arrange their lives according to their own ideas, answer it for themselves. But the question is not an idle one if it means " How can we help our daughters to put to profitable use such talents as they may possess, and so make a career for themselves ; and more particularly, how can the penniless girls, who are obliged to work, be placed in the way of earning a livelihood, and in what branch can they be assisted to achieve success without the expenditure of capital ? "

The first desideratum is to arrive at a really accurate idea of the special fitness of any individual girl for any desired career. A love of art, a certain facility and fluency in writing, a degree of mathematical power, an interest in science, or the study of medicine, by no means denote the possession of all the qualities that go to make a successful career in any of the pursuits represented by these tastes ; for to attain distinction in any one of them, a combination of special gifts is essential, and not the possession of one talent only, even if that be of a high order.

The ignoring of this fact causes many disappointments and many failures. Considering the enormous advantages women have enjoyed for many years, it is extraordinary how few have distinguished themselves, although the mental level of the sex is incomparably higher than that of our grandmothers. Take women-artists as one instance. Hundreds of girls attend schools of art, in countless cases chiefly through the advice of injudicious friends, who see genius in the most ordinary talent. How many of those girls arrive at distinction ? A few succeed as portrait-painters, a few more as copyists, although good copyists are very rare ; but the number of women-artists distinguished by creative power are singularly few.

Without going into the vexed question of the comparative weights and size of the brains of men and women, it must be confessed that where power and an original creative faculty are concerned, women's work often fails.

Nothing can be more deeply depressing than to go the rounds of the numerous studios with which London and most large towns abound, and to see girls—too many, as a rule, for the small space—industriously wasting their time in painting a prosaic model in a hideously prosaic way, studying ugliness with all their might,—which more often is feebleness—and forming a mutual admiration society amongst themselves in an atmosphere of bedaubed pinafores, smudged faces, and the smell of paint and turpentine.

It is perhaps still more saddening to walk down the Strand or any street where "pictures" are sold framed for a few shillings, the frame often being more meritorious than the picture, and to think of the work and hopes, of the days and hours of wasted time, of the painters—generally girls—buoyed up by dreams never to be realised ! For as regards real "Art" the saying that genius is "an infinite capacity for taking pains" is untrue, and a fallacy, if relied upon alone. There must be that divine spark which illuminates the mind of the artist and inspires his hand, which enables him to convey his meaning to others poetically as well as truthfully, which teaches him to idealise and elevate, and not to degrade, his subject—not resting satisfied with depicting the features correctly or emphasising the vivid tints or their absence, but by showing the mind, the spirit, and the very character, of the sitter.

As far as painting is concerned, it would be true kindness to discourage art as a profession for girls, though this is an unpopular thing to say, and many an embryo Raphael in petticoats will disagree with it.

There is, however, one opening for women for which experience proves them to be admirably fitted, and one of which English-women seem slow to avail themselves— Domestic Economy.

Many women have a special talent for domestic finance. From the palace to the kitchen there is nothing more necessary, and, I may add, more interesting. In England, where incomes so often depend on land, it is most essential, and if women would turn their real capabilities for business in this direction, not only would the well-being of their families be improved, but their incomes also. In Germany, in Italy, and in France, the question is thoroughly understood; in

Germany particularly so, where girls in all ranks are thoroughly taught all the branches of Domestic Economy, either in their own homes or in schools especially set apart for the purpose.

People talk of the difference in the expense of living in England and on the Continent, and many still go abroad to economise. Now, provisions are so equalised in price all over the world, that this is not necessary in reality. Every one should go abroad who can possibly do so, and the farther afield the better ; for change of air, change of scene, change of diet, and change of ideas, are all beneficial in every way. But in England you have the perfection of butcher's meat, and you have the command of every necessary for the same money as in France or Italy : only living and living comfortably is understood abroad ; in England no one troubles to study the question with the care and attention it deserves.

Why should not English girls who are obliged to leave home carefully study this important question and enter households in England on the same footing that so many foreign girls do? In Germany especially, where no daughter is available, almost every family has its "Mamselle." She has been trained, and perfectly trained, to understand how to balance the outlay of a family with its income ; how to arrange the work for the servants ; how, in short, to attain the maximum of comfort with the minimum of expenditure.

How many a woman in England would be relieved by such a girl in her household ; who is practically of the family, one of themselves, and yet watches carefully over the outgoings, and prevents the perpetual waste which, from the largest to the smallest households, is the rule almost without exception in England ! Schools of cookery have done much, and will do more. Why should not schools for Domestic Economy follow? Let parents who want the question answered, "What to do with our daughters ? " think over what may be a novel idea to them. In their own home or some one else's, Domestic Economy and its careful study will answer it most satisfactorily.

II. BY MRS. RENTOUL ESLER.

"She married happily instead, a better profession still."

GEORGE DU MAURIER.

TO the question "What shall we do with our daughters?" were the answer given, "Marry them off," it would be held by many to savour of farce. In the present instance it is, however, quite seriously intended. We covet for our daughters that which shall give them independence, a secure future, humanly speaking, and social status. The past quarter of a century has done greatly for women, has opened manifold doors for them towards all kinds of activities and industries, has rendered multitudes of them self-respectingly independent. But, considered from the practical point of view, what art, what science, what accomplishment, gives a woman the permanent and material things which will follow her union with the ordinary fairly successful man?

A woman's triumph in any practical calling must always depend, in a measure, on her youth, where she plays a public part. Does she sing? does she act? Let youth wane, and her chances go with it. Were positions ecclesiastical and legal open to her, the result would be the same. Average ability, with very good looks, will go far: great abilities, with a bad appearance, will, in the case of a woman, effect little in the open. It is so human to regard woman from the spectacular point of view, that age in her wears some aspect of the ludicrous. An old woman in the pulpit, on the platform, in legal wig and gown, would evoke laughter. It is inevitable. Average human· nature is not sympathetic, thinks of little but what it sees, and cares little for what it ignores.

Of course, art can be practised behind closed doors. A woman may write or paint, and, unless she has been freely interviewed in the days of her popularity, the world need never know if she is young or old, fair or faded. But fashions in art and literature change; it would be easy to indicate, could one do so without impertinence, two women writers who, twenty years ago, had names to conjure with, the one as a literary artist,

the other as a popular favourite: to-day if works, inferior to their early achievements by no single degree, go into a third or fourth edition, it is something for their publishers to make a song about. For the favourites of the present hour the same fate unquestionably sits in waiting. No doubt men rise to favour and fall out of it in a similar way, but that is beside the question. The obvious thing is that excellence in the art world does not ensure popularity, while popularity itself is an ephemeral thing.

Now, women constitutionally desire permanence. The admirers of Daudet's "Sappho" deplored that she was always striving to establish the transitory on an eternal basis. The average woman will labour and suffer patiently, provided she sees in the distance a promise of finality and reward. Marriage seems to woman a permanent condition: it is not natural to her to wish to abrogate it, annul it, abbreviate its duration. Where she sincerely asks to do so, it is because misery has forced on her the most cruel knowledge;—not only that her god had feet of clay, but that he was clay throughout.

Of course we all know that there are not men enough to go round, and that both men and women have spoken of marriage frequently as a condemned failure. Nevertheless, it continues to be the career which absorbs by far the larger proportion of women; it is the career to which only a very small proportion feel aversion; it is certainly the career which brings most honour and emolument in its train. How, then, can we secure the best thing available for our daughters, whom we privately acknowledge to be just ordinary?

The first thing to recognise is that the ordinary is extremely popular. We are all more at our ease with the wren species, neat, gentle, trim, unaggressive, than with the bird of Paradise. It is just the average girls, fairly intelligent, passably good-looking, amiable and anxious to please on the whole, who marry in myriads, while the beauties and the wits frequently swell the spinster ranks.

It is not very difficult to marry off our daughters, provided we set about it in the right way. First, the girl—we take them in turn—must never be allowed to realise the object in view, or instantaneously she will revolt, will think cruel things of her match-making mamma, and will render herself very unpleasant to every man who approaches her. It may be salutary, on the contrary, to indicate to her the various careers open to celibate women, so as to find out which of these she would fancy. The next step is to take the conceit out of her, without wounding her unnecessarily or unduly. The easy, pampered life of the average girl in comfortable circumstances tends to foster conceit or *ennui*. The latter is a serious drawback to a girl's attractiveness : the former is fatal ; it may be

forgiven in a great beauty, but it will not be forgotten, and with time the wounds it inflicted will be avenged.

To be attractive a girl should be natural, and her individuality should be cherished within limits. The girl who possesses a gay originality of her own, has a charm far beyond that of beauty. Should she lack this, then her special aptitude should be cultivated as far as it will extend. The girl who does anything well—sings, or sketches, or rides, or rows, or is even good at games—is certain to find herself in sympathy with some one some time, when the girl who does a little of everything, and has no individual tastes and no personal talents, will prove tiresome.

Intercourse is essential to partiality. Where intercourse between young men and young women is easy, the way of the match-making mother may be as pleasant as a path of roses.

III. BY MRS. HAWEIS.

WHAT to do with our daughters? This question is surely rather what our emancipated daughters mean to do with themselves. When they have made mistakes they are very glad to come back home and be picked out of the hole. There is no doubt about what we ought to do *then*—which is, our best. But my ambitious Editor appears to have fixed his eagle eye on that isthmic term previous to the "hole"—the term of restlessness, wing-stretching, finding one's level—what the Germans call the "*Flegel jahr*"—when parent and child require to become mutually acquainted under the new and more equal conditions—when childhood and tutelage are done with, and maturity and the wisdom-teeth yet to come. What to do with our daughters *then* (and make them think they are doing for themselves)? Ah, Mr. Editor, that too often depends on the defences of the home against the prowling hyena outside the home ; the prowling hyena who wants his or her nose in your larder, and can't let you be anyhow, whilst "I want to get out ! I want to get out !" says the starling.

The cure for most ills, whether restlessness, or the hyena, is work : and the question, "Ought our daughters to work ? and if not,

why not ? " has a vital moral bearing on the peace of the rather obsolete British home. We think too much of our children and of everybody else, as girls or boys, men and women, not human beings, with responsibilities as such. Boys in the sensible classes are mostly brought up to rely on themselves in the way of a profession, or at least prepare themselves to take a position in their parents' circle. They have competitive examinations which carry off some superfluous energy, and sooner or later something to support by their own efforts, if it be only the painful weight of a large income outside the bankruptcy court.

But girls are not so brought up ; they are taught to be nothing but the playthings of their parents—over-dressed, under-trained even for marriage ; and their equal energy, equal restlessness, equal ability with their brothers, runs to seed—and a very distasteful seed it sometimes is. By no means is this always the girls' fault. Too often in the upper classes the parents' conservatism deters young women of energy and social influence from becoming useful .members of Society. In their young days girls didn't do this and that, and therefore affection and strong associations both come in to combat their daughters doing it. In the minor classes, too often the parents, having risen in life, have ideas which it would be impolite to call snobbish, whilst the juniors really see more clearly than they where their own dignity and happiness lie, and bitterly resent obstructions to their reasonable activities. Walking out alone, bicycling unattended, working in the parish, and joining " debates," are amongst the innocuous novelties which the parent very naturally shies at, because at one time such doings would have been really dangerous and unseemly. What to do? Well, if the girl will not yield to affection, let her go. Let her bicycle be stopped by tramps, and her character developed, and even tarnished, by her originalities, and her eyes well opened by working amongst the poor. Let her " live her own life,"—no life is worth living that is not self-developed, after all—and pick her up when she tumbles, and squeals like the cross baby. Not till then. Else, she will have a grievance, and the hyena will push harder at the half-open door. In these particulars the humblest and the highest classes have very similar trials. After all, the tramp may *not* stop the bicycle.

But given parents judicious enough to see that work means happiness, duty, and even status, in these feverish, almost hysterical, days—the fair *frondeuse* may still manage to be a victim, and feel the pea beneath twelve feather-beds. Seriously, the daughters are not all ready to work. The fair *frondeuse* is as often the idle as the active daughter.

Parents hardly allow sufficiently for the reactionary element in Nature, the architectural principle which Nature employs to keep her balance, as in the tree or the flower —and are always equally surprised and grieved when busy children result from torpid parents, and idle children from busy parents; open-handed, unselfish progeny from close-fisted and selfish progenitors, whilst (as has constantly been noted) the parents who have sacrificed so much, thought so much, prepared so much for their young people's happiness, frequently find the young people with their pockets full of money, surly, inconsiderate, hard to please, and unhappy—just *spoilt*. Surely there is no keener condemnation of the mistaken in-

dulgence with which many young men and girls have been brought up, than the way in which we see the father have to retrench, take a poorer house, give up his carriage, his quiet dinners, all the autumn pleasures for which he has worked, and which he deserves in the twilight of life, because the children are " so dull " unless they are at the Empire every night, or because he has to pay Jack's debts, or set up Jack again after he has been *chassé* : or worse (for selfishness seems worse in a young woman), because he must keep up a separate establishment for Gladys, since Gladys will not behave at home, and find her in trips and fancy dresses, and pretend he approves, to stop the neighbours talking. Yet how often the most terrible stories reach our ears ! Perhaps the worst I ever heard hails from San Francisco. I read it the other day :—

" James Brusie, formerly a wealthy ranch owner at Sanjuaquin, died in the poor-house under somewhat painful circumstances. Mrs. Bauska, his daughter, refused either to keep him or to pay for his board at the sanatorium, at which he had been staying, so the doctor of that establishment sent him to the poor-house. His removal caused his death." That was a spoilt daughter.

What to do with our daughters is, I suppose, to implant in them a sense of duty a sense of dignity, and that other old-fashioned quality, a sense of religion—and trust to the seed coming up to colour; for liberty, like " love " (says Chaucer),

"too wyde y-blowe,
Yelte bitter fruit though sweetë sede be sowe."

If the good seed does come up healthy, the daughter, like the son, will not coldly watch father and mother growing older and older, weaker and weaker, with the busy decades, and live and sponge upon their goodwill, their whipt-up energies, their credit even, and do nothing to lessen the burdens and the boredoms of old age. The eager, warm-hearted, right-minded daughters of England are a force of incalculable power and importance. Let them feel their feet and balance their own steps ; leave the final disposal to God.

ROYAL ETIQUETTE.

THERE are many people whose good breeding or education prevents their ever making a mistake in ordinary society, who know little of etiquette with regard to members of the Royal Family. This knowledge, however, is not so superfluous as may at first sight appear. Of this fact I could give countless proofs, but I will confine myself to real instances that have come under my own knowledge.

1. It is the most ordinary occurrence for a nobleman to entertain Royalty at his country seat ; and although, as a rule, the house-party would be composed of those with whom the Royal guest is more or less acquainted, most of the neighbouring gentry asked to a ball or reception have possibly never been brought into contact with a Prince or Princess before.

2. A clergyman becomes a bishop, and his wife is possibly before long called upon to entertain Royalty.

3. A clergyman is appointed to a chaplaincy abroad, and is unexpectedly brought into contact with Her Majesty or one of the Princesses. In more than one instance he has even been honoured with an invitation to dinner by the Queen. Although strict Court etiquette is to some extent in abeyance abroad, to know the right thing is to feel more or less at one's ease.

4. Members of Parliament and their wives, irrespective of any social status, are constantly invited to receptions where Royalties are present, and occasionally receive invitations to State concerts and Royal garden-parties.

5. Men of all sorts and conditions are made baronets (to say nothing of knights) for public services rendered, and their wives would naturally attend at least one Drawing-room.

6. A girl marries, and her husband's military or naval position may necessitate her going to Court.

7. Girls are often presented, although their mothers may never have been to Court ; for Society has changed very much during the last twenty years, and presentations are much more common than heretofore.

8. A Princess opens the wing of a hospital or a bazaar, when the matron and the stall-holders are usually presented.

9. An author or artist has the honour of presenting personally a book or picture to the Queen.

10. A traveller in out-of-the-way regions is suddenly requested to show his sketches to Her Majesty, and describe the peculiarities of a hitherto unexplored region.

11. A gifted singer or actress is commanded to perform before the Queen, and after the performance may be presented.

12. A Princess presides at a committee meeting.

13. A letter asking the favour of Royal patronage for a concert, etc., has to be written.

Taking nothing for granted, I shall venture to tell the uninitiated some points of etiquette connected with the various occasions I have mentioned. I well remember, long ago, how grateful I was to a friend (a well-known lady-in-waiting) for similar hints the first time I had the honour of being invited to meet some of the Royal Family then staying with her.

The host and hostess thus honoured are generally personal friends, and therefore *au fait* with regard to the etiquette to be observed. This, however, is not invariably the case, for a newly elected mayor may have regal rooms at his disposal, in some of our palatial town halls, admirably fitted for the entertainment of distinguished guests.

With regard to the arrangements of a house-party to meet a Royal guest : a Prince is usually asked to suggest names of friends he would like invited. In any case a list of those to be asked must previously be submitted. A host and hostess would naturally like the house-party to consist only of those their Royal guest knew personally. Sometimes, however, State and political reasons necessitate a few additions. It is customary for the host and hostess to meet a Royal guest in the hall on their arrival if they are driving. If they arrive by train, they will of course be met by the host and hostess at the station. Foreign princes would be met at the station by one of the Royal Family. The Queen herself would welcome distinguished guests at the principal entrance to the Palace. Reigning sovereigns, even if near relatives, would be greeted with a deep curtsy, as well as an affectionate kiss. Only the other day some one who was near the Queen at the Jubilee service in the Abbey told me the deep reverence and the warm, loving kiss from her children, to their sovereign and mother, at the close of the service, was one of the most touching ceremonies ever witnessed.

To return to the house-party. Any friend not personally known to the Prince or Princess should be presented at an early opportunity. When others are invited to meet them at dinner, a person of rank would be presented as a matter of course, but if it were only a person well known in the county, a few words of explanation would preface the request, "May I present Sir A—— to you, sir?" The guest would make a low bow. He would of course not dream of being the first to enter into conversation with His or Her Royal Highness.

Very frequently our Royal Princes and Princesses (even including the Prince and Princess of Wales) very graciously join the house-party, not only at dinner, but also at breakfast and luncheon ; but it should never be taken for granted that they are likely to do the latter.

In the days when the Queen stayed at a few English and Scotch country seats, one of her ladies thus honoured told me, "The Queen always commanded —— and I to dine *every* night." I gathered that this did not include all the house-party, or even all my friend's children. When the Queen intends honouring any of her neighbours at Balmoral by a visit about tea-time, with her usual forethought she sends a message to that effect in the morning. If other folks are staying in the house, the host and hostess would receive the Queen alone, unless by her special permission.

Guests invited to dine and stay the night at Windsor usually arrive late in the afternoon, and leave before twelve the following day. Men and women alike speak with enthusiasm of the Queen as a hostess. An intellectual friend, who had travelled much, had the honour of sitting next the Queen at dinner. "Were you not rather nervous, as well as immensely interested, in talking to the Queen?" I asked afterwards.

"Perhaps I was a little shy at first," he replied, "but the Queen so quickly put me at ease, by talking on the subjects of which I happened to know something, that I could only think what an exceptionally interesting *woman* she was, apart from being a Queen. She grasped every point so quickly, and seemed to take in at once a difficulty in the Colonies."

At Windsor guests assemble in the corridor before dinner, of course in full evening dress. It goes without saying that questions of precedence are strictly adhered to. Before some great occasion, such as a Royal wedding, there are many fine points to be considered. Perhaps one of the most graceful stories in connection

with precedence, tells of when the Queen insisted on the Empress Frederick (when the late Emperor was alive) preceding her into the dining-room. Seeing her Royal mother was determined, her daughter walked backwards.

After dinner the guests sometimes wait in the corridor until the Queen retires to bed ; sometimes she leads the way to the drawing-room. In old days the Queen would go round to each and say a few kindly words. Nowadays, owing to her lameness, she remains in her chair and *sends* for any one she wishes to speak to. Some one (who had not been at Court for several years, until recently) told me only last week, that it was quite wonderful how the Queen asked after each child individually, and remembered all that interested her. No wonder the eldest girl's eyes glistened with pleasure that she had been early at the Drawing-room to be presented to the Queen, for they had a vivid recollection of dolls and presents to suit each one when they were small children.

In conversation you say "ma'am," to the Queen and her Royal daughters, "sir," to a Prince, although "your Majesty" or "your Royal Highness," would be used instead of the personal pronoun "you." Persons who cannot be called *gentry*, would always say, "your Majesty" or "your Royal Highness." In conversation with the granddaughters of the Queen, a slight acquaintance would say, "Your Highness" ; friends, "Princess."

The most delightful evenings are arranged by the Queen at intervals, when distinguished *artistes* come down to perform. The programme is of course submitted to the Queen beforehand. On these occasions the upper servants are permitted to be present. Their regulation dress to appear at these performances is a black silk, a cap, and black gloves.

Invitations from Her Majesty are *commands*, consequently you do not reply. It is a command, and you take it as such. Only illness, or the death of a near relative, would be an excuse. We must all have heard of dinner engagements cancelled with very short notice for this reason. An invitation from any of the Royalties is treated by courtesy as a command, although the word is not used in replying. The answer is of course, in the third person, even though the invitation be a friendly note. Princess Louise, who had been extremely kind to a child of a friend of mine abroad, graciously invited the boy to luncheon in the holidays. Having been well drilled by his military father to keep all engagements, to the Princess's great amusement he declined, having "a previous engagement with a schoolfellow."

Decorations for the Season

BY MISS SHERSON.

ALTHOUGH Christmas-time, there are many flowers to be obtained serviceable for table decoration, also foliage in variety; and I propose giving a few hints to hostesses suitable for the present season. For number one, take a long scarf of scarlet silk and arrange it in loose knots and folds down the table—there need be no centre-piece; saucers can be filled with damp moss, and white chrysanthemums wired and stuck into these with only their own foliage. On the silk, fronds of fern must be laid, and if this decoration be in Christmas week, an artistically arranged border of ferns and holly-leaves and berries has a cheerful appearance. Silver *bonbonnières*, filled with red and white sweets, finish the table nicely.

A "scarlet" table is very effective. Make a centre-piece of moss, into which put shaded red leaves, caladium begonia, and other stove plants; these must be lightly wired, and not packed too closely. At each corner of this centre have a wheelbarrow in white china or green rush-work, filled with red Christmas roses. At each end of the table a lyre of red roses, based with shaded leaves; silver candelabra, with the candles shaded with scarlet butterflies; and on the table small red kaga bowls with fancy *bon-bons*. When flowers are scarce, a good effect is obtainable with lengths of fine material called Eastern Crêpe. Choose two or three shades that blend well together, twine them in and out, and dispose them in graceful folds; in the folds place red and yellow Oriental china, filled with small ferns or shaded chrysanthemums. Have a centre-piece of ferns, mounted in any low dish that can be hidden by the drapery. Sprays of green foliage, knotted with shaded ribbons (orange to red) fill up the table very well; and the candles should have alternate shades of orange and red. This might be called an "Oriental" table.

A "frozen lake" is rather a novelty. A mirror down the centre of the table, edged with cotton-wool raised to uneven heights to represent snow. The lake fringed with sprays of ivy, sedge-grasses, or other suitable foliage, and little ferns peeping out from the "snow"—maidenhair fern can be used, but must be artificially blanched. Small "bushes" of holly lend colour, and a miniature sledge or two on the ice adds to the effect. Small easels, composed of scarlet geranium, on which to place the menu-cards, add the desired colour. The decoration must be finished off with a dusting of "Jack Frost," and some scattered over the mirror to represent frozen water.

The old-fashioned epergne is coming into fashion again. Many of these have the little hanging baskets attached. I think some of my readers might find the following arrangement novel and pretty. Fill the centre of the epergne with fern and allamandas; then arrange the little silver baskets with Tangerine oranges. Twine smilax round the epergne, and carry the sprays from this to the different candelabra that may be on the table; at the base of each of these arrange ferns and allamandas, with trails of smilax on the cloth, connecting small clusters of the flowers and ferns. At one end of the table a pine, at the other a yellow "laced" melon, dishes of oranges, and other fruits of yellow tints.

A green-and-white table is pretty, and at this time of year might be carried out thus. Arrange a centre-piece of moss in the form of a diamond or star, and fill this with white Roman hyacinths and small ferns. Down each side of the table arrange white china candlesticks entwined with smilax, and based with ferns embedded with moss. At each end, large horseshoes of hyacinths on a bed of ferns and fancy moss, and lengths of narrow green ribbon connecting each candlestick. This arrangement would be equally pretty with pink hyacinths and pink ribbons; and lyres might be substituted for the horseshoes.

I think I may suggest one more table decoration furnished from hot-house plants — the table to be entirely covered (only just leaving room for the plates and glass) with caladium begonia, choice small palms, and any of the hundred and one delicately tinted leaves to be found in the stove-house. Some of these would have to be wired, and the groundwork would be an undulating bank of moss—not too high— the whole thing to be bordered with a light arrangement of stephanotis and maidenhair fern—electric lights arranged among the leaves ; but if other light is used, it should be shaded with pale yellow or green shades.

Before I finish with table decorations, I will give an idea of one suitable for a children's party at this particular season. A log of wood in the centre, snowflaked and frosted, Father Christmas sitting thereon, and liberally supplied with crackers and little sacks of sweets, small palms, with clusters of holly well berried, bowls and dishes of fruits and cakes, and sugared almonds—these arranged on a long table, with pretty jellies, creams, etc., make a fascinating *tout ensemble* for young folk ; and this brings me to the decoration of rooms for a children's party.

Festoons of greenery, caught up alternately with bunches of holly and mistletoe, and frosted design, with welcoming mottoes in scarlet berries, should be the predominant feature in the ball-room ; whilst in corridors or on landings might be found Santa Claus, with his sack of Christmas gifts for the assembled guests. At other points of vantage might be discovered drums and tambourines, filled with crackers and bags of *bon-bons*—and " Pierrots " dispensing dolls and other toys to the little ones would be a change from the old-fashioned Christmas-tree ; whilst in the ball-room, the cotillon would afford a good way of disposing of the wares. The hall and staircase should be decorated with holly, flags, and all sorts of greenery. Palms and plants are out of place

at a children's party, and are liable to get upset and damaged.

For a " grown up " party the decorations must be more elaborate. The hall, corridors, and staircase arranged with tall palms, grouped with variegated foliage plants, hanging balls and baskets of shaded chrysanthemuns, the rooms hung with holly, and in the dancing-room, wall-baskets filled with poinsettias, ferns, palms, etc. Mirrors draped with trails of greenery, and these (if flowers are scarce) caught up with large butterfly bows of scarlet ribbon. The supper-table might be decorated with poinsettias and scarlet geranium, with small pot palms and maidenhair fern, and in front of each guest a spray or buttonhole of holly. One very large bunch of mistletoe should hang in the hall. In the cotillon the opportunity would be afforded of distributing the gifts from a gaily decorated wheelbarrow, well frosted, and propelled by two smart pages : the presents would all be marked with the owners' names.

Home decorations for Christmas vary according to variety and quantity of material to hand. Ropes of green stuff composed of evergreen, ivy, any variegated leaves, and holly ; when the latter is devoid of berries, the imitation ones, put together in small clusters, serve the purpose for colour. These ropes are generally made on ribbon-wire ; they can then be twisted and turned to suit every nook and corner, also for the balustrades, pictures, etc.—and the rope should not be made too thick. Of course, where flowers can be had, much prettier effects can be obtained—chrysanthemums, camellias, poinsettias, cinerarias, hyacinths, Christmas roses, or any plants of this kind to be found in large greenhouses through the winter. For flat decorations the flowers and ferns should be sewn on to stout brown paper, or stiffening such as is used by dressmakers.

Snow and frost are represented with cotton wool stuck on to cardboard or stout paper with a little paste, the wool fluffed out, and sprinkled with gum-water ; then powder it over with " Jack Frost."

Mistletoe must not be forgotten on these occasions, but be suspended in large bunches in the hall and other places, as much fun is got out of the ancient custom of " kissing."

A great deal of lighting is requisite where much green stuff is used. The electric light to be found in most large houses now leaves nothing to be desired. But where this is not numerous candles will be necessary.

At a musical reception the rooms, including that in which the concert is held, should be prettily arranged with flowers and floral emblems. The platform should not have too many flowers in front, to hide the performers, but the boards should be hidden with green-stuff and chrysanthemums tacked on with small nails and ferns, arranged so that there is no appearance of stiffness: at each corner facing the audience, a graceful palm well grouped with variegated foliage plants. If there is an upright piano, the back should be entirely hidden with a trellis-work of flowers, or draped with pale yellow silk, and a large lyre of shaded chrysanthemums in the centre, ferns outspreading from the base, and the strings of the lyre of gold silk. Mirrors could be draped with trails of green or with light silken hangings caught back with floral tambourines, small Irish harps, banjos, or violins. The edge of the tambourine could be made of yellow chrysanthemums and shaded leaves, and suspended with two or three shades of ribbon to correspond with the flowers. The harp might be of scarlet geranium and feathery moss, the strings formed by twists of green silk round the wire foundation. A violin of mauve asters, the strings gold thread and the pegs also coloured gold. The banjo of stephanotis, with the handle of small ferns and stephanotis marking the pegs. On console or other side-tables place lyres and harps of different flowers and hanging-baskets in the doorways, with festoons of natural flowers. Landings and staircases can be decorated in either of the following ways :—Liberty art muslin or silks, caught with sprays or trails of flowers or ferns and tied with large knots of coloured ribbon, or garlands of foliage with big bows of ribbon at intervals, or draperies of the lovely Oriental materials so much in vogue, and caught up with Japanese baskets, full of flowers, fans, or Moorish hanging-lamps. All this gives colour and adds to the fantasy of the moment.

As a rule the supper-room is not much decorated, but if it is arranged with numerous small tables, each one could have a centre-piece of glass filled with ferns and flowers, every one a different colour ; and the sideboard might be rather extensively decorated—all very high and at the back, in the centre there being the coat-of-arms or crest of the host in coloured flowers and a tall thin cocus wedeliana at each end, mossed in with delicate-shaded leaves —the lighting being electric, and under pink or yellow shades.

These winter decorations lead us to the hunt breakfast-table ; and the flowers make a pretty addition to the, probably, numerous trophies of the sporting host. The centre-piece a large double horseshoe of white Roman hyacinths, the nails marked with blue of the same flower ; and in between the various viands white china dogs, rabbits, and other animals, filled with flowers and ferns. This white china can be bought at almost any fancy shop, and looks better on the breakfast-table than the more elaborate bowls or vases. Designs in horns, hunting-caps, and stirrups made of moss on wire and stuck with hyacinths of different colours or with miniature chrysanthemums, serve to frame the menus. To make the table complete, the china should depict hunting and other sporting scenes, and goblets should be used instead of tumblers.

The old-fashioned wedding-breakfast is a thing of the past ; but with the introduction of luncheons and teas comes a much more elaborate floral display. The cake should have a table to itself, and be arranged with real flowers, and the table covered with pretty moss, daintily decked with white flowers ; from the table depend trails of asparagus and smilax, intermixed with choice white blooms— camellias, hyacinths, gardenias, stephanotis, daphne and bouvardia. The bridal couple stand by this table, and down each side of the room there is a long one laid with various seasonable dainties, and on these tables satin bags with the initials of the newly wedded pair worked in silver thereon, and filled alternately with small ferns and white flowers in variety ; also silver shoes or *sabots* filled with flowers. Occasionally a slender cocus or phœnix in white basket-work china pot, and connecting each of these pots streamers of white corded silk, knotted in the middle with a small spray of orange-blossom and white heather. Small wax figures dressed as pages, and holding a scroll of satin, on which is inscribed in silver lettering the *dejeuner menu*. These should be placed down the tables at intervals of about one to every four persons.

The entrance-hall will have large palms : the tall, thin ones are much more graceful and effective here than the heavier latanias and dracænas ; and pots of white heath, hyacinths, and chrysanthemums, put the finishing stroke to the decorations. Two children, dressed as heralds, should stand on either side of the doorway, and hand a button-hole of white flowers to the guests as they enter.

Before speaking of the decorations in the church, it would perhaps be as well to describe some of the most fashionable bouquets for the bride and her *dames d'honneur*. The latest combination of flowers for the bridal bouquet is lilies-of-the-valley, white moss-rose, orange-blossom, and gardenias. Myrtle is always used, and in the centre of the bouquet is a piece of white heather. There should be no ribbon, but long trails of asparagus, with small knots of white flowers to reach to the hem of the skirt; it should be a large and rather wide bouquet.

For the bridesmaids, unless it is a military wedding, and regimental colours are introduced, "foliage" is more effective at this season, especially if the dresses are of cream or white material. These foliage bouquets are composed of caladium begonias, colus, crotons, and variegated aspidistra of the dwarf kind. These look very well tied with shaded ribbons, but the latter are not so popular as they used to be.

With regard to floral arrangements in the church on these occasions, with the exception of white flowers on the altar and bordering the Communion rails, tall palms look the best— two of these at the entrance to the aisle, and two extra tall ones on each side of the chancel. If they are not in tubs, the pots must be hidden with white flowers. If there is a good attendance of bridesmaids, intead of receiving the bride at the entrance of the church, they should line the aisle near the chancel, and close round her as she advances. When the attendants are all in white, bouquets of poinsettias, with double scarlet geraniums and crimson leaves, are very effective, and give a lovely touch of colour, especially if the church is at all sombre.

I would now offer a few hints for Christmas Day church decorations—although, for this special work, certain rules have to be observed, and devices and emblems must be symbolical of the festival. The materials to be collected are chiefly various evergreens, berries, variegated leaves, and natural flowers. Devices with appropriate mottoes serve to hide blank walls and bare spaces, and can be made in the following way. Take a strip of stiff paper or cardboard sold for the purpose, and edge it with ivy or other evergreens. If berries are to be had in plenty, form your letters of these, but if not, cut

out the lettering in any red material, and to each capital attach a small spray of holly, Maltese crosses and knights'-shields of red-and-white stuff, edged with greenery, may be attached to each pillar, and can be wreathed with ropes of green. All imitation materials should be employed for the massive work, and the font, pulpit, chancel, and choir-stalls, should have the real flowers and berries. For the chancel and choir, an ordinary lattice-work, such as is sold by any ironmonger, is a most useful foundation, as it can be so easily attached. On to this is fixed the fern and moss, and then the flowers are carefully stuck on, or arranged thereon in devices, such as anchors, stars, *fleurs-de-lis*, crosses, wreaths, and sprays. At each end of the chancel, grasses and ferns mixed with tall lilies, white heath, and Christmas roses, forming the base. On the altar Eucharis lilies, with here and there a poinsettia to give colour. If the pulpit be white, an edging of these crimson flowers, with their long-shaped leaves, and a cross of the same, has a grand effect. The reading-desk might be done with evergreens and scarlet geraniums, or, if flowers are scarce, variegated leaves and holly, with Cape flowers, will answer the purpose and look very well. Pots of flowers hidden in moss form a very good base for the lectern. The font should, if possible, be decorated entirely with white flowers. Church designs for covering with flowers can be purchased all ready for use, and if money is no object this saves an immense amount of time and trouble. The windows can be framed with moss, and holly, or other scarlet berries, arranged thereon; and in the moss on the sill, a *fleur-de-lis*, a Maltese cross, or star, would mark the centre, when greenery is very scarce. The edging of the window-frames and the sills can be covered with some red material, and designs in holly- or ivy-leaves placed on it. This is most effective as a substitute, but not so satisfactory as the fresh green leaves and branches. There are various other modes of decoration, but want of space forbids my entering into further details at the present time.

BY MRS. DE SALIS.

DARK December is here, and Christmas will be with us shortly. With its advent, balls, dinners, private theatricals, and other festive functions, will be in full swing. Wishing all our readers a happy "Yule-tyde," we trust that a few of the following recipes may help those convivially and merrily inclined.

Oyster Soufflé.

Take two dozen small oysters; mince them and rub them through a wire sieve. Blanch and beard a dozen large oysters, and cut each one into four pieces. Put two ounces of flour and one ounce of butter into a stew-pan, and mix well together over the fire; then a quarter of a pint of oyster-liquor, and stir all together till it thickens.

Put this sauce and the pounded oysters into a mortar and pound them well together, adding two yolks of eggs, one at a time, a little salt, cayenne pepper, and a gill of cream. When these are thoroughly mixed, beat three whites of eggs to a stiff froth and stir them into the mixture very lightly; then put in the oysters.

Butter the mould, pour in the mixture, cover it with buttered paper, and steam gently for half an hour. Strew lobster coral over it.

Oysters and Bloater Roes.

(*A Savoury.*)

Cut some pieces of bread three inches long and one wide, half an inch deep. Hollow out the centre and fry crisp; fill with the soft roes of bloaters with three oysters in each, which must be *sautéd* in butter for a minute or so.

Add just one squeeze of lemon, and a dust of cayenne, and serve up *very* hot.

Iced Oyster Soufflé.

Prepare the *soufflé* according to recipe above for oyster *soufflé*, adding half a pint of whipped aspic jelly into the sauce, and after it has been steamed and turned out, it should be put into a mould which has been lined with clear aspic jelly. Put on ice till ready to turn out.

Garnish with chopped aspic, chervil, and the Lilliputian tomatoes.

Woodcock with Anchovies.

Cut a cold woodcock into neat fillets, fry them in sweet, clear dripping, and boil up some good brown gravy. Arrange the fillets *en couronne* in a dish which has been previously buttered and dusted with grated Parmesan. Upon each fillet place a fillet of anchovy, pour a little gravy on each and sprinkle over more Parmesan, and some breadcrumbs. Just before serving add a little champagne.

Ballotines of Turkey.

Bone a small turkey; poult and farce it with half a pound of pounded tongue, and the same of pounded pork. Pass through a sieve; then spread it out, chop up two or three truffles in it, and place a layer of *foie-gras* on it. Sprinkle on a little salt and pepper, with a few drops of sherry. After stuffing the bird with this, flour and tie it up in a cloth. Simmer it in a stewpan with some stock for an hour to an hour and a quarter; then leave it to get quite cold in the stock. When cold, cut it into neat slices, and mask over with pale liquefied aspic. Decorate by strewing alternately finely chopped truffle and pistachio nuts, and dish on a border of aspic cream, garnished with little mounds of chopped aspic, sprinkled with paprika.

Sardines au Parmesan.

Warm up the required number of sardines in their own oil, with a little salt and cayenne, also a teaspoonful of the juice of a lemon. When they are hot, lift them from the oil they have been warmed up in, and thicken it with a little cornflour and the yolk of an egg. Dish them on fried *croûtens* the length and width of the sardines, and sprinkle over them liberally some grated Parmesan cheese, then pour over the sauce, and serve very hot.

Boules à la Copenhagen.

Boil a Finnan haddock, then remove the flesh, taking care not to leave any skin or bones, pound it in a mortar with one and a half ounce of butter and a small pinch of cayenne; then rub it through a sieve. Next take two tablespoonfuls of breadcrumbs, a teaspoonful of finely chopped parsley, and the yolk of a small egg, to form a paste. Roll this into small balls, drop them into *boiling* butter, and fry a pale, delicate gold colour. After draining, pile them up high on a dish, sprinkle them with grated Parmesan, and garnish with watercress.

LONDON SOCIETY IN THE DIAMOND JUBILEE YEAR.

By Mrs. Humphry ("Madge" of *Truth*).

THE London Season of 1897 will for many long years stand out distinctly in the memories of those who took part in it or merely looked on. From the earliest beginning of it, when the first drawing-room was held on the 24th of February, there was a most wonderful efflorescence of loyalty to the Queen in the sixtieth year of her glorious reign. The word "Jubilee" must have been spoken millions of times every day. The Prince of Wales gave the year its name of "Diamond Jubilee," and took an active part throughout in all the arrangements for the celebration of the longest reign on record. The Queen herself, imbued with the inevitable sense of the mutability of events and the uncertainty of life, would listen to no plans or suggestions on the subject until June was drawing very near. Her Majesty would say to the Prince, when he asked her if she would like such and such arrangements to be made, "There are four months between this and June 22nd. Let us wait awhile." The usual testimony of popularity was awarded to the event in the naming of articles of dress, of food, furniture and household gear after the Jubilee. The word was displayed everywhere, heard on all sides, and constantly appeared in newspapers and magazines.

It was rather amusing to note how the word was utilised by tradespeople to puff their wares. In one instance, circulars were sent out with red, white, and blue Union Jacks on the cover, and the dates 1837-1897 emblazoned to match. The legend within began, "Our bacon, in both quality and prices, will compare favourably with——"

And another sign of the times was that everyone who could manage it painted his house afresh, aiding and abetting in the universal desire to make everything look its brightest and freshest for the joyful occasion.

It was about the middle of February that a novel and extremely pretty skating fête was given at Prince's, the performers being ladies and gentlemen of high position. The Prince of Wales and the Duchess of Teck were present, and a crowd of fashionable people filled the long corridor to overflowing. Twelve couples of skaters came upon the ice immediately after the arrival of the

From Photo by]   [*Hughes & Mullins.*

THE QUEEN WITH HER GREAT-GRANDSON PRINCE EDWARD OF YORK.

Royalties. The men were all in evening dress, and the ladies were clad in bright cardinal red from head to foot, black fur hemming their dresses, and forming zouaves upon the bodices, a little of it being introduced in the red toques. Lady Randolph Churchill headed the procession, and led the graceful evolutions of the party, which were much applauded by the Prince. In the intervals, Lady Randolph always sat by the royal party, which, by the Prince's invitation, had been joined by the Duchess of Devonshire.

While the Queen was at Cimiez, the Prince of Wales decided on several matters connected with the Jubilee celebrations, and throughout the whole of the ensuing months his perfect devotion to his royal mother, his tender consideration for her, and his studious care in every matter that could affect her convenience, were conspicuous, and served to increase the feeling of affection with which His Royal Highness has always been regarded. The careful planning of the procession in every detail was chiefly carried out by the Prince, the military part of the pageant falling upon the Duke of Connaught; and, as after events showed, the two royal brothers achieved what the executive has frequently failed in, i.e., arranging the minutiæ of the day's programme so perfectly that not a single hitch of any kind occurred to mar the proceedings. The sole approach to anything of the kind was a delay of twenty minutes, when the military procession had proceeded partly on its way to St. Paul's; and this was owing to over-punctuality on the part of the officials who timed the start.

The Queen is the most punctual of women, and even in her ordinary daily life Her Majesty has her time planned out with unvarying regularity, and, being well aware of the value of the fleeting minutes, none are lost in waiting for the tardy, who are to be found in every household. On one occasion, the Queen's drive had been given up on account of a snow shower, but on its clearing up half-an-hour later, a message reached Princess Beatrice: "The Queen drives in ten minutes." The Princess had changed her out-door dress when the carriage was countermanded, and had to be very brisk in order to be ready. But ready she was. It may, then, be imagined that on Jubilee day, when Her Majesty was informed that her carriage was at the door twenty minutes before the appointed time, she utterly declined to step into it one moment before the hour arranged. Consequently a messenger galloped along the whole distance already accomplished by the troops; and the mile or two of spectators, noting the delay that followed on his passing, became apprehensive of some catastrophe having happened.

This was the one solitary hitch in the whole day's proceedings, and it was, after all, of a most trifling kind.

The excellent organisation of the procession was the result of three months' deliberation and consultation between the Queen's two sons, the heads of the police, the Lord Mayor, and the Dean and Chapter of St. Paul's.

And besides this portion of the work, there fell also upon the Prince of Wales the task of arranging for all the royal and other distinguished guests who came to London to attend the Jubilee. Several journeys to Windsor had to be made in order to consult the Queen, and once or twice the Prince himself was too busy to go, and the Princess went in his stead. The Queen is not only the most experienced politician in England; she is also the first authority on all matters relating to kingly etiquette and social precedence in the highest circles. Her excellent memory informs her as to the observances in the case of previous royal visits, and there are few persons living who understand the various strata of German sovereignties as Her Majesty does, from the great dignities of the Empire down to the smallest little principality.

One of the triumphs of Queen Victoria's reign has been the way in which, by dint of sheer good sense, she has combined a strict regard for etiquette—which may, in this instance, be defined as rendering to everyone the deference that is his due—with an affectionate regard for those about her that has won for her sincerest love. The Queen is well-served, because she is well-loved.

On the first of June, London presented a most remarkable and extraordinary appearance. The whole line of the route to be followed by the Jubilee Procession could be traced, at least, as far as London Bridge, by the miles of boards that hid the fronts of the buildings and provided seats for the expected invasion of spectators. Piccadilly was lined with wood from Hyde Park Corner to St. James's Street, and Pall Mall presented a similar aspect on both sides of the way. The noise of the hammer was incessantly heard in the land, to say nothing of the saw and the plane, and the air was full of sawdust. The extreme drought of the weather, while it favoured the operations of carpenters (who improved the occasion, by the way, by striking for higher pay), prevented the laying of this dust, and the atmosphere soon became impregnated with it. On the whole, the lot of the Lon-doner was not a very enviable one just at that time, and much of theWest End was rendered absolutely hideous by the ugly yellow of the wooden seats. Never was the Whit-suntide recess more gladly welcomed, and by the 6th of June,Whit Sun-day, everyone who could pos-sibly manage it was enjoying rural delights or sea breezes. But by the 18th most of the wooden erections were finished off and covered with red cloth. Bal-conies and win-dows were decorated. Public build-ings were pre-pared for illum-inating and or-namented with flags and ban-ners, crimson hangings, and devices appro-priate to the occasion. Clubs and private

From Photo by]　　　　　[London Stereoscopic Co.
LORD ROBERTS OF KANDAHAR.

houses were lavishly decorated, and one of the most remarkable was the residence of Baroness Burdett-Coutts in Piccadilly, the whole of the frontage to that thorough-fare being draped with English printed velveteen. The balconies were filled with flowers and the illuminations were among the handsomest to be seen.

London was in a state of congestion. The traffic in the roadways was so heavy that walking would have been much quicker than driving, only that it was almost impossible to get on, so crowded were the pavements. Never before had London been so full. The newspapers had been pro-phesying for some weeks that a scarcity of food would be a consequence of the in-pour-ing crowds, but the timely warn-ing thus given served to avert the inconveni-ence.

Ascot was shorn of its glories by the Jubilee, which kept the Prince and Princess of Wales in town and prevented their taking a house at Sun-ningdale as they usually do for the race week. Their Royal Highnesses had so much to do in receiving and visiting the royal and other distinguished guests who came to England to attend the Jubi-lee celebrations that they could not get away for a whole week and went by special train on the occasion of their visit. The Prince's horse, Persimmon, won the Gold Cup, and there was a scene of popular excitement and joyful congratulation, the Prince receiving an ovation. The royal party was immensely pleased, and the Duchess of Saxe-Coburg was observed to give her royal brother-in-law a very hearty hand-shake.

At Sandown, when the great race for the Eclipse Stakes was run, there was a remarkably crowded and brilliant assemblage. The royal pavilion was occupied by a distinguished party of royalties, who had come to see the Prince of Wales' horse, Persimmon, run for the great prize of £10,000. The Princess of Wales never looked lovelier than she did in her flowered mauve muslin, with toque composed of heliotrope. The Duchess of York looked remarkably well, too, in an écru gown and very becoming bonnet of a new shade of blue, half mauve.

The bad manners of some of the ladies present were the subject of comment. They crowded round the barrier in front of the royal pavilion and stared at the Princesses, not two yards distant from them, as though the ladies had been shows at a country fair. The Princess of Wales, always ready to smile and bow when she is greeted in the usual respectful way, is quick to notice this sort of rudeness. Her expression becomes grave and she looks straight before her in a manner that contrasts with her ordinary genial style.

When the great race was about to be run, two ladies on the Lawn were heard in the following dialogue : " How shall we manage ? Will you look at the race while I watch the Prince's face?" "Oh, no," was the reply, " *I* want to watch the Prince's face," and so it was amicably settled that the gaze of both should be fastened on the countenance of Persimmon's owner. The Prince's horse won, and a roar of delighted congratulation went up from the crowded Lawn, to which H.R.H. responded by raising his hat and bowing and smiling. Persimmon has a favourite stable companion, a brown horse, and this animal preceded him to the course, and again, after the race, from the course to the paddock. One would like to know what the equine friends said to each other after the victory.

The serious illness of the Duchess of Teck about six weeks before Jubilee Day made many apprehensive. No one is better loved than the kindly, handsome Princess Mary, and next to the Queen herself, no one received heartier greetings on Jubilee Day.

At last the great day dawned, and found London very early astir. The sky was overcast and the light was grey, but no one feared that it would rain. "Queen's weather" was confidently expected and duly appeared upon the scene in good time for the pageant. As early as seven o'clock a bird's-eye view of London would have revealed its inhabitants pouring in from the suburbs in crowds, the greater part on foot, though the roadways were well filled with omnibuses, cabs, and brakes. The prices charged for vehicular conveyance proved deterrent to the majority. Five pounds for the day was the charge for omnibus or cab, fifteen for a brougham. The imaginary spectator in the air would have seen trains pouring in at every terminus and on every line of rail, all crowded with passengers, who, on alighting, converged towards the line of route. At eight o'clock the military and police were being stationed along the route, and in Trafalgar Square, suitably enough, the blue-jackets were placed. By the time the first procession started, everything was in order.

The decorations along the whole line of route were of the gayest and most imposing description. St. James's Street probably offered the most beautiful, as well as the most tastefully conceived and executed display among all the West-end thoroughfares. The tall Corinthian pillars at either end of the street, with their gilt capitals and the thickly-set Venetian masts which lined the roadway, with cork fern baskets filled with real flowers, combined, with the scarlet and gold draped balconies and many floral embellishments along house fronts and windows, to give an almost continual air of gaiety to the scene. Pall Mall was, of course, superb with its lordly clubs, and the War Office, plain enough in its military scarlet and gold, was brightened by rows of beautifully-dressed ladies. The narrow thoroughfare of the Strand had rather a mixed effect, owing to a want of unanimity in the decorations. A beautiful note of coolness was struck in Fleet Street by the pale green silk bordered with ropes of laurel leaves, which contrasted agreeably with the grey stone front of the *Daily Telegraph* offices. Festoons of pale green leaves were hung from the Venetian masts from Fleet Street to Ludgate Hill, and though no special decorations were to be seen about St. Paul's itself, the crowds assembled there, closely packed together, were in themselves a sight to remember for long years. Cheapside suffered from the same lack of consistency as that displayed in the Strand, but the sight of the Mansion House, the pillars of which were wreathed with coloured lights ready for the illuminations in the evening, the Royal Exchange with its trophies of flags and long lines of yellow lamps, and, above all, the Bank of England, decorated with festoons of tinted lamps and bearing the legend " She wrought her people lasting good," offered a display worthy of the wealth of the greatest money-centre of the world. The Monument had for once lost its severity of aspect, the rigid outline being broken by flags which waved from every loop-hole of the difficult ascent.

As to the procession itself, who shall venture to describe it? A mere enumeration of its component parts may suffice to suggest its comprehensive grandeur, and the idea it conveyed of the extent and glory of the British Empire. First came the Colonial Premiers in royal carriages, conspicuous among them being Sir Edward Braddon, Sir Gordon Sprigg, Sir W. Whiteway, Sir Hugh Nelson, the Hon. W. Laurier, and Sir G. Turner, most of them occupying the back seats, having given their wives the place of honour. The Premiers were headed by Lord Roberts, V.C., Colonel in Chief of Colonial Troops, on his beautiful white Arab, which has carried him in his campaigns for twenty-five years. Each Company followed the Premier of his district, and one knew not which to admire most, the Canadian Hussars and Dragoons, the New South Wales Mounted Rifles, in their distinctive slouch hats with feathers, and Lancer Volunteers in khaki tunics with broad-brimmed hats turned up at one side, all very tall men; or the Victoria Mounted Rifles in their soft felt hats, earth-brown tunics, turned up with scarlet, corduroy breeches and yellow gaiters. Following these were the giant Maoris; then came the Cape Mounted Rifles, in khaki tunics, the South Australian Mounted Rifles, in light-brown uniform, faced with scarlet, and brass helmets with puggarees. No less admired were the Natal Mounted Carabineers, in their broad slouch hats, followed by the Trinidad Light Cavalry, the Ceylon Cavalry, and the Rhodesian Horse, led by the one-armed Maurice Gifford, Lord Gifford's brother.

These by no means exhausted the list of Imperial and Colonial Forces, but will serve to convey some slight idea of their variety and numbers.

The Royal procession had an effective naval and military prologue, beginning with bluejackets, followed by artillery, dragoons, guards, and accompanied by the most telling music in the world. And how the people cheered the colours as they were carried past! We could read the names of Malplaquet, Waterloo, Sebastopol, Alma, Inkermann. Roars of cheering went up for the 17th Lancers, the "Death or Glory Boys," and few, amidst it all, forgot to note the beauty of the horses. Afterwards came ten minutes of marvellous military millinery worn by aides-de-camp, staff-officers, field-marshals, equerries, and naval and military attachés. But bright as it was, it paled before the magnificent Oriental colouring in the procession of native Indian officers of the Imperial Service Corps, the special Envoys from Hawaii, Roumania, and Corea, foreign ambassadors from far lands, and among them, distinguished in his plain citizen dress, the Hon. Whitelaw Reid, from the United States.

From Photo by] SIR EVELYN WOOD. *[Walery.*

The carriages containing the Royal Family were preceded by Princes and representatives, the former riding on horseback in groups of three abreast, and the latter in carriages, a most brilliant item in the programme.

The Queen's grandchildren wore bright faces, and bowed right and left with a little jerky movement that made everyone smile. Princess Henry of Battenberg had left off her mourning and wore pure white, but her face was pale and sad. The high rank of the Empress Frederick was denoted by the two equerries who rode by the side of her carriage, drawn by four black horses. An imposing escort of Indian Cavalry followed it, with Lord Wolseley immediately preceding the eight cream-coloured horses with their splendid trappings that drew the carriage of the Queen. Opposite Her Majesty sat the Princess of Wales, and on the fair Alexandra's left was Princess Christian, the former wearing mauve and white, the latter a white dress and red flowers in her bonnet.

The Queen has never, since her hair turned

grey, looked better, nicer, or more sympathetic than, on her Diamond Jubilee Day, when she bowed her acknowledgments to her people for their loving greetings. Her Majesty had lightened her mourning with white lace laid on her black dress and cape, and her black and white bonnet was of a new and very becoming shape, rather long behind the ears. Her beautiful white hair looked its softest as she smiled on either side with a glance of gentle kindliness.

It transpired afterwards that Her Majesty was deeply affected by the affectionate greetings of her people, more like those of sons and daughters to a beloved mother, and kept repeating in a low voice: "God bless them! God bless them!"

The Jubilee procession can scarcely be said to be over. It can be seen by all who wish to see it, perpetuated by the science of photography, in the Cinematograph and the Velograph; and it is worthy of notice that the crowds who gaze on this realistic pictorial and panoramic representation of it, always rise to their feet and cheer heartily when Her Majesty's carriage comes into view, though little of the Royal lady herself can be seen for the white parasol she carries.

The words of the prayer offered up at St. Paul's are as follows: " O Lord, our Heavenly Father, we give Thee hearty thanks for the many blessings which Thou hast bestowed upon us during the sixty years of the happy reign of our Gracious Queen Victoria. We thank Thee for the progress made in knowledge of Thy marvellous works, for the increase of comfort given to human life, for the kindlier feeling between rich and poor, for the wonderful preaching of the Gospel to many nations; and we pray Thee that these and all other of Thy gifts may be long continued to us and to our Queen, to the glory of Thy Holy name, through Jesus Christ our Lord. Amen."

A very few distinguished persons were given the privilege of viewing the Jubilee procession from the windows of Buckingham Palace on the great day of celebration, and among those was Miss Florence Nightingale, who was provided with a good place at the express wish of Her Majesty by the Earl of Pembroke, the Lord Steward.

Just before the Queen left Buckingham Palace on her way through her capital she telegraphed to her people a message consisting of these simple and touching words:
" From my heart I thank my beloved people. May God bless them."

A few seconds later the message was flying

under oceans and through the air to forty different stations on the globe where floats the Union Jack.

The Queen's dinner on Jubilee Day was a simple one, Her Majesty's gastronomic taste being unspoiled by indulgence in high-flavoured foods, one of the secrets of her excellent health. The meal opened with two soups, one Brunoise, the other potato; and these were followed by salmon and whitebait. Afterwards came a couple of entrées, then roast beef and fowl, with which green peas and potatoes were served. The sweet course consisted of two simple puddings, and the dinner closed with a savoury and strawberries with cream.

No one who was present at the gala performance at the Opera on the 23rd of June, in honour of the Diamond Jubilee, is ever likely to forget it. The beauty of the house was far beyond anything that had ever been achieved before. Veils of roses hung from all the boxes, the flowers being strung on trails of smilax, which were looped back at the sides, curtain fashion, and made exquisite frames for the occupants, consisting of the high aristocracy, the men in uniform or Court dress, the women glittering with jewels. A beautiful touch was the shading of the roses from pale to dark as they drooped towards the floor of the house. The three tones were amber, so tender of tint as to be almost white, pink, and damask. The royal box, composed of ten ordinary boxes thrown into one, was canopied with gold silk and framed in flowers, orchids, roses, and stephanotis, clustering along the ledge amidst feathery spirea blooms and broad begonia leaves in palest green with dark markings.

A royal crown, composed of orchids, was arranged above the heads of the occupants.

Below the box, which filled the whole space opposite the stage, the scheme of decorations became concentrated and centralised, as it were, the woven veil of roses hanging deep below it, and showing red below, pink in the middle, and white above. The royal ladies wore white or pale-tinted dresses, and all, except the unmarried Princesses, wore tiaras

From Photo by]   *[London Stereoscopic Co.*
THE RIGHT HON. SIR EDWARD BRADDON.

and splendid necklaces. The Princes and Royal Dukes were in uniform, and in the background was visible a further crescent of scarlet uniform, belonging to the Lord Chamberlain, the Master of the Horse, and other State officials who were in attendance.

The stalls and boxes contained a superlatively brilliant assembly. The duchesses were present in full force, and almost all the dresses were white, one or two were black, but pale tones of green or blue or yellow were numerous. The display of jewels was wonderful. Scattered among the pretty women were men in uniform, in Court dress, in levée dress, Oriental magnates in scarlet velvet coats, richly embroidered in bullion gold, and wearing white and silver turbans glittering with precious stones, and, altogether, with the swaying veils of roses and the perfume of exotics, the delicious music and the universal sentiment of rejoicing, the scene was one to be ever remembered.

Prices ran high indeed on this occasion, as much as two hundred pounds being paid for a single box, and the lowest price of a stall being six guineas. Some of the visitors were over an hour in getting to the Opera house, owing to the crowds of people who were out in the streets looking at the illuminations. Those who went in carriages saw but little of them, for the traffic soon became blocked, and we

From Photo by]   *[Chancellor.*
HIS EXCELLENCY LORD CADOGAN, VICEROY OF IRELAND.

know of one party who spent two hours opposite Apsley House, their carriages being blocked there all that time.

Small wonder that the one word "Repose" formed the Court programme for the Sunday that followed upon all the fatigues of Jubilee week. It was an eloquent, if brief, injunction.

The opera season was a very brilliant one. It had been feared that the death of Sir Augustus Harris would cause it to decline, but never has the house been better patronised by subscribers. The Princess of Wales had a box of her own for the first time last season, and with Princess Victoria was a constant attendant.

The Jubilee celebrations, as far as Her Majesty was personally concerned in them, may be said to have been concluded with the garden party at Buckingham Palace on the 28th of June. The beautiful grounds, which, in extent and the variety of trees they contain, are always such a surprise to those who see them for the first time, have never witnessed a more brilliant scene. The Oriental potentates and officers, in snowy turbans and crimson velvet, gold-embroidered coats, gave some notes of richest colour to the assembly, which included almost all that is distinguished in society, arts, letters, and the drama. The tent reserved for the royalties was visited by many specially invited and favoured persons during the afternoon. The Queen, who had very perceptibly lightened her mourning for the Jubilee celebrations, wore black silk, the front entirely veiled with black chiffon, embroidered in a design of jasmine sprays, and laid over white chiffon, which gave it a very light and cool effect. The black grenadine bodice was partly hidden by a black chiffon cape lined with white silk, rounded at the back, and finished with square ends in front. The royal bonnet was also black and white. The Princess of Wales wore white silk muslin, and had some mauve in her toque and a glitter of silver on the bodice of her dress.

The Queen drove through the grounds in a victoria drawn by a pair of grey horses, stopping every now and then to talk with some of her more favoured guests. Her Majesty was looking remarkably well, and seemed in the best of spirits.

The Princess of Wales showed great unselfishness during the eventful fortnight. No one could have guessed from her manner that Her Royal Highness was a prey to anxiety of various kinds. Her mother was far from well, and the Duchess of Cumberland was again suffering from her old complaint, while the unsettled condition of Greece must have made all the Danish Royal family anxious.

The Queen's favourite flower is the lily-of-the-valley, and she was extremely pleased with two floral offerings from some of her godchildren in Jubilee week. One was a chariot in pale green straw, with the wheels outlined in lilies-of-the-valley, and a flight of miniature white doves carried out in orchids. An imperial crown appeared on the panels of the little coach. The other present was a basket all red, white, and blue, with flowers in the same colours, and tied with ribbons, also in the national tints.

It was a wonderful season for fancy dress balls, Mrs. Arthur Paget leading the way before Easter with her very successful *poudré* dance, and Mrs. Oppenheim following suit with her flower-ball. The glory of these was overshadowed, however, by the brilliant historic and fancy ball given by the Duchess of Devonshire, and attended by many members of the Royal family. Even in anticipation this ball created a sensation only second to that caused by the Jubilee itself, and it is said that there were ladies who prepared their costumes for the great occasion, but never received an invitation. Great ladies are sometimes capricious, and the fact of being on their visiting list and having been invited to previous entertainments does not at all ensure a continuance of favours.

From Photo by]   *[Chancellor.*
HER EXCELLENCY THE COUNTESS CADOGAN.

On July 2nd the great event came off, and the fact that *The Times* devoted four columns to a description of the ball is indicative of the stir it made.

In tissue of silver and cloth of gold, and richly jewelled from head to foot, stood the stately Zenobia, Duchess of Devonshire, at the head of her marble stairway, to receive her guests of all the ages—queens who had stepped out of history to grace the scene, queens from the idyllic stories of long ago, queens from ancient Persia and Abyssinia, and queens from Fairyland. Was not Titania there herself, with glittering wings and lily wand? And the beautiful fair-haired queen, before whom all other queens bent and performed obeisance as she passed, fair Marguerite de Valois, in gleaming snowy satin and high lace collar, with silver-lined train of cloth of gold, was she not our own Princess, the queen of hearts? Her jewels were magnificent indeed, the diamond crown reflected in multitudinous bands and rivers of quivering light from the diamonds and pearls upon her neck. The Princesses in her suite were her own daughters and her daughter-in-law—Princess Victoria in palest citron, the Duchess of Fife in white, Princess Charles of Denmark in pale pink, and the Duchess of York in blue. The Prince of Wales, as Grand Master of the Knights Hospitallers of Malta, in black velvet and white satin, led the Princess to the dais prepared for her, and the glittering processions began to file past, according to their historic period and date. Among the Royal spectators were the Duke of Connaught as an Elizabethan general, looking extremely well in his steel cuirass, inlaid with gold, and dark grey velvet

THE PRINCESS OF WALES AS MARGUERITE OF VALOIS.

a Danish gentleman of the last century, and the Duke of Fife, in royal blue, was a courtier of Marguerite de Valois, as in duty bound. The Marchioness of Lorne was at her best and brightest in red wig and Gretchen white. The Duchess of Connaught was Anne of Austria, in amber velvet brocade, her hair arranged in short ringlets under a jewelled cap; the high Vandyck collar was thickly sewn with pearls and gold. The Duchess of Teck, as Electress of Hanover, looked every inch a queen in her lovely Frédéric gown of orange velvet, the full skirt sewn on with rows of large pearls. Fine old point and royal ermine made the bodice a thing of beauty, and ermine also trimmed the skirt; a very picturesque arrangement of lace falling from one side and caught up in the hair, with a splendid necklace of pearls and diamonds, completed an exact reproduction from a miniature at Hampton Court.

Among the various courts were those of King Arthur, the Doge of Venice, Queen Marie Thérèse, Queen Elizabeth, and Catherine II. of Russia. Enid was personated by Lady Ashburton in white cut velvet. Mrs. Willy Walker was a pretty Vivian in lurid and sinuous draperies. Her husband, Major Walker, was Merlin, and the knights, in chain armour, white tabards richly broidered, crested helmets, and velvet mantles, were Lord Ashburton, Earl Rodney, Earl Bathurst, Sir Lister Kaye, and the Hon. G. Hood.

Lady Tweedmouth was gorgeously arrayed as Queen Elizabeth, and was surrounded by a numerous Court, including Lord Tweed-

doublet, and trunks slashed with gold-embroidered grey satin; the Duke of York, in the character of the Earl of Cumberland of Elizabeth's reign, also in grey velvet cape and doublet, the trunks crimson velvet slashed with grey, the high grey suède boots rolled outwards at the top, and in the front of his grey felt hat a jewelled cordelière glove, representing that given by good Queen Bess to her faithful Cumberland. Prince Christian, as Earl of Lincoln, wore white satin and velvet, his black velvet cape being lined with ermine. Princess Christian, in eighteenth-century costume of pink and gold, had her hair looped with pearls. Prince Charles of Denmark was very handsome in purple and mauve as mouth, Lord Battersea, the Earl of Sandwich, and Lord Frederic Hamilton, to say nothing of six stalwart halberdiers, one of whom was the Duke of Roxburghe, whose Duchess was bravely attired as an Elizabethan lady of high degree. Lady Raincliffe, as Catherine of Russia, was a marvel of millinery in yellow and gold, ermine and rubies. Her lords and ladies emulated her splendour, and among the most successful were the Duchess of Newcastle, Lady Yarborough, Lady Henry Bentinck, Lord Raincliffe, and Mr. Cresswell.

The Countess of Warwick, as Queen Marie Antoinette, in white and blue, with golden fleur-de-lys upon her velvet train, was the centre of a picturesque group, among whom were the Earl of Essex dressed as his ancestor of that period, and the Earl of Mar and Kellie as Sir Walter Raleigh.

Lady Edmonstone was a perfect picture as Mary, Queen of Scots. The Duchess of Sutherland looked prettier than ever as Charlotte Corday in revolutionary red. The Duchess of Hamilton went as Mary Hamilton in Elizabethan days, all in white satin and gold embroidery.

There were three Queens of Sheba, and Paris himself could scarcely have decided to which the apple of beauty should have been awarded. Lovely Lady Cynthia Graham was one, in white satin embroidered in gold and silver and bright rose. Princess Henry of Pless was another, and her dress was absolutely magnificent in its barbaric splendour of turquoise, emerald, amethyst, and ruby, caught in a web of finest gold, and spread thickly upon the dress and train of diaphanous gauze

in purple and gold, its shifting light seeming to mingle with that of the jewels. Black attendants bore her train along, and among her girl attendants was her pretty sister, Miss Cornwallis West, in an Ethiopian dress of snowy crêpe, girdled with jewels under a flowing robe of gold tissue. A drapery of gold and pink shot tissue was held round

THE DUCHESS OF DEVONSHIRE AS ZENOBIA

the hips by jewelled wings, and the pleated Liberty silk underdress was hemmed with pink roses, repeating the flowers in the hair.

Lady Archibald Campbell wore a beautiful dress as "Artemis," goddess of the chase. It was in palest green crêpe de chine, embroidered by hand with glittering silver thread and crystals, which resembled dewdrops. The tunic opened at the side to show an underdress of pale, steely-blue crêpe. Floating scarves of pale blue and green chiffon suggested moonlight. The green chiffon sleeves were held together by crystals. The headdress consisted of a star of crystal on the forehead, and a crescent moon in mother-o'-pearl, lit by electric light.

The Duchess of Leeds wore a lovely dress as Lalla Rookh. Tommy Moore would have beheld his ideal realised. But where was Feramorz? Lady Meysey Thompson, as Elizabeth, Queen of Bohemia, was in orange velvet, yellow satin, and old lace collar; the orange velvet cape sewn with silver, had a garland of lilies slung at the back.

Countess Clary, Countess Kinsky, and Countess Isabel Deym went as the three sisters of Napoleon I. in dresses which were perfect copies of an engraving by Isabey. All three being tall, handsome, and graceful, the effect was excellent. Lady Angela Forbes also was Queen of Naples. Miss Muriel Wilson made a splendid Vashti, in white crêpe and silver, with bands of diamonds in her hair, a lotus flower at one side, and a pomegranate at the other.

The Princess of Wales, as Marguerite of Valois, looked quite lovely, but H.R.H. refused to wear the quaint coif of the period, and consequently had a rather modern air. The Duchess of Devonshire was not very well suited as Zenobia, though dressed with the utmost Oriental magnificence. The truth is that many were overweighted and overshadowed by their clothes, the wearers sinking into insignificance in comparison with the splendours of their array. Another circumstance that rather marred the occasion was the disproportionate size of the rooms to the enormous company assembled, and the consequent impossibility of gaining an adequate idea of the scene. A very large hall would be needed in order to display to proper advantage the various quadrilles in which the characters belonging to the different courts joined. This idea was borrowed from the fancy ball given at Marlborough House several years ago.

Many of the dark-haired ladies chose to wear light wigs, while numbers of fair-haired beauties donned dark hair for the occasion. The Duchess of Portland was ill-advised to abandon her own beautiful auburn hair, which is one of the most charming points of her appearance. She spoiled herself with her fair curls. The Duchess of Sutherland, on the contrary, never looked prettier than in the dark locks of Charlotte Corday. Mrs. Ronalds, as the Goddess of Music, made a sensation with her electrically lighted headdress, but had constantly to retire to be lighted up. Princess Charles of Denmark was very much admired. The Countess of Dudley wore a marvellous dress as Queen Esther, a mass of embroidery under a floating robe of peach-tinted gauze, with pale poppies and superb jewels almost covering her head. Every woman there seemed to have emptied her jewel casket over herself, and many of the men were wonderfully jewelled. Lord Rosebery had five hundred pounds' worth of diamond buttons on his Horace Walpole costume. The manner in which serious-minded statesmen and others, who might be supposed to be, like the Laird o' Cockpen, "ta'en up wi' the things o' the State," dressed up for the ball, spending very high sums on their costumes, was nothing short of surprising. The average price of their costumes was £200 apiece, and in some cases the hire of the jewellery amounted to considerably more. Lord Kenyon and Mr. Montagu Guest were the finest men in the rooms. The Hungarian National Anthem was played as the Marchioness of Londonderry's procession passed the Royal dais. The beautiful Marchioness represented the Empress Marie Thérèse, surrounded by a brilliant court. The Duke of Devonshire was Charles V. of Germany, and among other well-known men were Earl Spencer as a Florentine noble, Mr. Chaplin as General Lefebvre, Mr. Joseph Chamberlain (in rose-coloured silk) as a Louis Quinze seigneur, the Hon. Gathorne Hardy in Louis XV. dress, Mr. Asquith a Roundhead, Lord James of Hereford as Sir Thomas More, Lord Halsbury as George III., and Viscount Peel as a Doge of Venice.

Of the beauties, the most conspicuous were Lady de Grey, a magnificent Cleopatra, Lady de Trafford, a too-lovely Semiramis, Mrs. Jack Menzies as Titania, the Countess of Westmorland as Hebe, and the Duchess of Leeds as Lalla Rookh.

The Countess of Suffolk's dress was copied from the painting of a Countess of Suffolk—Maria Constantia—date 1766, skirt of black moiré, with hanging sleeves and draped bodice of chiffon sparkling with embroidery. The Duke of Somerset went as the Protector Somerset, in jetted black velvet; Lord Ellesmere as James I., in grey satin trunks embroidered in large pearls, jewelled grey velvet mantle, etc.; Lord Hyde as Romeo; Lord Winchester as an officer of the Coldstream Guard, 1700; Lord Stavordale as Petrarch when young, in violet crêpe robe, doublet slashed with damask rose velvet and gold laurel wreath. Lady Muriel Fox Strangways, as Lady Sarah Lennox, one of Queen Charlotte's bridesmaids, wore the identical bodice, white satin and silver. The Hon. Bridget Harbord, as "Bride of Abydos," had a lovely clinging robe, all silver and white, and a little cap embroidered in pearls. Lady Belper, as Ann Page, was in pale blue broché, the slashed sleeves filled in with large puffs of lisse, and a white front to the gown. The Hon. Mrs. George Beckett, as Marie Leczinski, wore a very handsome brocade with chiné roses, worked over with sprays of leaves in gold, emeralds, and diamonds, set in with gold embroidery; the white brocade trainmantle was lined with pink. Mrs. Rupert Beckett's white velvet train of the same period was lined with pink. Her gown was silver and white brocade trimmed with lace and crystal embroidery.

Lord Burton, as Cardinal Dubois, was one of the successes of the evening. The different courts had to advance in fours to pass before the Royalties, but the master of the ceremonies thought Lord Burton and Lord Lathom, as the Doge of Venice, so imposing in themselves that they came past alone, or with only their train-bearers.

Sir Henry Irving looked in late, as Cardinal Wolsey. The Royalties did not leave until three, or past. The Duke and Duchess of York were the first to go. The Duchess of Teck walked round with Lord Lathom. The Duke was dressed as an Austrian officer. Prince Francis wore the red coat and uniform of an officer of the Dragoon Guards, and looked very handsome, as did Prince Alexander in the blue coat of a Gentleman of the Guard. Lord Basil Blackwood was in the blue and red uniform of a German officer, date 1818. The Duchess of Marlborough looked very pretty in her pale green Watteau dress wreathed with roses, her hair slightly powdered, with black feathers and roses. Lady Westmorland, as Hebe, was greatly admired, but the enormous eagle on her shoulder was considered by some to be too heavy. The Orientals salaamed. The Hon. Mrs. Talbot, as Brunhilde, was much cumbered with her shield and spear. Lady Gwendolen Cecil looked very well as Portia, in a red robe. The Hon. Mrs. George Curzon was a perfect picture in white and blue, with a blue velvet hat at the back of her head. Many of the guests were unable to sit down, so unwieldy were their dresses. A Joan of Arc slipped on the stairs, not

From Photo by] SIR PERTAB SINGH. *[Walery.*

being able to manage the marble steps in her iron or steel shoes. Mrs. Asquith, either intentionally or accidentally, prostrated herself at the feet of the Royal party.

Several ladies got very much out of temper with the heavy properties they had chosen to carry, and the wearers of velvet and fur-trimmed dresses felt the tropical heat of the night very much, even in the gardens, which were beautifully illuminated. One or two great ladies were observed to be in a frightful passion. Perhaps this was in some degree owing to the heat imparted by white wigs.

In taking leave of the Duchess, the Prince remarked that it was the prettiest ball he had seen for five-and-twenty years. Earlier in the evening, while the Prince was talking to Lady Randolph Churchill—who was so exquisitely dressed as Théodora that someone said that her portrait should be sent to

THE DUKE OF YORK AS THE EARL OF CUMBERLAND.

Sardou—a tall and handsome man came up and held out his hand. The Prince took it, and asked, in a puzzled tone, "Who are you?"

Lady Randolph laughed. "It is your son-in-law," she said, "Prince Charles of Denmark."

Dawn was just beginning to break, when

the Princess of Wales went out on the terrace in the garden and sat down, admiring the lovely light in the sky. A gentleman bent low before her. "Your collar is crooked, sir," she said, and with her own pretty fingers Her Royal Highness straightened it for him. He was Mr. Arthur Balfour.

At half-past four the Royalties left, and soon the rooms were empty, after having been filled with a crowd that suggested a scene out of "The Arabian Nights."

After the ball some scarcely recognisable people were going about in London, owing to several of the men having sacrificed moustache, and sometimes whiskers as well, to the exigencies of fancy dress. The Marquis of Lansdowne was one of these, and his friends scarcely knew him, so great was the change it made in his appearance.

The other most notable balls of the season were those given in July by the Duchesses of Westminster and Sutherland at Grosvenor House and Stafford House; Lady Derby's two splendid balls at Derby House; the Duchess of Portland's in Grosvenor Square; Captain Holford's at Dorchester House; and Lady Londonderry's in Park Lane. The hostesses of Royalty in Jubilee season compose a group of very beautiful women. The Marchioness of Lansdowne, who, with the Marquis, entertained the Prince and Princess at a regal banquet at Lansdowne House, is one of the "handsome Hamiltons," as the Duke of Abercorn's family is called in the North of Ireland. The Duchess of Portland is well known as a beauty of dignified mien and great height. Lady Londonderry is of a most winning type of loveliness, and her manner is so fascinating, her gifts as a hostess so excellent, that her ball was unanimously pronounced the most enjoyable of the season. The Duchess of Westminster is a pretty woman, with a sweet, childlike face, and the Duchess of Sutherland has a loveliness all her own.

For Jubilee time the Colonial Premiers were all lodged at the Hotel Cecil, where they were guests of the State. Royal carriages were placed at their disposal, and, with their wives and sometimes their daughters, the Premiers were often to be seen, seated behind the scarlet liveries of the royal servants, in the Park and the West-end. London was all bustle and joyful excitement. The weather was superb, and the first fortnight of July was the gayest the capital has known for many years. The picturesque attire of the foreign troops was a distinct factor in the gaiety of the crowded West-end. So full was it that on one occasion the Prince and Princess of Wales were blocked in their carriage in the Park, and on a memorable night, when their Royal Highnesses essayed to attend a party given in Piccadilly by the Right Hon. Joseph Chamberlain, they were unable to do so, owing to the enormous crowds, not only outside the house, but in the doorway and passage.

The Colonial troops will long remember the entertainment given them at Ranelagh under the management of Lord Ava. They are as little likely to forget the scene as are the great lords and ladies who were present and who witnessed the picturesque assemblage of Chinese with their white soup-plate head-gear, turbaned Orientals, khaki-clad Rhodesians with slouch hats, Africans in dark blue with red caps, Sikhs from Hong Kong, British Guiana Negro police, huge Maoris with immense heads, and giants from Sierra Leone.

In the first week of August the heat was so tropical that the judges in the Law Courts took off their wigs, Lord Russell of Killowen (the Lord Chief Justice) removing his, after a vain attempt to reduce the temperature in his court by having doors and windows opened. His sensible example was immediately followed in other courts.

On the 6th of August the newspapers published a reply made by the Queen to an address presented to Her Majesty by the women of Great Britain, Ireland, and the Colonies, on the occasion of the completion of the sixtieth year of her reign. The address asked for " one Royal word of sympathy with the progress which women have achieved during your Majesty's illustrious reign, one expression of gracious confidence and hope in the happy results which may be expected to follow from still further enlarging the area brought under the influence of women."

Sir Matthew White Ridley, in replying, wrote: "I have to inform you that Her Majesty was pleased to receive the same very graciously, and to express her confident belief that the women of the British race will, in the future as in the past, exercise zealously and faithfully for the welfare of her people the powerful influence that by Divine ordering they must ever possess."

Extravagance in the matter of private entertainments reached an extraordinary pitch during Jubilee season. Melba sang thirteen times at private houses at a fee of £300 on each occasion. Madame Eames had several similar engagements at £200 a night. At one concert Paderewski played twice, at a

cost of £1,000 to the host. Mr. Astor almost always has Paderewski at his splendid concerts, and Melba as well, with sometimes Plançon and Ancona at £100 apiece. The American millionaire gave, towards the

THE PRINCE OF WALES AS GRAND MASTER OF THE KNIGHTS HOSPITALLERS OF MALTA.

end of the season, two evening concerts each preceded by a dinner party at which his little daughter, not yet " out," presided. He gave as a reason for this unusual proceeding, his objection to see anyone else occupy her late mother's chair. Mr. Alfred Rothschild gave several of his noted concerts, and now that he has bought the house built by the late Barney Barnato in Park Lane, next to the one he has occupied for so many years, he will have more room than ever for his hosts of friends. Mr. A., as he is universally called, is one of the best-liked men in London society. Mrs. McEwan's concerts are famous for the excellence of the music heard at them, and the one she gave in July surpassed all previous ones. Mrs. Ronalds had Melba singing at a smart " tea " at the end of May, and Mrs. Uzielli came to the front as a giver of first-rate private concerts of the costly order.

THE SEASON'S HERESSES.

As fortune-hunters know well, London is always the happy hunting-ground for heiresses, and Jubilee season saw quite a remarkable number of wealthy girls assembled in London society, both American and English. The fortunes of our transatlantic sisters are in solid cash, not sunk in land, and they are unaffected by any laws of entail, so that financially, as well as sometimes for other reasons, American heiresses are often preferred to English. Their wonderful flow of sprightliness and frequent beauty are no mean factors in their undoubted success. Miss Ogden Goelet was the principal among them last season. Her father died in August, and she is heiress to enormous wealth. She is a nice-looking girl, very bright in manner and a great favourite. Miss Burns is another great heiress, and will also inherit her father's great jewel collection. The two daughters of Senator Morton are said to be very rich, and were well entertained, and Miss Leiter, sister of the Hon. Mrs. George Curzon, is also a great heiress.

Lord Ashton's daughters are the richest English heiresses, and Lady Clifford's girls are also well dowered.

The revival of the game of croquet among fashionable folk was a circumstance of the Jubilee season. Several croquet parties were given, and some of the prizes for the winners were very pretty. A new game, "lawn billiards," was also introduced, and promises to become a favourite pastime at Ranelagh and other clubs where there is good turf and plenty of it.

THE DUCHESS OF MARLBOROUGH.

Broken engagements were quite the fashion last season. There were quite twenty. Shortly after the announcement of a betrothal, there would follow the formula usual in such instances : " The marriage arranged between Mr. Dash and Miss Blank will not take place." Towards the end of July, generally a busy hymeneal time, there was a singular dearth of marriages.

The matrimonial sensation of the season, however, was the marriage of Miss Violet Grey Egerton, a pretty, gentle, and charming girl, to Lord Romilly, on the day before that appointed for her wedding with Mr. Cunard. The announcement of the event appeared in one daily paper in the next column to that containing a paragraph giving the hour and place of the lady's marriage to Mr. Cunard. She had been engaged to Lord Romilly some years before, but circumstances intervened to prevent the marriage. The bride wore her travelling dress, and was given away by her maid, and the bridegroom's solicitor acted as best man.

THE CHILDREN'S OWN CORNER

TO THE YOUNG READERS OF "THE LADY'S REALM."

MY dear Children,—
Is it not nice to think that the Editor is going to spare us a page that we may call our "very own"?

By this means I hope you and I may soon come to know each other very well; and as the only chats that we are likely to have together will be pen-and-ink ones, I hope you will write to me from time to time letters which, when suitable, and of sufficient interest, we may find space to print.

For my own part, I shall be delighted to hear from you, and trust you will tell me all about yourselves, your pets, your home and school life, your favourite games and occupations; and thus, I am sure, we shall soon become fast friends. That, dear children, is how I want you to look upon me, as your own special friend, who will be always ready and glad to hear about what is of interest to you, and to help and please you in whatever way is possible.

One and all, then, I bid you welcome to our corner, and, in due course, I hope to receive, in my turn, words of welcome from some of "my children."

I do not want you to let me do all the talking, month by month. That would be a very one-sided affair, would it not? Besides which, it would not be half so interesting as the news you young people will be able to send me.

I want to hear all about that grand cricket match from Harold, in which he made so splendid a score, and about the school examination from Doris, in which she has done so well; and the wee laddies must tell me what wonderful castles they can build with their fine new bricks, and what famous battles their smart tin soldiers can fight; while the tiny girlies will whisper to me the name of their last beautiful baby doll, and the colour of her hair and eyes.

Big and small I shall welcome alike; and if some of the tiny ones are too young to write, no doubt some kind elder sister or brother will sometimes spare a few minutes to guide the dear chubby fingers in their efforts.

Later on I hope to be able to arrange some competitions for you; but first I must get to know you all

a little, and then I will hint to you something of the many plans I am forming for your interest and amusement during the winter months.

I often find that you dear little people are rather shy of making a beginning; you can most of you chatter away fast enough when you have once begun, but sometimes you find it rather hard to make a start, do you not? And it seems to be the same with regard to letter-writing.

I can fancy I hear some of you say, "I should like very much to write to 'our own' page next month, but I don't quite know what to say." Or, perhaps, another will go a step further and, with paper before her, and pen in hand, get so far as "My dear Flora." Then the old cry comes again: "I don't know what to say next."

So, dear children, I am going to make a suggestion—give you a start, as it were. Suppose next month you each tell me something about your favourite pet—for I am sure most of you will have one of some kind or other, dog or pussy, bird or rabbit; and, to me, there is scarcely anything more interesting than to hear about their funny ways.

I have a whole host of dear, four-footed friends, and some day I can tell you many curious stories about them which I know will amuse you very much.

And now I must say good-bye until next month. Do not be afraid to write to me; remember that this is "your own" page, where "your own" friend will always be waiting to give your letters a hearty welcome, and to be of use to you in any way she can.

I am, dear children,
Affectionately your friend
"FLORA."

P.S.—If you address your letters as under:
"FLORA,"
5, *Throstle Bank*,
Old Trafford,
Manchester,

and let them reach me before the 6th of the month, I will do my best, dear children, to let you have your answers as soon as possible.

"Her form so lightly slender and so fair."

I HAVE touched lightly once or twice upon that most important subject, the figure, how to preserve and how to make the best of it ; but it is a topic that is well worth repeating, as my fresh readers increase every month, and find, so it appears, much consolation in my little article.

The average Englishwoman does not possess, by any means, a bad figure. Nature, in fact, has been kind to her in this respect ; but, with a wilful disregard of the artistic, she, nine cases out of ten, entirely spoils what Providence has given her, simply by wearing cheap and ill-made corsets. Indeed, I need not have taken the trouble to have written ill-made, for a cheap corset must of necessity be this : let a woman stint herself in her frocks, coats, and hats, but if she will religiously wear under her dress a well-cut pair of stays, she will be able to pass muster in the proverbial crowd without much difficulty.

In the first place, every woman should carefully consider what type of figure she has—if she be short-waisted or *vice versâ*, if her shoulders be square or sloping, if she be thin, plump, or really stout—and then have her corsets built to her requirements.

Few women may perhaps be aware of the immense amount of fatigue caused by the wearing of cheap stays, not being moulded to the figure, and in fact the figure being made to fit them ; they press on bones and ribs, bestowing an everlasting sense of weariness and discomfort, which leads to other ailments. It should be remembered, too, that the same kind of corsets cannot be worn on all occasions ; for instance, for riding, skating, bicycling, etc., a very small, short stay is required, lightly built to give full play to the muscles. It is a great relief to take off one pair of corsets and put on another, and every sensible woman should possess at least three pairs to don in change.

I recommend the employment of one good *corsetier*, who understands one's figure, and knows how to make the best of it. Round backs and square waists are, I think, the greatest failings of the English figure, and these failings are very frequently made, and not born with the owner. I will not be so prejudiced as to say that no graceful and easy-fitting corsets can be purchased ready-made. There are some reliable makes which suit certain figures ; and these, when once tried, may be always worn to great advantage.

And now what are the attributes of perfect-fitting corsets ? Well, they should be soft and yet supporting, moulded to the figure, and so cut that they will diminish its bad points and bring out its good ones. They should not be too tight, as this is bad style ; and for beauty and refinement's sake, they should be made in soft silk or satin, in some bright and pretty hue.

I have been asked to give my opinion on those who condemn stays as unhealthy instruments of torture. These folk refer triumphantly to the beauties of classic days, who knew not the meaning of such garments. I can only say that the conditions of life are utterly different now to then. Modern feminine dress does not lend itself to a stayless form, and I ask my masculine readers (and I know I have a good many) to tell me what they really and truly think of the "New Woman," who, stayless and shapeless, faces the world and defies Fashion. She may be extremely hygienic, but she certainly is not beautiful. For my own part I am ready to declare that well-fitting corsets are the greatest comfort and boon to womankind, putting aside all thought of loveliness. Let any of my readers try the experiment of leaving off her stays for a week or two, and she will soon find out the truth of my statement. Still, once again, let me say that if a good figure is to be preserved, cheap stays must never be worn, while to find one make or maker, of the same, is the golden rule.

POWDER PUFF.

THE HOME BEAUTIFUL.

BY K. WARREN CLOUSTON.

SCHEMES FOR DECORATION.

IN modern furnishing the main object should be to combine the really good and beautiful of every style and time. Love of the new must not ignore what is beautiful and substantial in the old. But if it is only substantial, ignore it as much as ever you like. Some people are inclined to run after an antique, simply because it is an antique, without looking at the beauty or worth of its design and workmanship. Then others go to the opposite extreme and purchase anything novel, so long as it is pretty and cheap, notwithstanding its flimsiness. I always feel that if a thing has nothing but its novelty to recommend it, we shall get tired of it in a few years, when its one attraction has worn off, and shall be glad to dispose of it anyhow, to make way for some more " up-to-date " attraction. But many purchasers prefer to buy only cheap articles, to last for a time, so that they may have the pleasure of re-decorating at an early period; and for these my second scheme is devised. But my advice is to buy really good furniture—furniture with some character if possible, and not the tables and chairs that are duplicated in every emporium in London. Let a house show traces of its owner's mind and taste, and not merely exhibit the latest thing in suites.

An artist friend had picked up by degrees, in the North of England, any bits of furniture which took his fancy. Now, by taking time, using your judgment, and being content with what is not the fashion, you will do wonders—not only in the North of England, but even in the counties round London: nay, in London itself. My friend's things were not all antiques — they were a judicious mixture; but there was only a modern house to put them in. It was not one of the stained-glass, white-painted, semi - Queen - Anne achievements of the jerry-builder, but a house erected about fifty years ago. The mantelpieces were plain wood,

simple even to commonness; the walls covered with ancient marble papers; and the fireplace, built across one corner, had a large expanse of bare wall above, which was rather apalling. My friend was in despair, but to me there seemed great hopes of success in the struggle; and I warmed to the fray.

Hearing of a quantity of old panelling which had been removed from a village church, in the Vicar's thirst for " improvement," we went off to explore. We found the timber outside a builder's shed, piled up in a heap and washed white with exposure to the weather. My friend's spirits again went down to zero; but hope rose in mine, as they evidently did not put too high a value upon the oak. Further examination revealed carved boards among the

OLD OAK CHEST AS WASHSTAND.

heap ; his spirits went up, so did my offer, and the bargain was concluded.

When we got the panelling home, had it carefully cleaned and rubbed up—and such a rubbing ! for of stain we would have none—the full value of the acquisition revealed itself. Not only was there enough wood to panel the space above the obnoxious fireplace, but sufficient to make a settle into the bargain. The best pieces of carving were reserved to support the shelf, and the old sides of the oak mantelpiece remained. We produced the effect of an overmantel, by twisted pillars below and above, finished by a cornice. Such pillars are easy to obtain, and most country dealers sell them for a few shillings. They were originally the legs of gate-tables, or bedposts ; but these latter are usually in mahogany. They are generally transformed into lamp-stands, though the shorter posts come in for mantelpieces, while those of greater length appear to most advantage at the sides of the room door, supporting a shelf.

Before deciding on wall decoration, a large piece of each paper or fabric should be fastened against the wall. The little scraps of paper in the pattern-books are quite useless, so it is best to choose the most likely and then have several large pieces supplied. No one can tell how the light and shade, or the furniture and colours already in the room will affect the wall-hangings, and yet half the harmony of the room depends upon them. Our next task was to render the walls suitable to the panelling, and arras cloth proved most satisfactory. We selected a dull, pale brown paper shade, perhaps rather low in tone for ordinary tastes, but a wonderful background for the pictures and bright touches of colour which were afterwards added. It is always much easier to brighten a room afterwards than to tone it down, as I daresay most furnishers have discovered.

Perhaps some of my readers are rather horrified at the idea of a made-up settle, but I fear most of those offered to the public are of the same nature. There are very few originals, especially carved originals, to be had. Settles are picturesque to a degree ; but as regards their comfort opinions differ. They are comfortable up to a certain point, or they would never have filled the ingle-nooks of old inns and farmhouse kitchens for so many centuries. But when the luxurious classes adopt the furnishings which have been in use by working people, they generally find they need some embellishment before they satisfy all requirements. Hard and angular in their ordinary form, pad

and drape them and they would not disgrace the most luxurious room—for what are our elegant cosy corners but glorified settles ? We covered the oak seat with a long cushion the exact size, encased it in old brocade, placed one or two small cushions against the dark wood, and threw Indian embroideries about —adding a thousandfold to its comfort and beauty.

It may be well to mention, while I am on the subject of antique adaptations, how a washstand can be made out of an old oak chest. No one for a moment would think of doing this with a really finely carved or inlaid specimen, but there are many plain panelled or wainscoted chests, which it would not be sacrilege to treat in the manner described. We are all acquainted with the difficulties of obtaining anything antique in the way of wash-stands, and such a thing in oak has become almost an impossibility. Yet oak chests-of-drawers, "tallboys," and carved and panelled wardrobes are numerous, and the bedroom from which my illustration is taken did not cost five pounds.

If the chest is not high enough for a washstand, have the legs lengthened, or raise them on plain feet like those on a gate-table. Add brass towel-rails at the side, and nothing further is wanted—unless a carved board is hung against the wall for a splash-curtain. The one illustrated is of modern work, stained to match the chest, and the wooden curtain-rod rests on brass hooks from the lower side. This can be easily made by the furnisher herself, or I can tell my readers where they can be had to order.

In contrast to all this antique, let us take a modern room which a lady wishes to decorate for her own private use, as a *boudoir* or anteroom ; for the style is best suited to apartments of moderate dimensions. I wonder if it is because women have had economy dinned into them for centuries that hardly one in a hundred can bring herself to pay a good price, even for a good article ? Pausing for the reply, which I fear will not be forthcoming, I must go on to say that our lady furnisher was like the rest of her sisters, and did not want to spend more than she could possibly help, yet desired the room to appear to the best possible advantage. She had a little of the lighter modern furnishings to put in—some white enamelled tables, chairs, and screens. As the room was not required to be durable, but must be smart, it seemed the best thing to use as much white as possible. It could not be all white, however—touches of colour had to come in—so the idea was adopted of a willow-pattern plate, as squares of this design in deep blue and white can be had at most of the art emporiums. The walls were hung with Japanese *crêpe* in blue and white, slightly fulled at the top on white willow-pattern blue as the cushions, but both had huge frills of pure white pongee silk, to give a lighter appearance to the room and prevent monotony. The little casement windows, opening outwards, were screened aside by sash

A
MODERN BOUDOIR.

enamelled bamboo. No pictures were to be hung on the walls, so this gave a decorative appearance. The folding screen was covered with white *crêpe* of a blue pattern, and soft silk cushions filled the chairs and lounges. The table-covers were made of the same deep, curtains of a blue-and-white silken fabric, cool and pleasant, and an arched recess in the walls was hung with large dishes and plates of the design which our grandmothers considered only suited to the kitchen, but which we reverence as a household god.

GAMES FOR WINTER EVENINGS.

BY LAURA ALEX SMITH.

MANY of the new games which have been invented for the beguilement of the long evenings this winter have a distinctly athletic trend, and bring before us the delights of summer's golden days which may be enjoyed by the cheerful hearth.

"NICOLAS," OR PUFF BILLIARDS.

The invitation conveyed in the words of the song "Boys and girls come out to play," might be paraphrased "Boys and girls stay in and play," and even then they are not likely to find time drag, for there is simply a plethora of entertainment devised for indoor recreation. Golfing, cricketing, bicycling, racing, and football, are now recognised parlour pleasures, and even the exhilarating sport of yachting is achievable over the drawing-room fire.

Americans are more enterprising with their inventions, and our embryo military men may learn much of the strategy of war in the nursery, from a clever game known as "The War in Cuba." Budding girl journalists will doubtless be fired with enthusiasm for globe-trotting by one which depicts "Nelly Bly going round the World." The best of all these *jeux* is that they are equally amusing for the grown-up members of the household and for the little folks; and invalids and old people will find plenteous distractions in any of them. Messrs. Parkins & Gotto's of Oxford Street is one of those firms where one is quite certain of finding all the novelties of the world of games, their choice this season being exceptionally good. One of the best is "Nicolas" or Puff Billiards, of which we give an illustration. This is entirely new and equally amusing to onlookers and operators; it is quite original in the manner of playing, the balls being of cork, and cues being substituted by "Pipettes"; these are ingeniously arranged to be directed at any angle. Another capital game, which is already a great success, is "Lamplough's Model Cricket." This is a portable, virtually collapsible game, which is set out on a green baize pitch capable of folding into three. There are a neat

boundary, batsmen, "fielders," wickets, and every accessory for the great national game, and the batsmen and bats are worked by means of a needle-spring; the bowling is effected by means of a spring, the ball being held in the hand. At the base of each fielder there is an enclosure into which, if the ball be driven, it is considered caught. "Byes," "Wides," "Leg hits," and, in fact, all the regulations of ordinary cricket, are observed. The figures are beautifully made, and we are glad to learn from the clever inventor of the game, Mr. Henry Lamplough, that they are English. Little boys and girls, too, may easily prime themselves by this in England's king of games, and old folks will by its means be able to re-achieve their fielding triumphs. A very amusing and up-to-date affair is "Bikee," by the same makers (Messrs. Faulkener & Co.) as the popular "Upidee." Very entertaining are the incidents *en route*. The game is played with little figures on the ubiquitous wheel and with cards. One enterprising firm has conferred a positive boon upon all households where there are children to be kept entertained on Sunday, by a "Sunday Pictorial Loto." The Gramophone at Messrs Parkins and Gotto's is something to conjure with in the matter of quelling nursery or school insubordination. The absolute distinctness of the singing and speaking voices, and of the instruments, has to be heard to be believed.

At Mr. Morrell's, Oxford Street, there are also

LAMPLOUGH'S MODEL CRICKET.
(*From* MESSRS. PARKINS & GOTTO.)

many novelties to be seen, and a special collection of games suitable for quite young children is a speciality here. For children of larger growth there is "Nansen's North Pole Voyage," in which any number can take part, ten or fifteen counters paid into the pool procuring the privilege of being a party to this voyage to Polar regions. There is for this a map marked with numbers, and these are aimed at

GRAMOPHONE.
(*From* Messrs. Parkins & Gotto.)

with pips. The person who first reaches Spitzbergen takes the pool ; but should he or she overshoot the mark, then they must retrograde to the extent of the surplus numbers. "The Waterloo Cup" is quite a scientific coursing game, played with one hare, and one dog to represent each player, on a divided and numbered course. Artists are not forgotten in this multitudinous variety of interests, and there is a really instructive game of "National Gallery," played with cards on which the name of the painter, and a short biography of him, are inscribed. "Skits," is a new geographical card game, consisting of eighty cards lithographed in colours, representing the English counties in picture and map form ; appropriate verses and caricatures are on each. In commemoration of the Diamond Jubilee we have a new series of the favourite "Who Knows?" the questions and answers naturally relating to events and facts of Her Majesty's reign. This, like "Skits," "The National Gallery," "The Waterloo Cup," and many others, is publishing by Messrs. J. Jaques & Son, Hatton Garden, E.C.

Another firm celebrated for their original games of skill is that of Woolley & Co., Finsbury, the publishers of "Halma," "Ludo," "Funny Families," etc., This year they have brought out the "Penny Post." A letter-box is placed in the centre of the table, and the players have to attempt to post as many letters, *i.e.* round cards, as they can from the opposite ends of the table. The player who first gets all his letters (six) into the box is the winner. The cards are of a different colour for each person.

At Hamley's, that most delightful emporium for toys, games, and conjuring tricks, there are of course many novelties to be found, either at 64, Regent Street, or at "The Noah's Ark" in High Holborn. Indeed, it is quite difficult to make a selection where there is so much to choose from. A capital game is entitled "Shuvette." This is played on an oval-shaped, brightly polished board, with discs. Two, four, six, or even eight, may join,

partners sitting opposite to each other, and holding discs of the same colour. The skill of the game consists of trying to lodge the discs in the centre recess on the board in the case of the first player, and of forcing his opponent's one into the ditch in the case of the second ; indeed, the fascination of forcing as many as possible of your enemy's discs into the ditch is great. Sometimes three are ditched at a single shot, by cannoning from one to the other. Each plays in turn, till all the discs have been discharged. There are numberless rules to be observed in "Shuvette."

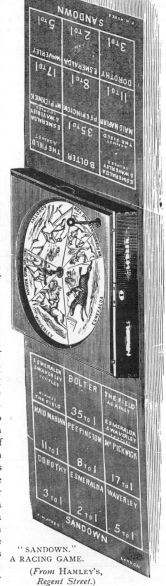

"SANDOWN."
A RACING GAME.
(*From* Hamley's,
Regent Street.)

"No-Karms" is essentially a game of skill, which must be most fascinating to yachting people in general. It is very simple in construction ; there are no pieces of delicate or intricate mechanism connected with it. There is a chart, and small blocks of wood carrying distinguishing flags, which are meant to represent yachts : two tiny spikes on the bottom of them, fix them in their various positions on the chart. The other requisites are a foot-rule, and a tee-to-tum marked with the principal points of the compass. If properly played, this game will teach all the much-disputed points in the rules of the Y. R. A.

The many lovers of the turf will find endless charm

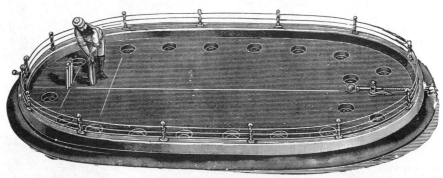

and excitement in " Sandown " which, as its name indicates, is a thoroughly up-to-date miniature race. The machinery of this consists of a revolving disc, round the circumference of which there are thirty-seven divisions, one of which is in favour of the table. Two horses, " Esmeralda " and " Waverley " occupy eighteen divisions out of the lot. The winning horse is that which occupies the division which is opposite the winning-post line when the disc comes to a stop. A judge must be appointed at the outset of the game, whose decision as to " dead-heats," etc., must be accepted as final. The disc has to be spun with sufficient force to cause it to revolve at least six times. Failing this, it is a " false start," and does not count. The game is beautifully got up, being in a polished wood case, and the divisions gaily painted with horses, jockey-mounted. Players may be of any number.

Another racing game of an undoubtedly popular nature is " Bicycle Distance Riding." Here we have a map of England and Scotland and tickets bearing numbers on them dotting it at intervals. The ride is from Plymouth to Glasgow, touching *en route* such towns as Exeter, Bristol, London, Birmingham, Liverpool, Manchester, Newcastle, etc., There are six little bicycles and riders, and their progress is intimated and directed by throwing a fair-sized wooden die with eighteen sides. The die may be turned up at " Rest," " Uphill," " Re-

quite an enjoyment by thus bringing the links to the home.

For those with a bellicose taste there are innumerable amusements, the before - mentioned

CLEVER MECHANICAL PIG.
(*From* MESSRS. PARKINS & GOTTO.)

American invention, " The War in Cuba," deserving special mention. Several players make of this an exciting affair. One side takes the Spanish soldiers, including the commanders, Generals Weyler, and Munoz, the other the Cubans, at whose head are Generals Maceo and Gomez. The soldiers, in the now well-known uniforms, are of card on wooden stands, and there are strong little pistols with wooden projectiles.

The opposing troops are placed some eight feet apart, and then the firing begins. The game is entirely without danger, provided that the shooting takes place alternately, and that the players do not remain behind their troops during the fusillade.

CHAMPION MODEL CRICKET.
(*From* HAMLEY'S, *Regent Street.*)

freshment at Inn," " Tyre-pumping," " Light-up," or any one of the exigencies of wheeling, and according to the rules of the game this means going back or forward a few paces. For golfers there is " Putting golf," which, by the way, may also be enjoyed out of doors, a good smooth gravel drive being an excellent *locale* for it. The implements, besides the putters, drivers, and balls, include metal discs to act as holes. The object is, of course to do the round of discs in the least number of strokes. If played in the house, the best way is to make the course longer by setting the discs in the hall and in one or two rooms off it. A wet afternoon in a country house with a large party would be rendered

" Eureka " is another shooting game, played, this time with a numbered target. The implements used for this are darts, with india-rubber tips, which, when slightly moistened, stick anywhere. There is, of course, the usual belt around the waist to hold the darts. Another mechanical contrivance consists of a triangular green baize-covered board, and a little platform, from which rises a cylindrical pole. At the other end of the triangle there is a small spring cannon and each time the projectile hits the target a little sailor springs a step or two up the pole. Ten turns should send the man to the top, but the player who succeeds in doing so with the fewest turns is the winner.

LAURA ALEX SMITH.

LADY LAVENDER'S THREE CHANCES

A STORY OF THE OCCULT.

BY ADELINE SERGEANT.

I.

LADY LAVENDER was pain- fully conscious that she was in a false position. She had a suspicion that she was doing something very wicked. She had always been told that it was foolish and perhaps a little bit blasphemous to have anything to do with the Occult, and yet here she was, on a fine May·morning, in the waiting-room of a well-known professional palmist, while her young cousin and *protégée*, Lil Fennimore, interrogated the wizard in a private room. It was Lil who had insisted upon coming, and Lady Lavender devoutly hoped that Lil would bear the responsibility. For every- body knew that she had no will of her own where Lil was concerned.

Lady Lavender was a widow. She had been persuaded into marrying a millionaire, who had opportunely died six months after the wedding-day, and it was now considered probable that she would complete her social successes by marrying a duke. In the mean- time she was an excellent chaperon for a pretty girl like Lil.

And as Lil wished to consult the palmist about her own private affairs, Lady Lavender obediently accompanied her to the cave of the oracle, and was much relieved when Lil emerged, radiant, from its seclusion, and in- formed her cousin triumphantly that she had had a splendid fortune predicted for her, and would not Muriel herself follow her example and have her fortune told?

"Certainly not, Lil," said Lady Lavender,

with a touch of dignity. "My fortune was settled for me long ago ; and I do not want to hear anything more about it."

The palmist, a pale, striking-looking man, with very dark hair and eyes, glanced at the speaker and smiled.

"Not yet, madame," he said, in an under- tone.

And Lady Lavender would have been more than mortal woman if she had not asked impulsively, "What do you mean ? "

"The crisis of your life is approaching, madame," replied the palmist suavely. "Will you not permit me to glance for one moment at your hand ? "

Muriel drew back at once. "I would rather not," she said.

"It is no matter," he answered quietly. "The trained eye, madame, sees further than that of the ordinary observer. To-morrow is the day on which madame's future fate will be decided. She will have three chances of happiness or of misery, and all will depend upon the choice she makes."

He turned away with a bow, and Lady Lavender impatiently drew Lil out of the room. "What nonsense ! " she said, as they went downstairs, in rather an offended tone

"Why do you think so ? You have no idea how much he told me about myself.

142

You would have thought that he had known me all my life."

"He could not possibly know anything about you," said her cousin; "and I am rather surprised, Lil, that you should attach importance to what he says."

Lil laughed cheerfully. "Well, we have an excellent proof at hand of his skill, Muriel. He has committed himself to prophecy about your future. It is not often he does that, I believe. If your whole fate should be decided to-morrow, would you not believe in him?"

"How can my fate possibly be decided in one day?" said Lady Lavender, with an air of mild exasperation. "Do not let us say anything more about it, Lil."

Lil laughed and abandoned the conflict. Muriel was an irreconcilable, and Lil shook her golden head wisely over the prejudices of people who had been brought up in the country and belonged to a parson's family. "I do believe that young people know best, after all," she reflected, putting into words what many another young person has felt before her. "It is a great pity that the old ones won't listen to us a little more. Why, it was perfectly wonderful what that man said to me about Jack—for of course it was Jack he meant, although he did not mention the name. All about my marrying a man with a title, and the opposition of my friends, and the number of men who had wanted to—oh, well, that was nonsense, of course; but on the whole, he was wonderfully correct, and perhaps what he said about Muriel may be equally so. I wonder Muriel would not listen! She is terribly obstinate sometimes, and very old-fashioned, too."

But Lady Lavender was perhaps less obstinate than she wished to appear. At any rate, she devoted a good deal of time to

"THE CRISIS OF YOUR LIFE IS APPROACHING, MADAME!" REPLIED THE PALMIST, SUAVELY.

consideration of what the palmist had said to her. "I would not have Lil know it for the world," she said to herself that night, when she had dismissed her maid, rather earlier than usual, and sat before her mirror with her magnificent dark hair about her shoulders still, "I could not bear to seem so silly; but I must say that I have rather a superstitious feeling about it, especially since I got this letter!" And she drew from a toilet-table drawer a thick, monogrammed envelope, which she had hidden there when she rang for her maid. "He writes nicely," she murmured to herself. "I think he is kind and good, and that I might perhaps be happy with him. Perhaps it is my duty to say yes." And she re-read the letter with a sigh. "I am sure that Aunt Agatha would say it was my duty," she added, with a somewhat humorous smile. But she was not naturally a very humorous person, so the smile soon faded away. "I will not look at it from Aunt Agatha's point of view, however. I did so once, and none will ever know what I suffered. No; I will only think of the great opportunities which a marriage with the Duke of Newminster might put in my way. How much good might I not be able to do in that position! And since I cannot hope to be happy with the man whom I—whom I thought I loved, and who seemed once to love me"—here her voice faltered, and for a moment or two she bowed her head—"let me at least do what I can with my life, and never think of Ronald again so long as I live. But it is no use: I can never forget him—never!"

This was what she said to herself, while she hid her face; then, quickly recovering herself, she drew her handkerchief rapidly across her eyes, and went on in a firmer tone. "No; I will not say that. It is an unworthy thing to say. Let me rather think of what Ronald proved himself to be—how false! how careless!—and then I shall have courage to do the thing which seems the highest, without considering my own happiness at all."

And then she said her prayers—for she was a thoroughly good and sincere woman, as all her friends acknowledged, though they sometimes added that she might be called a little "limited" in her views; and she prayed that if she married the Duke of Newminster, she might make him a good wife, and use her opportunities to the best of her ability— and it did not occur to Lady Lavender at the moment that she thought more about the opportunities than the man. After which she went to bed, and meant to go to sleep, but lay awake and cried until the dawn came stealing into the quiet, curtained room.

The Duke was to come at noon. Muriel, having no skill in diplomacy, was obliged to confess frankly to Lil that she wanted the drawing-room to herself that morning; and Lil, after opening her eyes in astonishment, decided upon going out to luncheon. "You don't mind being left, do you, dear?" she said; "and I shall be back to tea at four o'clock."

"I do not mind at all," said Lady Lavender. "I shall have plenty to occupy me, you may be sure."

"If the palmist's prediction is true, you certainly will," said Lil, laughing; and then she wondered why her cousin blushed. It looked as though Muriel herself expected something to happen, Lil thought lightly to herself, as she went upon her way.

II.

SOOTH to say, Muriel had not forgotten the palmist's words. She sat and meditated upon them, when Lil was gone. It was certainly a fact that her fate depended upon the events of the day, and it was a curious coincidence that the cheiromant should have happened to say so. She was a little bit disposed to give him credit for occult powers of a decidedly unlawful kind.

The Duke was late. Lady Lavender was astonished, for he bore the character of a most courteous man, who would rather die than keep a lady waiting. But on this occasion he was certainly twenty minutes behind time. He arrived at last, somewhat flurried and out of breath, but with no abatement of his usual urbanity of bearing.

"How can I find words in which to apologise for my unpunctuality!" he exclaimed. "Dear Lady Lavender, I must assure you that only a most untoward incident would have delayed me."

"I hope it was nothing serious, Duke," said Lady Lavender, with a smile. She looked at him as she spoke, and thought how handsome and manly he appeared, with his white hair, and stately figure, and beautiful smile; and her heart swelled within her at the very idea of becoming the wife of this venerable man.

"Yes," said the Duke, as he drew his chair nearer hers, and seemed disposed to enter upon a confidential statement, "I think, my dear lady, you will sympathise with me in the peculiar trials which Providence sees fit to send me. In fact, I know no one better fitted than yourself to soothe them, and even, if I may say so, to share them"— his voice grew solemn and tender, as if he were on the verge of a most important declaration. Lady Lavender knew what was coming, but was suddenly seized with a womanly panic, and a wild desire to put off the answer which she had resolved to give.

"Do tell me," she said, in her softest voice, "what has troubled you to-day? It would be such a pleasure to me if I felt that you could trust me, or that I could do anything for you."

"Dear lady, I have no claim to trouble you with my affairs, unless you give me the right to——"

"Then," said Lady Lavender, with a pertinacity for which she could not account, save on the ground of an unnatural nervousness, "you will not tell me why you were so late in coming to see me this morning?"

The Duke looked a little put out. He had prepared a speech, and he did not like to be interrupted. But he put a good face upon the matter, and smiled indulgently at the request. "Ah," he sighed, "like all the rest of your charming sex, you desire to soothe and sympathise! And why should you not have your wish? Indeed," continued the Duke, while a touch of vexation made itself visible in his countenance, "I shall be only too glad to impart my troubles to you. It is a family matter which detained me to-day."

"Oh, I beg your pardon," ejaculated Lady Lavender, faintly.

"Not at all—why should you? No doubt you have often heard reference made to the great sorrow and disappointment of my life—the marriage of my youngest son with a dancing-girl, and his subsequent death in America?"

"I have heard of it," said Lady Lavender.

"Conceive my annoyance, then," said the Duke, "when on coming back from my ride this morning, I was confronted by the woman whom my son unhappily married, and asked to contribute to her maintenance and that of a child whom she declares to be Alured's! Can you imagine anything more monstrous?"

"You mean," said the listener, with some natural confusion of ideas, "that she is an impostor, and that you will not assist her on that account?"

"By no means," the Duke answered, stiffly. "You misapprehend me. Of course she is my son's widow; I know her by sight perfectly well. What amazes me is the unparalleled insolence of the creature—to come to me and tell *me* that she is starving!"

"When you know she is not? Oh, now I see!" cried Muriel, with an expression of marked relief.

The Duke looked absolutely pained. "My dear Lady Lavender, you totally misunderstand," he remarked solemnly. "Under no circumstances, even if that wretched woman were starving before my eyes, should I feel justified in holding out a helping hand to her. But for her, my son would never have been unfaithful to the traditions of his order, and might even be living at this moment."

"It must be terribly difficult to forgive, certainly."

"Forgive! There is no question of forgiving. I shall simply ignore the creature's existence, and leave her to earn her living as she used to do. Let us dismiss this unpleasant subject from our minds, dear lady."

"One moment!" said Lady Lavender, with some agitation. "Surely I have misunderstood what you implied. You cannot possibly mean that you will allow this poor woman, your son's widow, to remain in poverty, when you—you——" she paused, unable to finish the sentence.

"I mean what I think I said," replied the Duke," with a sudden access of stiffness. "I mean that I shall not give this person a penny, and shall forbid all the rest of my family to do anything for her."

"Then I hope your family will disobey you," cried Muriel hotly. "What! Refuse to help your son's wife, when she comes to you for help? I never heard of such wickedness in all my life!"

"Madam!" Words seemed to fail the Duke as he looked at the flushing face and kindling eyes of the lady before him. "Madam, such language is—is—I think that if you intend seriously to maintain the views that you have just advanced, it would perhaps be better for me to withdraw!"

"I quite agree with your Grace, and I wish you good-morning," said Muriel, still too indignant to care what she said; and the Duke, accordingly, made her a very low bow, and took his departure. And then Lady Lavender realised that she had practically refused him, and would never be the Duchess of Newminster after all. "And I am very glad of it," she declared to herself, as she sat down to her solitary luncheon. "For if I had found out after marrying him that he could be so heartless and so cruel, I think I should have died."

But after luncheon she felt rather depressed. She knew that she had been expected by her friends to accept the Duke of Newminster, and that, even if they did not openly question her, they would gossip behind her back about the change in her prospects. Probably they would say that the Duke had not proposed after all, and that she was a disappointed woman. It was inevitable, of course, but she did not quite like the thought of it. "If only I had a true friend who would advise me!" she said sorrowfully to herself, as she sat alone in the drawing-room and waited for afternoon visitors and afternoon tea. "Mr. Hillingdon," the servant announced; and Lady Lavender looked up hopefully. Here at least was somebody who bore the reputation of being a clever man, and one who had a theory of his own about

MADE HER A VERY LOW BOW AND TOOK HIS DEPARTURE.

life. Perhaps he could give her the benefit of his experiences. So, as soon as they had settled down into their seats, and the hostess had poured out the first cup of tea, she amazed Mr. Hillingdon by saying,—

"I have been told, Mr. Hillingdon, that you think every woman ought to have an object in life?"

"Surely!" said Mr. Hillingdon, with gentle emphasis. "And not only every woman, Lady Lavender, but every man."

He was a very fair man, with arched eyebrows and dreamy brown eyes; he had also handsome features and a silky brown beard, of which he was reputed to be vain. His fingers were long and delicate, and he had altogether the appearance of those who toil not, neither do they spin.

"I wish that I had your secret, Mr. Hillingdon. I am haunted by the idea that my life is a very useless one. If any one would suggest to me some way of making it more—more serious," said Lady Lavender, rather doubtfully, "I should be everlastingly grateful to that person."

A sudden light came into Mr. Hillingdon's brown eyes. What could Lady Lavender's speech mean but that the marriage between herself and the Duke was "off," and that she was disposed to turn to him—Lancelot Hillingdon—for consolation? He was charmed. He sat up, and seriously considered the situation.

"There is but one way of perfect happiness and satisfaction, dear Lady Lavender," he said, in mellifluous accents. "It is the way of culture—the way of Art."

"Oh," said Lady Lavender hesitatingly. "But is not that a rather selfish way of living? I suppose, however, it depends a good deal on the objects on which the culture and art are to be expended?"

"With your usual perspicacity, dear lady, you grasp my idea exactly," said Mr. Hillingdon suavely. "No object can in these days be so noble as the furtherance of individual development. If you, therefore, were to devote yourself to the culture of your own mind, your own spirit, your own perception of what is beautiful, you would be conferring upon the world the greatest boon which it is in your power to give. You might begin," said Mr. Hillingdon dreamily, "with an exhaustive survey of the different picture-galleries of the world, and then endeavour—under proper guidance, of course—to make a selection of such works of art as are within your means, in order to form the nucleus of a new and unrivalled collection——"

The suggestion was not without its attractiveness. Muriel listened as a bird to the voice of the charmer.

"I think that *is* a worthy object," she remarked. "Your idea is, I suppose, that I should use my collection for the good of the nation; that I should throw it open to the public and endeavour to elevate their taste? Yes, that might be a worthy ambition!"

Mr. Hillingdon looked unfeignedly shocked.

"Dear Lady Lavender, who said anything about the public?" he asked plaintively. "The public is a brute-beast: you can do nothing for it but fling it a bone now and then. It is stupid, lazy, and vulgar. No, no; you should keep the public carefully out of your collection, and indeed, if I might advise, I should say, keep everybody out. Let it be a joy to yourself alone, and to the one or two friends whom you permit to share that joy."

"But think how selfish that would be," said Lady Lavender warmly. "My idea was to do something for the people!"

"Believe me, there is not the slightest use in trying to benefit the populace. Self-culture—pleasure in its highest form—is humanity's only good," said Mr. Hillingdon languidly. "May I not offer my collaboration in the great scheme that you have so nobly conceived? And my heart as well? Believe me, it will give me the deepest joy if you will accept my devotion! Together, Lady Lavender—may I not call you by your sweet name of Muriel?——"

"Certainly not," said Muriel, rather sharply. "I have given you no reason, sir, to think I should permit it."

"But, my dear lady, forgive me, did you not ask my advice?"

"I think your advice detestable," said Muriel frankly; but she covered her momentary lapse from good manners with a charming smile. Mr. Hillingdon was not,

however, to be so easily propitiated. He rose from his chair with a sour look, and bowed himself speedily out of the room. And Muriel reflected, in astonished dismay, that she had refused a second suitor, and thrown away, perhaps, another chance of future happiness. Was it possible that the cheiromant had been right?

"In that case," she mused, "I shall have a third offer before night to accept or refuse; and really I don't know anybody else who is likely to ask me; or anybody, indeed, that I feel at all inclined to accept. There is only one man in the world for whom I have ever felt anything like regard, and if he were here I should reject him instantly."

III.

AT this moment Lil made her appearance, and rushed into Lady Lavender's arms. She was glowing and radiant with delight, and before she opened her lips, Lady Lavender guessed that some wonderful bit of good fortune had happened to her.

"It's all right, dear, it is indeed!" cried Lil triumphantly, as she lifted her blushing face from Muriel's shoulder. "He was there!"

"Jack?" queried her cousin, who knew all about the little love-affair, which had not hitherto gone very smoothly.

"Yes," Lilian answered, with a tear in the midst of her smiles. "And that wonderful man, the fortune-teller, Muriel—do you know that what he said to me about Jack was perfectly true! He told me that Jack would have some great good luck within the week, and I hardly liked to think of it because I thought he might mean that Jack's uncle was going to die, and I did not wish to speculate on his death. But it is not that at all; it is just that an old friend of his has offered him a splendid appointment in the Diplomatic Service, and if he likes to take it there need be no further delay to our marriage. What do you think of that for a bit of palmistry, darling? Oh, I am so happy about it all! And now do tell me what has happened while I have been out. I hear that you have had two visitors—the Duke and Mr. Hillingdon. You know what everybody has

"RONALD, RONALD! IS IT REALLY YOU?"

been saying, Muriel; now do tell me if—if——"

"Oh, don't ask me," cried Lady Lavender. Then, rather inconsistently, "I refused them both!"

"Both! Why, I thought it was as good as settled with the Duke," exclaimed Lil; but seeing the mute distress in Muriel's face she desisted from any further expression of surprise. "But my dear, have you remembered that the palmist seems to be as right about you as he was with me? Did he not tell you that you would have three chances to-day of happiness? I wonder who the third man will be!"

"There is no necessity for any third man to appear, or any third thing to happen at all," said Lady Lavender, with dignity. "I am not so superstitious as you seem to be, Lil; and even if I were"—after a moment's reflection—"I should refuse to give way to such weakness. Really, I am quite tired out. I shall not go to Lady Kerr's ball to-night, Lil; you don't want me, for you can go

with the Malmaisons; and I shall have a quiet evening at home."

"For fear of another proposal, dear?" said Lil, somewhat maliciously; "but you must remember that if Fate means to send you another, the man may come here."

"Then he will have to go away again," replied her cousin, "for I am going to give orders that no one is to be admitted for the rest of the day."

And she held fast to her determination, sending Lil to dress soon after dinner, and betaking herself to the pleasant security of the library. She had said that she was not superstitious, but she had nevertheless a strong dislike to the idea that the palmist's prediction must necessarily be fulfilled.

"I am tired of proposals," said Lady Lavender, with as near an approach to a pout as she ever permitted herself. So she lay back in a comfortable chair, and opened the last Mudie novel.

But she was aroused from her occupation presently by the sound of something like an altercation in the hall. She listened in surprise, for her servants were all so highly respectable that she could not believe them to be in fault. She was certain that she heard her own name, and finally she went to the door and opened it.

"What is the matter, Stevens?" she asked.

Stevens advanced towards her with a distracted air.

"It's the fault of the new footman, my lady," he said impressively. "He said you were engaged, he thought, instead of saying that you were hout. Consequentially, this gentleman refuses to take 'no' for an answer, and won't be satisfied unless I give you his card."

"Of course I won't," said a man's voice at the door. "I am quite sure that you won't turn me from your door without at least speaking to me, cousin Muriel, although"—and he was inside the room by this time, and Stevens was shut out—"although you treated me so badly in the days gone by."

"Ronald, Ronald! is it really you?" cried Lady Lavender, stretching out her arms wildly to a very handsome specimen of a young naval man, whom Stevens had striven so resolutely to exclude. And then she fell forward upon his shoulder, and Lieutenant Ronald Graham, of Her Majesty's gunboat *Isis*, awoke to the fact that his cousin had fainted in his arms. With great presence of mind, he did not call the servants, but used such rough-and-ready methods of bringing her back to consciousness as seemed good to him.

"My poor little darling—did I startle her! Look up, sweet; it's only Ronald. There, I'm sure you're better now. I have only one day in London, and I made up my mind that I would see you this time at least, if I were hanged for it! What? Let you go? I—I beg your pardon—I had forgotten for the moment that you were not my Muriel any longer."

He had placed her on a sofa, and now regarded her with gloomily reproachful eyes.

"Ronald, it was you who cast me off," said Lady Lavender, going straight to the point without loss of time.

"That I swear I did not. You never answered my letters."

"You never wrote any."

"I wrote reams. I wrote six times."

"Do you think it is possible," said Muriel, in a hushed voice, "that Aunt Agatha intercepted the letters? She was so terribly anxious for me to marry poor Sir Peter!"

"I'll be bound she did," said Ronald cheerily; "but you're mine after all, aren't you, sweetheart?"

"For ever!" answered Lady Lavender, nestling into his arms with infinite satifaction; and it was not until Lil reminded her next day that she remembered the palmist's prediction, and saw that she had made her third—and last—choice between happiness and misery.

All her life afterwards she knew that she had chosen aright. But nothing would induce her to enter the palmist's door again, although Lil informed her that all the world of London consulted him, and that the Duke had paid him a visit only two days before his proposal. And Lil was exceedingly angry when Ronald said that, in that case, then, the seer's prophecy was at least partially explained.

From a photograph by Elliot & Fry.

Adeline Sergeant.

THE CHILDREN'S OWN CORNER.

BY "FLORA."

MY DEAR CHILDREN,—
Your letters have given me very much pleasure, and I should like to let many of them appear in our Corner, but have only room this month for three or four.

If I were to print all I have received, THE LADY'S REALM would contain little else but your letters; and this, I am afraid, would not meet with general approval.

RANSOM E. SEABROOK writes as follows :—

ST. WINIFRED'S,
PLASHET GROVE, EAST HAM.

MY DEAR FLORA,—
I am very glad you have put a page for children in THE LADY'S REALM. I have long wanted to be able to write letters to a book.

We have a lot of pets, a little toy terrier, black-and-tan, and about forty fowls, and eight ducks and a little canary. We have had the canary about nine years; he is nearly twelve years old. He came from India. One of our ducks has a crossed bill, and we call him "Crossbeak." He does look so funny when he tries to pick up seed. He is very small, because he does not eat so much as the others. We give him the measure to feed out of. We had six pigeons once, but some fantail pigeons came and enticed ours into a trap, and they were caught. It seemed a pity that they should go away, because we reared one of them up when its mother died. I am eleven and a half years old and go to the City of London School: there are seven hundred boys. We have our annual sports at Herne Hill Grounds. It has a very nice bike course. I can ride a bike, and hope to have one soon. I may be coming to Manchester next Christmas to see my auntie. I think I shall come and see you.

Wishing you a Happy New Year.
Yours affectionately,
RANSOM E. SEABROOK.

You have indeed a lot of pets. I am sure you will enjoy riding a bicycle when you have one, and I shall look forward to seeing you next Christmas. Tell Winifred that I cannot find room for her letter at present. I think she might teach her dog "Princie" many tricks, and some day I will tell her how I used to teach my little dog.

KATHLEEN MARY BOWRING sends the following little letter :—

ALSTONE HOUSE,
HUNTSPILL.

MY DEAR FLORA,—
I am sorry I have not any pets of my own to write about. Our dear old dog we used to have is dead. We have a dear little pony called "Judy," which we are very fond of. I have one sister; her name is Freda; she will be six years old next April, and I shall be nine in July. We had a governess at home to teach us, but she has gone away now. Will you please tell us of another nice one? We had a children's party last Wednesday. We had lots of games, dancing and fun; we had such funny things out of the crackers. I shall watch every morning for the postman until I get your letter.

With love from
Your affectionate little friend,
KATHLEEN MARY BOWRING.

I cannot reply by post, dear little girl. I wish I could have been with you on Wednesday to join in the games and fun, and to pull one of those famous crackers with you. I am afraid I don't know of a governess, but hope you may soon find a very nice, kind one.

I am delighted that you are all so pleased with "Our Corner."

AURIOL EDITH SOAMES says :—

MY DEAR FLORA,—
I am so glad to see that we are going to have a page in THE LADY'S REALM.

Now that we have come to London for the winter my mother always has THE LADY'S REALM, and I shall like very much to write to you. I sometimes look at *The Gentlewoman*, and those kinds of papers, but they always seem to be in the middle of something, so that I have never written to them yet.

I am rather good at guessing things, and I have written a good deal of poetry, and three or four stories which are supposed to be rather nice, so I shall like to do anything that is in THE LADY'S REALM. I can tell you a nice lot about animals. I am twelve years old. I have one brother and sister.

Yours affectionately,
AURIOL EDITH SOAMES.

As you are fond of writing stories, dear, I am sure you will be pleased with the competition announced last month. Do not forget that all MSS. must reach me by the 25th of this month.

ERIC ARTHY writes :—

MY DEAR FLORA,—
I think it will be very nice to have a corner all to ourselves in THE LADY'S REALM. I wish you a very happy new year, dear Flora, I had a very happy Christmas, and one of my presents was a magic-lantern, and I can work it all by myself. Some of the slides are very funny. I shall be eight years old next birthday, and when I am a man I am going to be a doctor, like Father, because I think it is so nice to be able to make people better when they are ill. I often go on the round with Father, and like that very much.

Your loving
ERIC ARTHY.

You are right, dear; it is indeed nice to make people better when they are ill. I hope you will be a very clever doctor when you are a man.

FREDA YOUNG sends an interesting letter. I am very sorry that I cannot possibly find space for it this month.

"VERA," aged eight, writes to me from Cork. "Wasp" must be a very intelligent doggie, I think, dear. There are no mistakes in your charming little letter.

MOLLY ROBERTSON.—Many thanks, dear, for your nice letter and pretty card.

MÉLANIE PARET tells me that she has been suffering from influenza. I hope, dear, that you will soon be quite better, and become much stronger. I am very fond of the books you mention. I think "Barabbas" is my favourite. Fourteen is not a bit too old to join our "Corner"; I am glad your mother is so pleased with it, and I hope you will write again.

GLADYS JONES sends a nice account of her many pets. I should very much like to see those pretty white "fantails." How tame they must be to come to your hands! What a clever big brother you have in Rupert!

I have also received interesting letters from Phyllis Flamank, Gertrude Tucker, Katie B. Perkins, Connie Standley, Frances Sullivan, Vera Shelley Rix, Kathleen Wren, May Harren, Madeline A. Stone, Florrie Barker, Daisy Mellor, Sybil G. Tilbrook, Muriel Treasure, and others. Later on I may, perhaps, be able to let some of them be printed.

Many thanks, dear children, for all your loving wishes. I am quite sure that you and I will soon become fast friends.

Affectionately yours,
"FLORA."

5, *Throstle Bank*,
Old Trafford,
Manchester.

SPRING FASHIONS.

ECHOES FROM PARIS.

BY ALINE D'ERVILLE.

NEVER, perhaps, at this season of the year have we had such variety of style and colour in dress.

Tailor costumes, Princess dresses, blouse bodices, with or without basques, are all equally correct.

The new cloths probably account for the favour which the Princess and tailor costumes are having, as these cloths are made in every variety of texture, and in the most exquisite shades of colouring. The

FIG. I.

FIG. II.

peau-de-gant and *peau-de-gazelle* have been chiefly used, but *cachemire* cloth seems to be the favourite at present; and certainly, nothing makes up better than this material.

The Princess dress is now cut all in a piece at the back, but frequently the bodice in front is of blouse style, and finished with a corselet.

There is a great tendency to define the apron width of the skirt, either by embroidering it or by letting in pleated panels on each side. Sometimes these panels are of the same material, and sometimes of taffeta silk, or of guipure lace.

The accompanying illustrations will give an idea of some of the newest styles. Nothing could be more dressy and becoming than the blouse (fig. I.) of china-rose velvet, trimmed with lace insertion and two shades of pink silk muslin to match the velvet. The bodice is slightly pouched, back and front, trimmed with the lace and edged on each side by a narrow quilling of silk muslin. The gathering of silk muslin down the side is of the paler shade, and the quillings round the bodice, collar, and sleeves are all of the deeper pink. The pointed waistband is of velvet. This style of blouse is also very pretty in pale blue, or pink taffeta.

For an ordinary walking - costume, the one in *cachemire* (fig. II.) trimmed with black mohair braid, is most practical. It is of the new shade known as *violine*, with a pleated waistcoat of white taffeta, and waistband and cravat of black taffeta. The hat is of the same colour as the dress, with white lacebow, strass ornament, and black aigrette.

In fig. III. we have two costumes of a more dressy kind. The one is blue *cachemire* cloth of the shade known as *bleu de France*. The skirt has the apron width of blue velvet let in and carried on round the skirt as a shaped flounce. The bodice has a velvet yoke let in, and the whole dress is braided with black.

Many of the dress skirts are now being made in this style, but the apron width carried on as a flounce is all of the same material and colour as the rest of the dress. It is merely outlined with a narrow cross-way band of taffeta to match, and a second band of taffeta round the bottom of the flounce. Grey, drab, and beige dresses are being made in this way, with a short tailor jacket opening down the front, over a waistcoat of white or coloured taffeta.

The second dress is of cream woollen material with applications of reed-green silk and trimmings of black satin. The apron-width is of black satin with narrow pleatings of same and two narrow pleatings of black satin round the skirt. Sleeves, collar, and waistband of black satin, and waistcoat to match the apron width of the skirt. The festoon edge is finished with green silk applications.

As regards the trimmings for dresses, never has embroidery of every kind been so much used, particularly spangled and bead work. Applications of guipure, silk embroidery, or bead *passementerie*, are sewn on to *revers*, waistcoats, sleeves, or plastrons. Mohair and silk braids are also used, and very narrow ribbon velvets.

FIG. III.

A favourite design for trimming is the Louis XV. bow in spangled applications. A very effective dress is of grey *cachemire* trimmed round the skirt with these Louis XV. steel embroidered bows put on at intervals. The bodice is blouse shaped in front, cut away slightly round the neck over a white satin *guimpe*, studded with steel spangles and finished in the front with a Louis XV. bow of strass.

FIG. V.

FIG. IV.

This same style is carried out in a new shade of heliotrope, with the Louis XV. bows embroidered in violet spangles.

Grey dresses are trimmed with white or pink taffeta. Drab and a new shade of fawn are frequently trimmed with guipure over white satin. Pink in every shade is very much worn, both by itself and as a trimming to mix with other colours.

The linings of dresses are more elegant than ever, and are always of silk. A contrast now seems to be preferred rather than a silk to match the colour of the dress. Violet is lined with heliotrope, soft shades of red with pale pink, sapphire blue with pale blue, and black dresses with any pretty colour.

As to sleeves, we have now gone from one extreme to the other. There is scarcely any gathering round the top, and even the epaulettes (which have hitherto served to give a wider appearance to the shoulders) are being put on with as little gathering as the sleeve itself.

For out-door garments the short tailor jacket seems to be preferred. It was said that capes would disappear entirely this season, but they are so useful, and there are so many of them in existence, that, with certain modifications, we shall still be allowed to wear them.

The redingote, in various new shapes and styles, is being made in light cloths. Some of them are finished with round hoods drawn over the shoulders to form a sort of cape, and edged round with silk muslin.

The one of which we give the illustration (fig. IV.) is of light beige livery cloth. It is tight-fitting, back and front, and opens over a waistcoat of heavy guipure. There is a guipure collar under the cloth one, and all the seams of this coat are finished with narrow straps of machine-stitched cloth. The hat is of beige, trimmed with taffeta and a black aigrette.

Ball and theatre cloaks are most costly items and nothing could be more beautiful in the way of wraps than the new ones of lace. They are of the old-fashioned circular shape from the neck to the bottom of the dress. A cream Chantilly was made in this way with half-inch bands of dark fur put round with about two inches of the

FIG. VI.

lace between each. This lace was lined with soft heliotrope satin to within ten inches of the bottom, and the remaining ten inches of yellow satin. Heliotrope silk muslin in accordion pleats was put between the cream lace and the satin lining, and two long ends of this silk muslin fell from the neck to the bottom of the cloak. The interior was lined with ermine. A more practical wrap of this kind was in very much the same style, but of green silk covered with black Chantilly lace. Old shawls of black lace are being used now for short theatre cloaks with the points back and front and a coloured silk lining over fur.

Lace dresses of all descriptions are to be very much worn, but Chantilly seems to be preferred. Embroidered nets, silk muslins, Greek and Russian nets, are all being shown. These dresses are made over coloured silk slips, and are most convenient, as by having two or three different-coloured slips with collar and waistband to match each one, a change is easily made.

The illustration (fig. v) we give is of embroidered net made over black taffeta. The taffeta skirt is made separately, and then the net is gathered and trimmed round the bottom with a *ruche*.

The bodice is covered with gathered net, and trimmed with rows of narrow ribbon velvet of lettuce-green. The collar, waistband, and bows on the shoulders are of lettuce-green velvet. The sleeves are of quilled net, and these sleeves show how little fulness is now allowed on the shoulders. The *toque* is of white satin with silver threads, a black velvet bow on the side, which turns up, and a black aigrette.

Toques of this style are being made in spangled net and *tulle* of all colours. Some of the black net with coloured spangles is lined with white *tulle*, and this gives a very pretty soft effect to the *toque* when made up. Hats and *toques* are of the most original shapes, and flimsy materials are more used than ever for millinery.

We now come to evening dresses, which are certainly more artistic than ever. *Tulles*, silk muslins, and laces, are all worn over white or coloured taffetas. The French art silks and satins are in the most exquisite shades this season. Long sleeves with low-necked dresses are still the favourite style, but a neckband of some kind is invariably worn—the pearl dog-collar, or a band of velvet with diamond clasps, or even a straight collar of quilled silk muslin to match the dress. Most of the evening bodices are slightly pouched over the waistband and many of them fasten over down the left side.

The dress in our illustration (fig. VI.) is of a lovely shade of turquoise blue art satin, with low-necked bodice and gathered sleeves of white silk muslin. The sash is of silk muslin, with a *chou* at one side and in the centre a diamond brooch. A dog-collar of pearls and diamonds and a blue-and-white aigrette in the hair.

The very latest thing is to have ball-dresses painted by some celebrated artist. A most magnificent cream satin dress was ornamented with sprays of roses on the skirt, a few loose petals looking as if they had just fallen into the folds of the satin.

Jewellery and fancy ornaments are worn in profusion. Belts, instead of being studded all round with stones, are now of ribbon or velvet, with about six clasps put on at intervals. Skirts are more elaborate than ever, and are often trimmed with one deep flounce upon which are two or three very narrow ones.

Veils are very much worn of the same colour as the *toque*.

Morning wraps of coloured surah are made with gatherings from shoulder to shoulder, back and front. They then fall straight down without any waistband. The sleeves have one small puff at the shoulder, and then fall very wide and square. They have a second sleeve inside of piece lace. There is either a flounce of lace or of silk round the bottom of the gown, and the neck is trimmed with insertion or lace.

AT MADAME KATE REILY'S.

THE ordinary English visitor to Paris may search and search in vain in all the *ateliers* of fashion for definite and lucid ideas as to what will and what will not be worn, for Parisian shops are like none other in the world, inasmuch as they seem always in a fuss and flutter, and almost regardless of their customers, who "catch as catch can" fleeting glimpses of the pretty women who come in and out at long intervals in the latest and the newest wraps, the smartest coats, and most enlightened *toques*. It really takes a month at least to shop decently in Paris, therefore our thanks are the more due to Madame Kate Reily, who goes sometimes twice a month across the Channel, and brings back to Dover Street not only the very newest and prettiest things, but also those which, by experience, she is aware are most likely to be most worn. The tendency is towards an upper skirt ; and one of the most exquisite evening frocks seen at Madame Reily's was made of white satin, veiled in white net embroidered richly round the edge in silver and mauve *sequins* representing sprays of purple and white lilac, while the edge is softened by the daintiest little frills of ribbon, and on the little cap-like sleeves of *tulle* (which fit the shoulders almost like a glove) are sprays of pale purple and white lilac. There is another evening frock of white, veiled in gold net, embroidered richly in gold, with a belt of mauve velvet, and bands of rich yellow velvet on the shoulders, with violets as prettiest contrasting colour.

But if Madame Kate Reily excels in one thing more than another (which all her admirers will doubt) it is in the manufacture of the exactly right dress to wear in the day-time, the little simple dress in which all women look most attractive, which can be worn at any time and not look too smart, and yet is equal to any grand occasion. She always has a very smart black dress, and a very smart dress in white, as well as exceedingly pretty creations in fawn colour, or putty colour and dark blue. Just now it is the fashion to have a scarlet cloth coat to wear with a dark skirt, and one of these, with white *revers*, is finished with black buttons and black belt.

The pretty shirts, new muslin collars, and new silk neckties have only to be seen to be immediately secured, for nothing better of this sort can be found anywhere in town. Last year Madame Kate Reily had a favourite sailor hat which everybody seemed to buy ; this year there is a new edition of the same, which is a wonderfully smart idea in drawn silk—say purple, with two spreading quivering purple wings and a few yellow roses tucked under the brim ; but another, in rose silk with rose wings, has Parma violets as flowers.

A Spring Idyl

BY ARABELLA KENEALY,

Author of "Woman and the Shadow."

I.

"The silver birch is a dainty lady,
   She wears a satin gown ;
The elm-tree makes the old churchyard shady,
   She will not live in town.

"Such a gay green gown God gives the larches—
   As green as He is good !
The hazels hold up their arms for arches
   When Spring rides through the wood."

"DID you ever see such a threadbare person ? " Madge demanded.

"He really is an absolute disgrace, you know," said Milly.

"He hasn't had a new coat for years."

" Three certainly. And one of his boots has a crack across the toes."

" And then his hat ! "

" And his waistcoat ! "

" It's a comfort he does not even attempt gloves. If he were to, they would be so absolutely shocking, we should have no alternative but suicide."

" Oh, Madge, do you think he would wear them with holes in *every* finger-tip ? "

" He'd wear them," Madge stated emphatically, " if there were not a finger-tip or button belonging to them. That's what poets are ! "

" And to think he's *our* father," Milly said, at the conclusion of a tragic pause, during which she had exchanged admiring and complacent confidences with a very pretty person in the mirror.

" If he were not so frightfully handsome— handsomer than every other man—we should be almost ashamed of him."

" And if he were not so fearfully clever— you forget that."

" Oh, no, I don't. I'm not likely to forget it after that notice in the *Times* this morning. What did it call him ?—' a genius of the highest order,' ' a poet of pellucid thought.' "

" Do you think it will sell his book ? He can't go through the spring without a coat, you know."

" Nor we without jackets. Oh, Milly, quick ! quick ! There is Mrs. Derwentwater driving past. And what perfectly delicious feathers ! There must be six of them at least in the front of her hat. And doesn't she look lovely ? And what horses ! And Milly, look ! She is turning down the station-road. She is going by train. And she will see father on the platform. Oh, you stupid, stupid idiot, why didn't you make him put on his best coat ? "

" Well, he looks very nice," Milly said composedly : " a thousand times better than any other man she's likely to see. And the crack in his boot doesn't show—as it's blacked."

"Of course his coat isn't so bad as we made out, and nobody can see his waistcoat when his overcoat is buttoned."

"And his hat quite shines now it's nicely brushed. I'm glad I brushed it myself."

"Yes. And it is a comfort he doesn't even attempt gloves."

There was a pause, during which the girls gazed diffidently into one another's eyes.

Then: "Do you think she admires him?" Milly whispered.

Madge nodded reflectively. "I think so," she said slowly. "I saw her watching him in church last Sunday. I had an eye on her all the time, to see what impression he was making. And he never once suspected why we changed our pew."

There was a longer pause. Then Madge adventured: "Do you think he admires her?"

Milly caught her breath. This were treading on sacred ground indeed. She shook her head dubiously.

"He said that first day she was in church that she was very handsome," Madge persisted.

"Did you ask him if she were not handsome, and he agreed, or did he volunteer it?"

"He didn't volunteer it," Madge admitted, with a sigh.

Both their pretty faces fell. There was a further lengthy silence.

Then: "I am afraid he is too much of a poet to be in love with a real woman," Milly asserted. "The women he writes about are not like women who live in houses and wear stays."

"Mother lived in a house, and she must have worn stays, or she could never have had a waist like that," Madge insisted, pointing to the portrait of a somewhat insipid blonde above the mantelpiece.

The girls observed it with disfavour. "I wish she didn't look so good, and simper. It's shocking form nowadays, for a woman to look good," Madge said.

"Father laughed when I told him. He said he didn't know that she was particularly better than other women."

"Well, that is a comfort," Madge sighed, relieved.

"Do you think he cared very much about her?" Milly questioned, under her breath.

"Why, of course he did. That lovely sonnet about 'hearts torn from their rootings' described what he felt when she died."

"He wrote it before she died," the other protested diffidently; "and you can see Mother's eyes were not hazel."

"He may have called them hazel to rhyme with something."

"If it had been that, I should think he would have left them blue. There are a hundred words to rhyme with blue, and I don't know one that rhymes with hazel."

"What colour are Mrs. Derwentwater's eyes?"

The girls' tones blended in a triumphal chorus: "As hazel as nuts!"

"It's a pity she is a widow," Madge submitted. "People don't write poems about widows."

"Nor about three thousand a year," retorted Milly. "But having it never stopped anybody from marrying that I've heard of."

"Father wouldn't marry for money."

"Father's a great deal more sensible than you think. And he knows we shall have to come out and perhaps have some seasons in town. Because I don't suppose even *we* shall both marry in our first season."

"That means only you will, I suppose! But thank goodness some men have the taste to like fair girls!"

"Well, it would be ridiculous to quarrel about it, considering that you are only fourteen and I am nearly sixteen. It is likely I shall marry before you. But we've got to settle Father first. I should like to know how a genius of the highest order would get his breakfast in the morning or his boots cleaned without two practical young women to look after Bridget. Do you think she would remember both? It might be boots without breakfast or breakfast without boots. Certainly it would never be boots and breakfast too. No. Our only plan is to marry Father comfortably before we think of ranging ourselves. And I call it an absolute Providence that sent a rich, handsome widow like Mrs. Derwentwater to the Grange, just as we are of an age to manage his affairs for him."

II.

Now the mind of the reader may disabuse itself of the impression that John Dillon's portrait has been faithfully presented by his daughters. Madge and Milly were sufficiently smart young persons, but they had their limitations; and—though limitation is scarcely the word to fit the expansive nature of their adjectives, yet in so far as any accuracy of application was concerned their descriptive powers may be faithfully described as having bounds. Dillon was neither aggressively shabby nor insuperably helpless, but it pleased his girls to paint him as being both. He did not spend largely on clothes — he had not the wherewithal to spend largely on anything. And such outlay as could be spared from his slender resources for the purchase of apparel was spared for the purchase of feminine apparel. Had the girls but exercised a little more discernment they would have known him for a less absent-minded genius than they portrayed him from the eminently practical results of his shoppings. Such frocks and cloaks as he procured for them out of the proceeds of his sonnets were chosen with an eye to fitness and durability, and with an appreciation of the prevailing *mode*, for which the readers of his sonnets would assuredly not have given him credit. For some poets, though they may lead you in verse to suppose them cognisant only of nymphs with hyacinthine locks and nebulous vestments, in real life are aware that their womenkind need muffs and woven woollens in the winter. So Dillon only smiled when the girls unrolled his packages and exclaimed with lifted hands and shrill staccato notes of admiration about the taste and discretion these disclosed.

THE GIRLS OBSERVED IT WITH DISFAVOUR.

"Now, how *could* Father have known that blue is being worn?"

"And that low hats with wide crowns are the latest thing from Paris?"

"The shopwoman told him. Now, on your honour, didn't she, Father? Confess that the shopwoman told you not to buy green hats to be worn with blue cloaks."

"Or purple frocks."

"Never mind how it came about. Only be thankful it did come about, and give me some tea for my pains," he said, smiling.

"Did you see anybody you knew at the station?" Milly inquired, with an overdone vacuity of eye and tone.

"Whom did you expect me to see?"

"Why, somebody drove by so quickly that we could only make out just the top of her hat," Milly fibbed breathlessly; "and *I* said it was Mrs. Derwentwater, and Madge said it was Miss Smith."

"You were both right," Dillon responded, unconcernedly drinking his tea. "Both ladies were at the station."

"And did Miss Smith get into your carriage?" Madge demanded truculently.

"Why do you ask?"

"Father," the girls cried in chorus, "if you were to marry Miss Smith, even though she is so rich——"

"Heavens, girls, what are you talking about?" Dillon protested sternly. "I am not likely to marry Miss Smith or anybody."

After he had gone the girls exchanged wary glances.

"We shall have to be very, very careful," they decided. "Father has the very sweetest temper, but——"

Dillon himself could have written no epic on anger more eloquent than the silence succeeding.

But alas for youthful machinations! Early next day, on the girls' return from a walk which had led them in ecstatic circuit of the lichened, ivied walls enclosing Mrs. Derwentwater's domain, they came face to face with a sign-board bearing the legend *To Let*, planted on the grass-plot of their own modest garden.

By the time they had learned that the sign-board was no ridiculous mistake, but a hideous reality, they were not so cast down as they might have been.

"There are over ninety days between March and June," they decided valiantly, "and a good deal can be done in ninety days!"

They forbore to probe the paternal decision.

"When Father says, 'I have decided to let this house because I intend to take another,' he means 'So forever hold your tongues,'" said Milly.

"Now, I wonder why we were not even consulted? Father has never before done anything without our consent."

Mrs. Derwentwater was seated in the window of her charming morning-room, gazing, to all appearance, toward the lovely greens and azures of a forest-fringed horizon. In reality she was looking into the shadow-flecked memories of a past which lay beneath the rippled arches of her own dark hair.

The meadow upland, billowing soft and undulant before her, the young trees shaking out their new green dresses, the blue haze clinging like the languor of awakening over all awakening things, the hush, the subtle sweetness, and fair promise of fair spring, whispered her apparently to little purpose. The story of Nature is read mainly by those who have no story of their own. A woman's smile, a man's frown, a child's laughter, a town's approval, the flow and ebb tide of finance—these are the motes which blind us to that sweetest smiling, perfumed pageant ever unfolding on a World's Stage.

And Mrs. Derwentwater met its revealment with darkening eyes and a fold between her brows. A freshly written letter lay before her. She came back from her retrospect to seal and stamp it with a capable white hand. "What a horrible—horrible coincidence!" she exclaimed, shuddering. "I shall let the place at once."

A card was laid before her. She stared at it, incredulous. "Tell him I am engaged," she said hurriedly. "Say Mrs. Derwentwater regrets that she is extremely occupied, but if——"

"It is a young lady, ma'am," the butler said. "She wrote her name in pencil on her pa's card."

Mrs. Derwentwater's hazel eyes were a trifle short-sighted. She read the card at a nearer angle. She gave a little abrupt laugh. "I will see her here," she said.

Milly came in with an air of assurance, tempered by a diffident blush.

"I'm afraid you will think me terribly—rapid," she broke out precipitately, "and mercenary," she added, "but I am one of the collectors for the Society for Cruelty to Children, and I thought if you——." She produced a shiny note-book with pencil appended, and took out a somewhat shabby purse confidently.

"Oh!" Mrs. Derwentwater said lingeringly. Her eyes dwelt with a strange, half-shy intensity on the pretty, unformed face and girlish figure. Her lids quivered for an instant as the large, clear eyes met hers. She seemed to thrust aside a memory. Then she said, with a slight smile, "The Society for Cruelty to Children does not commend itself by its title, but I suppose it is all right."

"Now how perfectly idiotic of me!" Milly cried, abashed. "I am always making that absurd mistake. It is such a frightfully long name. It is the Society for the Prevention of Cruelty to Children, of course. Oh, thank you. How lovely! I never had so large a subscription before. You *are* kind! And may I write the receipt for it here?"

She wondered why Mrs. Derwentwater was staring so strangely at her when she looked up presently from the final flourish she appended to her name. The elder woman's eyes were soft and humid, and there was a wistful look about her mouth, almost, Milly thought, in a burst of imaginative speculation, as though she had once had a pretty daughter of her own—a daughter who had died.

The widow accepted the receipt somewhat absent-mindedly, and Milly's obligation to make her good-byes and retire was obvious.

But she mustered her courage and sat down. "Do you think you will like Farmford, Mrs. Derwentwater?" she inquired bravely.

"It would seem not," Mrs. Derwentwater answered, with a glance toward the recently sealed envelope, "as I am leaving at the end of the quarter."

"Why, good gracious, so are we," cried Milly, in amazement.

Mrs. Derwentwater's eyes fastened on her with a sudden question.

"Father made up his mind all in a moment," Milly explained. "The board was put up yesterday. And we came here when mother died, ten years ago, and he had always talked as though he meant to live here all his life."

The widow's face had twisted again, with a sharp, abrupt movement, toward the blue and green horizon. "Perhaps the air does not suit him?" she said stiffly.

"He didn't give any reason," Milly asserted. "But he isn't strong. He broods you know; I suppose poets do. You might think he was frightfully miserable sometimes. But he laughs, and is himself again, and never admits he isn't perfectly happy. Of course he is a genius, and geniuses can't be expected to act like other people."

There was a long silence. Mrs. Derwentwater was slowly tearing up the recently directed letter. Milly noted the slender beauty of her hands, and the richly glittering diamonds upon them. Then:

"Oh, you are tearing the stamp," she cried impulsively, "an unused stamp!"

"Why, so I am," the widow smiled; "though, after all, it is only a penny, dear," she added, looking whimsically into the grey, ingenuous eyes.

"When she said 'dear,'" Milly acquainted Madge, later, "I could have choked—and kissed her. She is the loveliest, sweetest, most aristocratic woman I have ever seen. And she's as young as anybody need be. And—and her rings are superb."

But Milly had made a further move before rejoining Madge. Mrs. Derwentwater, assisting her shy, girlish leave-taking, moved across the room with an extended hand.

"Good-bye," she said graciously. "Thank you for giving me an opportunity with the Cruelty to Children Society. It was kind of you to think of me. See now, you are forgetting your book."

Milly turned a flushing face.

"Oh," she said, "it is only a volume of Father's poems. Father is John Dillon the poet, you know. If you have not read them," she persisted casually—"and—and would like to——"

Mrs. Derwentwater smiled, still proffering the volume.

"You are very good," she said, with an air of finality. "I rarely read poetry."

Yet when the girl had gone she crossed the room with the graceful, swift movement characteristic of her, and took down an identical volume from a shelf.

She held it tenderly in a hand, turning a page or two.

"As though I needed to read it!" she said, with fierce, wet eyes.

III.

"OH, you little Donkey! You Tremendous Cur! You Miserable little Monster! Why didn't you go at him again. No decent-minded dog would have allowed herself to be rolled over like a dumpling, and never even bark!" Madge stormed in undertones, the while her lips curved sweetly upward in a seraphic smile till Mrs. Derwentwater's carriage had whirled out of view.

The little dog so apostrophised sat up in the road and waved its two small fore-paws abjectly. It was a pitiable object. Its silken mane was wet and mud-bedraggled, its curly coat bristled with prickles and rubbish scraps; over its right brow went a brand of clay. It had done its diminutive best, and its best had been feeble fiasco. For nearly an hour before the time of Mrs. Derwentwater's afternoon drive Madge and Pompon had lurked in ambush by the road. During that time Pompon had been diligently prompted in her *rôle*; her temper had been set on edge, her nervous system harried, her tiny brain tormented with exhortations against an impending foe, who was to be "fetched" and "bitten," and torn in her most bloodthirsty fashion.

When at last carriage-wheels resounded, Madge, with a final rap of warning on the silken pate, had turned the small head sharply in the direction of attack. "Now then, bite him! fetch him! tear him," she insisted savagely. Whereupon the nervous creature, quivering with mingled bravery and trepidation, had shrilled one shallow war-cry, and, like a streaming ball of silken fringe, had precipitated itself upon the foe. There was a whirr of dust, a blur of outlines, and a short, despairing yap. Then Pompon was discovered lying prostrate in the road, while Nero, Mrs. Derwentwater's mastiff, went his way unmoved, strong, erect, and serene, in a manly consciousness of having disposed of his ridiculous assailant without unnecessary violence.

Madge fairly sat down by the roadside and shed tears at this frustration of her ruse, while the small humiliated ball of silk alternately sat up and waved its apologetic fore-paws and sat down and cleaned its damaged coat.

"Why, what is the trouble?" a voice said above her presently. A hand was laid softly on her shoulder.

Mrs. Derwentwater had returned on foot, and was standing beside her. Nero slunk at a distance, eyeing his floss-silk assailant with shamefaced looks.

"You would have it, little missie," he was deprecating. "A chap can't have his ankles snapped at when he's on duty, you know."

The truth being inconvenient, Madge prevaricated.

"Your enormous mastiff nearly killed my poor little Pompon," she said, with humane indignation.

Poor little Pompon immediately sat up and pawed the air pathetically. Whereupon Nero, reduced to the depths of canine abasement, sat down on his haunches and sniffed. Mrs. Derwentwater picked up the quivering atom and stroked its tiny head compassionately.

"Poor, poor little Pompon," she murmured.

Pompon, finding herself in a secure position, pushed her silken muzzle from amid the velvet of her protectress's mantle and yapped one shrill yap of contumely in the face of the mortified foe.

"We must enlist Mr. Nero's sympathies in the Society for the Prevention of Cruelty to Animals," Mrs. Derwentwater submitted, as she and Madge walked homeward side by side.

"Now how did you know I am my sister's sister?" Madge demanded.

The widow glanced down into the girl's eyes. They were large and hazel. They were not her father's eyes. But:

"I knew," she said softly.

"Won't you come in and let me brush you?" Madge proposed at the gate. "I am afraid Pompon has just covered your mantle with dust. Father is away I am sorry to say," she added ruefully.

Mrs. Derwentwater was looking so perfectly charming, she reflected with admiring glances, that no man—not even Father—could fail to fall deeply in love with her on the spot.

But Mrs. Derwentwater, with one long glance toward the face of the pretty cottage greening over with new leaves and buds, shook her head gently.

"I will not trouble you," she said. "I am only a few minutes from home."

She had nodded a smiling good-bye, and was moving off with the conscience-stricken Nero in her rear, when Madge, desperate to see her go without having advanced one whit in social acquaintance, blurted eagerly, "It seems so silly not to know you as we knew the Mortons who lived at the Grange before you, and not to be able to send you honey— we have the finest bees—and first gooseberries and parsley, just because Milly is two years too young to make formal calls."

Mrs. Derwentwater extended a friendly hand, her eyes softening upon the animated, girlish face.

"It would be very silly," she said, "if—if you were not leaving, and if we were to continue to be neighbours."

"Oh, but we are not leaving after all."

Mrs. Derwentwater paled during a perceptible silence.

Then she said slowly, "I thought your sister told me——"

"Oh, we were then," Madge cried ; "but that very same day she came home and told us *you* were going, Father had made up his mind that *we* were not."

Mrs. Derwentwater withdrew her hand abruptly from the girl's warm clasp. "It would be a pity to make friends only to lose them so soon," she said a little coldly, "because you know, though you are remaining, I am leaving."

Dillon came home that evening in high spirits.

"The whole of my first edition sold again before publication, girls," he said, "and a large demand for a second. We shall be able to take that trip abroad in the autumn."

"And I do believe we sha'n't need a rich step-mother after all," Madge insisted ; "and after all, she would very likely be an incubus."

"Oh, but Mrs. Derwentwater is such a darling!" Milly protested, "and—and I don't believe Father is nearly so happy as he ought to be."

However, Mrs. Derwentwater showed no marked desire for the *rôle* of Madge and Milly's step-mother. All their carefully constructed plots and strategies proved fruitless. By some strange perversity Dillon could rarely be persuaded to walk, as his daughters manœuvred, in the direction whither the widow was to be met. The widow was gracious and smiled pleasantly upon the girls in passing, but she made no advance toward further acquaintance.

Madge and Milly interchanged sombre confidences. "In a book they would have been married in less than six weeks. And we have scarcely got Father even to admit that she is good-looking."

And indeed, Dillon gave himself but little opportunity for judging, for when it so turned out that the girls contrived to lure him whither he would meet the widow, he studiously turned his head the other way.

The girls had never known him so obtuse.

"Mrs. Derwentwater !" he would exclaim. "What, the little old lady with spectacles and pattens !"

Madge declared once that she could thankfully have shaken him !

Finally they gave up in despair.

"I don't believe Father knows one woman from another woman," they determined irefully, and ceased from further plottings.

And then Fate, which had scorned to avail itself of their immature essays, stepped in at the last moment, as doubtless it had purposed doing from the first.

Dillon, summoned to town by a wire from his publishers just as the last van had drawn up at the door for its load of cottage furniture—for he had finally determined upon leaving—was re-summoned home by a telegram from Milly.

She met him on the platform, her pretty face tear-stained and white.

"She is getting on all right, Father," she broke out. "It was the piano you know. The men were bringing it downstairs, and Madge was passing underneath, when one of them stumbled and loosed a corner of it, and it fell against her ankle, and the doctor says a bone is broken. Mrs. Derwentwater met them as they were carrying her to the doctor, and she insisted on having her taken to the 'Grange.'"

IV.

DILLON was awaiting Mrs. Derwentwater in the morning-room. During the week wherein Madge and Milly had been her guests he and the widow had not met.

Now, however, Madge was sufficiently well to be moved, and he had driven over from the hotel for that purpose. And farewells and courtesies must be exchanged. These he had determined should be as brief and distant as civility and obligation would permit. Lover of books as he was, in the interval of waiting in the charming Chippendale room, he had moved to the glass-paned, silk-draped bookshelves lining the walls. A key stood in a lock. He turned it and lifted aside a silken curtain. He dropped it abruptly, and, crossing the room, investigated the shrouded volumes of the opposite wall. Then he walked to the window and stood looking out. The dew of heated, rapid breathing blurred the pane before him. His hands moved restlessly — till he faced round suddenly to the sound of silk. They stood one minute interchanging searching glances. The widow uttered a faint exclamation.

"It is difficult to thank you sufficiently ——" he began, labouring with his breath.

"Don't," she cried, shivering and stretching out a hand. "Blame me, revile me; but, if you have any mercy, don't treat me as a stranger."

"Whose fault ——?" he began sternly.

"Mine—all mine," she confessed. "There is no word to say in my defence."

He laughed bitterly. "Oh, I have never deceived myself," he said. "You had reason enough on your side. You are not the first woman who has deserted her children and a book-worm, for a rich man and a man of fashion."

"And yet—and yet," she murmured, more to herself than to him, "I loved the book-worm."

There was a pause.

"You patronise his books I see," he said, with an ironic smile, sweeping a hand in the direction of the curtained shelves. "So it is you to whom I am indebted for the sale of my first editions before publication."

"It was not patronage," she returned sadly. "I wanted them all, John."

He made an impatient gesture. His eyes, resting on her beautiful blanched face, glowed with strange light

Suddenly he moved to the door. "It is useless to prolong this—this horrible interview," he said strenuously. "I am grateful for your kindness to the girls."

"Oh, you will let them come to me sometimes," she cried out, stretching trembling hands to him. "John, you were always pitiful and kind. If you knew—if you knew what a lonely, miserable woman I am!"

She read his eyes. She moved toward him with a lifted head. "Oh, not that," she cried. "I am ashamed — abased; but God or merciful fate spared me the worst. In intent—if so mad and reckless a proceeding can be said to have had intent —I have forfeited my wifehood. In reality, I am the woman who left you ten years since."

She unlocked a drawer in a desk and took out a letter. "The train we travelled in ran off the lines an hour from home—it seemed like some horrible, swift vengeance overtaking us," she said. "He was hurt— terribly hurt before my eyes. He died that night. Before he died he wrote this for you. He thought—he thought when you knew—you might take me back. I dared not face you. I went abroad, and have been living, till a few months since, with the de Lisles."

He was standing above her with a set, white face. His breath came in swift gasps.

"If it were only true!" he said between his teeth.

"John, it is true. We had never intended it. I was vain and thoughtless. I thought you neglected me for your books. But I never intended it. It was a sudden, mad impulse. We repented almost while we did it. And then came horrible retribution."

"If it were only true!" he said again, transfixing her with fierce, insistent glances.

"It is true," she said, touching his hand timidly. "If it had not been true, John, do you think I could have met my girls?"

There was a pause.

SOME MINUTES LATER THE BUTLER ENTERED.

"When you divorced me——" she began, in a low voice.

"I never divorced you," he said.

She remained a minute staring at him. Then she faltered to a chair. "You wrote that you would divorce me," she protested helplessly, drawing a hand before her dazed eyes. "I was abroad. For a year I dared not look into the papers."

"I never divorced you," he said again. "Where was the use? I had no wish to try marriage a second time. And you—I heard, of course, that he was dead."

"Then I am——. John dear?"

"You are still my wife," he said.

She was kneeling at his feet. She was covering his hand with tears and kisses.

"Take me back," she whispered hoarsely. "John dear, take me back. I was but a girl. It was but a mad impulse. And thank God, thank God, there is nothing between us but intention. I am rich. When Father died, a year since, he left me everything. If I cannot share it with you

and with the girls—oh, John, if only for the girls' sake, if you have no love or pity left for me—for the girls' sake, for your girls and my girls, take me back."

Some minutes later the butler entered. His shrewd ear gathered a swift sweep of silk as he opened the door, his shrewd eye noted his mistress standing with a discourteous back upon her guest, who in his turn was showing inordinate interest in a very ordinary paper-weight. The tones of his voice were exceptionally suave as he submitted, "The cabman, sir, is getting anxious about the time; he is afraid you may lose your train, sir."

Mrs. Derwentwater, standing looking from the window, questioned softly,—

"Do you not think it would be better for Madge to remain another week?"

The poet took two half-crowns from his pocket. "Give the man these," he said practically, "and tell him he may go."

Whereupon Robson departed briskly to

inform the kitchen that the household had taken on a new master.

"And to think," Madge commented, "to think she was our own Mother all the time, and that horrid pink-and-white faced person over the dining-room mantelpiece is only a ridiculous 'Study of a Lady' by Greuze, and it was merely father's fun to tell us it was Mother. Still, there certainly was a likeness to me about the nose, and to you about the chin."

"And to think Father and Mother should have quarrelled, and should have been separated all these years only because— what did they quarrel about, Madge?"

"It was such a trifle, I've forgotten it already. Shall we go and ask them? They are just crossing the lawn."

The two girls sought one another's eyes.

"Aren't they fearfully in love!" they whispered.

"Perhaps, after all," Milly said sagely, a minute later, "perhaps it will be better not to mention the quarrel again. It isn't of the slightest consequence, you know!"

Arabella Kenealy

ENTRANCE COURTYARD, WORMWOOD SCRUBBS, SHOWING ANGLICAN CHAPEL AND COLONNADE.

WOMEN PRISONERS.

[ILLUSTRATED FROM PHOTOGRAPHS TAKEN BY THE AUTHOR.]

BY THE VISCOUNT MOUNTMORRES.

WHEN she disappears from the dock, down the narrow winding staircase to the cells below, all the excitement and anxiety of the long, wearisome trial ended in hopeless despair, what becomes of her? She cannot yet realise that she has bid a long farewell to the outer world, that she is a common convict, before she is ordered into the prison-van and secured in one of the small compartments, or else hurried with a female warder into a four-wheeled cab to be driven to the gaol to which she has been assigned. If she is an old hand, she will merely give a sigh of disgust at having been caught again, and take it all as an annoying episode—she will look forward to the coming imprisonment with a philosophic resignation, and settle down at once in sulky indifference to laze through her term with as little inconvenience to herself as possible. She will be the well-behaved prisoner—silently, uncomplainingly she will do as she is bid, and get her full quota of marks each day, for she already has learned that the less trouble she

gives to the officials the less trouble she will have herself. But the novice, sentenced for the first time—she will probably, as soon as the first crushing sense of utter numbness has given place to a realisation of what has happened, become hysterical and violent. She remembers it is Harry's dinner-hour and that there'll be no one to give him his dinner —how anxious he looked at the trial, and she'd never seen him cry before; what'll he do the whole time she's put away?—and there was just a heap of things she wanted to tell him that she forgot at that brief farewell. It is all very sad, and the wardress, whose heart —God bless her!—has not grown stony or callous, though she has seen the same painful scene times and oft before, tries to calm her. But it is of no use—she shrieks and struggles, and the female officer sees that the only way to deal with her is with firmness and severity; though it pains her, experience has taught her that that way true kindness lies. Gradually the prisoner is cowed and grows submissive; it is her first lesson in having her spirit broken, and the sooner that lesson is known by heart the better for her. Then they reach the prison; and as the great creaking doors swing slowly to, behind them, there is, perhaps, another little scene; but she is tired by now and somewhat dazed. All she wants is quiet and rest and to be left alone to herself to think. And so she is soon subdued, and goes through the rest of the ordeal mechanically.

She is taken to the receiving-room—a small room, with whitewashed walls and a deal table, at which sits another wardress. The only other furniture is a weighing-machine and a measuring-machine. The wardress who has brought her, hands over the committal note and gives the necessary particulars as to the case, receives a receipt for her, and from that hour Emma Smith becomes No. 77. She has to undress, and is led into an adjoining room, in which several baths with wooden partitions round them are let into the floor; the floor itself is covered with a bath-sheet. A wardress bids her enter one of the baths, and asks her whether it is hot enough. Yes, it is all right. After her bath she is anthropologically examined in the receiving-room: her weight, height, measurements, are all duly recorded, together with notes as to the colour of her hair and eyes, any peculiarities in her features, any disfigurements or marks upon her. She notices meanwhile, upon the table, all her clothes set out, the contents of her pockets ranged side by side. Whilst she dresses in prison garb she is asked to check all these her possessions as an inventory of them is read over, which she has to sign.

The preliminaries are soon at an end; she is taken to her cell, and on the morrow she will begin the regular routine of prison life. If she be a first offender, her uniform will differ from that of other prisoners in that in the cap and on the sleeve is a white badge with a great red star upon it; otherwise it will be the regulation drab-brown shapeless dress of coarse serge, with apron and cap. The "red star" women are all kept to themselves, in work and in leisure, so that they may not become contaminated by intercourse with their more depraved sisters.

The first evening she will no doubt receive at five o'clock—supper time—a tin basin of rich cocoa, or a bowl of stirabout, and an eight-ounce loaf of bread; it is more than the regulation allowance, but she needs it after the strain and excitement of the day, though probably she has not the heart to taste it, and so the cocoa grows cold and the "butter" rises and sets in a thick white layer on the surface. She mechanically takes in the details of her surroundings with a vacant eye, as she sits staring upon the edge of her narrow bed, or walks feverishly round the confined apartment like a caged animal.

The cell is about twelve feet in length by seven feet in width, and about nine or ten feet high. The floor is either boarded or else flagged, and in the latter case it is black-leaded until you can almost see your face reflected in it. The walls are whitewashed. In the heavy door through which she entered is a small peep-hole, so that she can be kept under observation from the outside. On one side of the door is a small window of thick, opaque glass, behind which a gas-jet burns and serves to light the cell until 8.30 p.m., when all the lights are put out. On the other side of the door is the heating apparatus, by which hot air is let into the cell. Immediately opposite the door, high up near the ceiling is a closely barred window, one pane of which opens by a lever under the prisoner's control. Beside the window is the ventilating apparatus, which exhausts the cell of foul air. The monotony of the walls is broken only by a corner bracket, on which stand the prisoner's slate, salt, comb, etc., and a small wooden bookshelf containing a Bible, prayer-book, and hymn-book. The only furniture in the room is a little wooden stool, a low table, the bed, and a set of utensils—basin, slop-pail, water-can, mug, food utensils, etc. The bed is merely a sloping plank, at present standing up on end in one corner of the cell, with a mattress hanging over it, and a couple of blankets folded on the top of it.

The whole gives one the idea of extraordinary, brand-new cleanliness. The floor is—if wood—white as though the boards had just come from the carpenter's bench, the stool and table the same; the tin-ware glistens

TAKING DINNERS ACROSS THE EXERCISE-YARD.

CLASS IV.

Breakfast : Bread, 6 ozs ; gruel, 1 pint.

Dinner : Same as Class III., with the addition of 2 ozs. more of potatoes in each case, and 1 pint of soup instead of ¾ pint on soup days, and 10 ozs. of pudding in place of 6 ozs. on pudding days.

Supper : Same as breakfast.

If a prisoner is sentenced to seven days only, she is on No. I. diet the whole time ; if she is sentenced for fourteen, twenty-one days or a month, she is on No. I. diet for the first week and No. II. diet for the remainder of the time. If sentenced to over a month, but not exceeding four months, she has No. II. diet for a month and then No. III. for the remainder of her term ; if her sentence is for upwards of four months she gets No. III. for the first four months and No. IV. afterwards. Her diet may be varied by the following substitutes : Tin cooked beef or mutton served cold, beans and bacon, frozen meat, fresh fish, salt fish or salt meat, may be given instead of cooked beef ; and cabbage, turnip-tops, parsnips, turnips, carrots, dried potatoes, leeks, or rice in lieu of potatoes. After nine months of imprisonment, a

like polished steel ; not a speck of dust or dirt can the eye discern.

Next morning No. 77 has to rise at 6.30. Her cell must first be cleaned and tidied, with infinite pains, until its appearance is, if possible, even more glitteringly new than when she entered it. At 8 o'clock comes breakfast — and here a word about her diet. This will depend upon her sentence. There are four different classes of diet, as follows :—

CLASS I.

Breakfast at 8 : Bread, 8 ozs.

Dinner at 12.30 : Stirabout (a kind of gruel made with oatmeal and Indian meal), 1½ pints.

Supper at 5 : Bread, 8 ozs.

CLASS II.

Breakfast : Bread, 5 ozs. ; gruel, 1 pint

Dinner : Bread, 5 ozs., and either suet pudding, 6 ozs. ; or, potatoes, 8 ozs. ; or, soup, ½ pint ; —according to the day of the week.

Supper : Same as breakfast.

CLASS III.

Breakfast : Bread, 6 ozs. ; gruel, 1 pint.

Dinner : Bread, 4 ozs. ; potatoes, 6 ozs. ; suet pudding, 6 ozs. : or, bread, 6 ozs. ; potatoes, 8 ozs. ; cooked beef, 3 ozs. : or, bread, 6 ozs. ; potatoes, 6 ozs. ; soup, ¾ pint.

Supper : Same as breakfast.

IN THE REPAIRING-ROOM.

prisoner may, if she prefers it, have one pint of cocoa and two ounces extra of bread instead of gruel three mornings in the week.

These diets are not of course either luxurious or excessive, but they are sufficient and nourishing, and the bulk of prisoners thrive on them. All the food supplied is of the very best quality that can be obtained, and thoroughly wholesome, whilst the very great latitude allowed in the substitutes provides that variety in feeding so necessary to health ; at the same time the regularity of the life, the constant employment, the systematic exercise, all tend to improve a woman's physique, and the prison records bear ample testimony to the benefit which women receive from a course of prison treatment. It may be recommended as superior to a visit to any health resort on the Continent, for building up one's constitution and generally restoring health.

A prisoner's occupation in prison will depend very largely upon her own conduct. Life in prison is divided into four stages, or classes. Every prisoner on entering is in Stage I., and during the first month of her term she remains in this stage, the principal feature of which is that she works her whole time in her cell, and only leaves it for her "exercise" of one hour per day, and for her attendance at chapel. Each day she can, by good behaviour and industry, earn eight marks ; if at the end of a month she has earned the full tale of two hundred and twenty-four marks she is advanced to Stage II., when her work will be with the other prisoners in the workshops, the laundries, the kitchen, or in the general work of the prison. At the end of her second month, if she has earned four hundred and forty-eight marks, she advances to Stage III., and a further two hundred and twenty-four marks during the third month entitles her to Stage IV., and to the privilege of writing and receiving one letter, and of receiving a visit, at which three people may be present, for twenty minutes. For every further completed six hundred and seventy-two marks she may write and receive a letter, and have a visit of thirty minutes. In addition to this, after she has got into Stage II. her marks have a monetary value ; that is to say, that for every

completed two hundred and twenty-four marks per month, she has a small sum, which gradually increases, credited to her to receive upon her leaving prison, until this sum totals ten shillings, the maximum which she can thus receive. In Stage II. she is credited in this way with a penny for every twenty marks, or a shilling for the whole two hundred and twenty-four. In Stage III. her two hundred and twenty-four marks are worth eighteenpence, and a penny is earned for every twelve marks up to the two hundred and twenty-four. In Stage IV. and onwards (until the maximum is reached) ten marks bring her a penny, or each completed two hundred and twenty-four two shillings.

To return to No. 77. Having done her best to swallow some of the essentially wholesome breakfast, she cleans the utensils in which it is served, and is soon set a certain tale of work. In former times this principally consisted in some wholly barbarous and useless employment, devised with no other object than that of killing time. Such occupations as oakum-picking are fast disappearing, and the usual forms of work nowadays for cell employment are doll-dressing, Japanese reed and bead blind-making, mat-making, Oriental rug-weaving, and other very technical and refined work, in which prisoners can take an honest pride, whilst learning a trade that will in all probability be useful to them later on, and undergoing a salutary discipline which will in most cases have a beneficial moral effect. During her first morning she will no doubt receive two visits—one from the minister of the religion to which she belongs. Prisoners are very particular about their religion. The other visit is from the schoolmistress. And these two phases of prison life require a little explanation. Each prisoner has to acknowledge to some form of faith, be it Anglican, Roman, Jewish, or Nonconformist. They must all attend "chapel" once every week-day, and twice on Sundays, unless they belong to some creed which conducts no religious service at that particular prison. In most cases there is a Church of England chapel, which is also used by dissenters, a Roman Catholic chapel, and a synagogue. The religious

GOING IN FROM THE WORKSHOPS.
(Notice most of them turning their faces away from the camera.)

attainments of the readers, and it is extraordinary what an enormous number of prisoners, in these days of free education, are absolutely untutored. A very large proportion can neither read nor write, whilst the majority probably can only just read. All these are systematically taught until they can pass the third standard.

The first morning in prison is further broken into by visits from the matron and the head wardress, probably, to make arrangements about the prisoner's occupation; possibly also by the doctor, to see wnat her state of health is. Then there is chapel and the walking exercise; and as No. 77 leaves her cell she is able to gain some idea of her surroundings. Her cell is one of some scores, opening down each side of a long, lofty corridor lit from the roof; gallery after gallery,

ministers of these various faiths have free access to the members of their community, and prisoners are very ready to discover which minister is the most acceptable visitor, which is the most kind-hearted, amusing, good-natured; and hence prisoners are very particular about their religion: it means so much in the dull tedium of prison routine to have a really pleasant visitor dropping in now and again.

The scholastic side of prison life is interesting. The schoolmaster has the library under his control, and the hope of getting a really exciting or interesting book, a collection of short stories, a magazine, is a keen incentive to his pupils to make good progress. Each prisoner is entitled, if well conducted, to a change of book every week, one volume at a time; and as there is a great run upon some books, they are naturally reserved as rewards of merit. Of course, the schoolmaster must, in giving out books, have consideration for the

THE ANGLICAN CHAPEL.

rising in successive storeys, one above the other, run round this corridor, each with its long row of narrow cell doors. As she is marshalled into line with several other prisoners by a wardress—they are never called wardress, by the way, always female officer or female warder—she sees that at a table in the corridor a prisoner told off for the duty is handing out warm frieze capes with hoods to such of her party as feel the need of them. She is then conducted out into the exercise ground —a large grass plot of from a quarter to half an acre in area, intersected by a very maze of asphalted paths, along which the p r i s o n e r s have to walk in and out, u p a n d down, round and round, at a regular pace of from three to four m i l e s a n hour, keeping two yards always between each prisoner and the next, for an hour by the clock under the eagle eyes of four officers.

A GROUP OF WARDRESSES.

rate, she will be in the presence of others of her kind ; and if, under cover of the noise of the sewing-machines in the workrooms, or of the mangles and the hiss of escaping steam in the laundry, she venture to say a few words to her neighbour, who can blame her ? And if the wardress in her neat blue uniform checks her, she does so kindly—for they are a good-hearted, large-souled body of women, these wardresses, and understand tempering discipline with tact.

The work of the prisoner in the repairing rooms, or laundry, or kitchens, is obvious. In the workrooms she is engaged upon making the prison dresses, the uniforms of the officers or in doing jobs for the War Office and Admiralty and Post Office— s h e e t s , b l a n k e t s , bags, sacks, etc.—and it is not long before the most idle, d r u n k e n loafer becomes proficient with her needle under the patient tuition of the superintendent of the room.

Exercise over, comes dinner, and then the excitements of prison life are at an end for the day. Until chapel next day No. 77 is shut in her cell with her doll or her curtain, nothing but supper at five to relieve the monotony.

If she behave herself, in a month she will be privileged to pin a badge on her breast with a large II. in Roman characters, to signify that she has reached the second stage ; and now she will leave her cell during the day to work in the repairing rooms, or the tailoring shops, the laundry, the kitchens, or in other parts of the prison where, at any

If it ever fall to the lot of No. 77 to be in the infirmary she can have little to complain of—a bright, cheerful little dormitory where the doctor is king, where she receives the most careful and attentive treatment that it is in the power of humanity to give her, where all prison regulations as to diet or routine fall to the ground before the requirements of an invalid's fancy, and where probably she comes as near her ideal of paradise as ever on this earth. There she will see the prison mother, whose sole occupation is to tend to her little convict offspring—that poor little mite whose misfortune in first seeing light in a penal establishment is certainly more than compensated by its being the idol of all who see it, by its receiving attention and feeding in its earliest life which would be far beyond the means of its mother in her ordinary condition in life, by everything being done for it which can be done to give it a good start in life and a set-off on its journey through the world which it would never have had, had it been born in the slum garret which its mother looks to as home.

They are very careful of their prisoners in this country. The doctor can, with a nod of the head, ride rough-shod over the governor's most peremptory orders : he is supreme, and neither "diet-table" nor "stages" have any weight with him. Prison life, as a whole, is essentially healthy — a physical as well as a mental and moral training ; but if in any individual case it does not come up to expectations, the doctor sends the whole system to the winds with a single word. And any prisoner can see him whenever she wants to—or any other officer of the prison either for that matter : whilst she is one of Her Majesty's guests Her Majesty's servants are her servants, from the Governor downwards. Has she a complaint to make or a request to ask ? A card with the word "Governor" is slipped in a slot on her door and the Governor waits upon her at "inspection" during the morning. Or has she an ache in her little finger ? A similar card with the word "Surgeon" is put up, with a similar result ; and so with the others. In this way it is quite impossible for a prisoner to undergo any real or injurious hardship. Prison life is a punishment, of course, but the object which is made paramount in the English system is the bodily, mental, and moral reclamation of the individual ; and the best testimony to its efficacy is to watch, on the one hand, the arrival of a batch of newly convicted prisoners —seedy, broken-down sluts—and then to witness the discharge of a batch after a lengthy term of imprisonment—finely set-up,

strong, healthy women, women who, one knows, have all acquired some useful knowledge, have all learnt some trade, have all undergone a course of systematic routine and constant employment which cannot fail to have a beneficial effect upon their characters, unless they be—as it is to be feared many of them are—nothing but criminal lunatics. Prison life is monotonous, of course : all routine is, and well-disciplined routine such as is found in prison is especially so. Day after day to rise at six-thirty, work till eight o'clock, breakfast at eight o'clock, then to work on till chapel, exercise for an hour by the clock, work on again till dinner at twelve-thirty, work on afterwards till supper at five o'clock, finish work and have a little well-earned quiet and leisure till lights out at eight-thirty, and go to bed looking forward to exactly the same next day—when one knows that such a life is to go on week in week out from month's end to month's end, each day as like any other as two rococo doves— then one realises the monotony, the dreariness of it. Sunday alone differs from other days — unfortunately, not to Sunday's advantage in the eyes of prisoners : it is a long, dull day in cells, with no work and with two chapels, with nothing to do but to sit and watch the shadows cast by the window-bars creeping across the floor and up the wall and on to the ceiling. But all said and done, it is to be doubted whether life in prison is really any more dull and monotonous than that of the majority of industrious artisans who from January to January, from the beginning of life to the end of their days, tread the same daily road of toil and sleep. Certainly prison life is healthy, the food wholesome and the effect beneficial ; and it is doubtful whether those soft-hearted philanthropists who would make prisons pleasant and the life in them enjoyable would really be benefiting their species by rewarding the lazy and the criminal with a life easier and more comfortable than can possibly fall to the lot of the honest mechanic.

SIMPLE HOMES, AND HOW TO MAKE THEM

V.—SITTING-ROOMS

By Mrs. J. E. Panton, Author of "From Kitchen to Garret"

ERHAPS the most difficult room in the whole house to arrange well and yet simply is that chamber which the owner thereof generally calls the drawing-room : that is to say, unless she is an adept at the art of furnishing, then she knows just what is suitable, and in consequence makes a success at once of the pretty place. Let no one who has a really small house be beleaguered into buying the regulation drawing-room furniture. I do not use the word suite, because those abominations are never now met with in any lady's house ; but what I do mean is that no one should have a great cabinet, very large arm-chairs, and those terrible "occasional" chairs on which it is quite impossible to sit, and that are neither ornamental nor useful in the least. The ordinary small suburban sitting-room has usually a bow window, and if so, this can always be made a feature ; while in the especial room I have planned in my "simple house" (which, drawn to scale by a kindly architect, will duly appear when these articles are reprinted in book form), we have not only a square window, but a capital recess, either or both of which can have an appropriate seat put in, fixed if the house is our own, but not attached to the wall in any way if we are only temporary tenants of the structure. I may say that I do not personally advise a seat in the recess on the lines of the cheap and uncomfortable cosy corner, which as a rule is more like a stool of repentance than anything else ; but I do advise a window-seat either after the design of the one illustrated here, or as a fitted seat placed straight across the window and not shaped at all. This latter is the more comfortable of the two designs, but the one given here is the least expensive, and can be managed at home if we are the lucky possessors of a home carpenter, and have clever fingers, which can really sew, at our disposal. Ample directions how to make such a seat

are found in "From Kitchen to Garret," so I will not repeat them here. It will be seen at once how much space is obtained in a small room if we use the window in the manner shown. In olden days a long brass pole would have been placed across the window and dark curtains hung therefrom to draw at night, while hideous blinds would have further added to the expense and trouble of furnishing. The small curtains, arranged as shown, serve all purposes at once, and the room is the same size at night as it is during the day, when as a rule the room is little used, except by an occasional afternoon tea-party, which, except on very stiff occasions, would be far more pleasant and less formal if held in the hall.

Here let me digress for a moment, and beg the would-be owner of a simple home to carry out the idea of simplicity all through her beings and doings ; and above all let her never pretend to have or to be anything save what she really has and is. I would always have the means of getting my tea for myself close at hand, were I obliged to economise on every detail in household life ; for if I were, and were beginning life again, I would far and away sooner economise in the domestic servant line than in any other I could name. This is easily done by a young wife who really likes her home and her pretty possessions, and sees no more harm in washing her china and glass herself and laying her table daintily and neatly than in mending her husband's socks and re-trimming her hats. I have no sympathy with pretence of any sort, and the pretence that insists on two inferior maids when one superior one would mean happiness and comfort, is a pretence that means so much, that I hope these days of "servantless mistresses" will bring about in due time a really healthy state of affairs in our kitchens and servants' rooms. I have found it very difficult to have what I consider proper illustrations for these articles ; and none of them are to be taken as my idea of perfection, for I cannot find a really simple room which would suit the folk for whom I more especially design these words of mine. I have a couple of old photographs I shall have to have reproduced; but one is about eighteen years old, and though the effect is still excellent as a whole, there are faults naturally that one would not tolerate now. Why, even on the chairs in one of the photographs I print here are to be found antimacassars! These, of course, are never used now: albeit I must say I still admire them,

readers would, I am sure, have written at once to ask where the simplicity came in. So all I can do is to print "hints," not copies to be followed slavishly in the pictures here submitted to you, and trust you will take from them and add to them just as you think best. At the same time no one can improve on that special bow-window arrangement, try as hard as they will to do so! That room, too, was really the very prettiest and daintiest room I ever had or did in all my life.

The walls were decorated with a beautiful

A CHARMING WINDOW-SEAT.

and think the little drawing-room here illustrated looks quite sweet with them still. I then looked over at my dear cottage, simplicity itself as far as the furniture is concerned, but we are a family which collects endless odds and ends. We have many friends who give us charming gifts, and we can afford to have them dusted and put straight for us. Please don't think me a snob for mentioning this: I only do so to account for my not being able to obtain a photograph of just the very room I want my young folk to have, and had I reproduced the cottage home sacred to the boys, my

yellow and green and white paper, while the dado and loose furniture linings matched exactly; the pattern on the cretonne used for this purpose ran round the room, in contrast to the paper, which ran up, and altogether the effect was just lovely. The little window curtains were of stamped yellow linen at $7\frac{1}{2}d.$ a yard, edged ball-fringe, and the carpet was a blue-patternless pile. The surround was flatted ivory paint, which we painted on an oilcloth surround left by the last tenants, and which lasted the four or five years we lived in that special house without being so much as touched up. It always scrubbed clean, and was a constant joy to me; and I advise any one who has a shabby oilcloth anywhere to try painting it with really scrubbable paint. There are two kinds of which I know: Aspinall's Water-Paint, and Hoskyn's Ben Trovato Paints. These really last well, and enable one to still use our shabby oilcloth, should we be un-happy enough to possess such a bugbear in our house. When that special room was furnished, it was in the height of the rage for using enamelled furniture, and I had as

themselves or allow a "handy man" to do it, taking care that he follows directions im-plicitly, and does not work on the lines of his own sweet will. To satisfactorily paint new furniture, one coat of ordinary white lead paint should be given, and this must be allowed to dry thoroughly. If the wood be rough, a second should be put on; and then, when that is really dry and hard, it should be scrubbed, to ensure perfect cleanliness. Then one coat of enamel must be put on: that dries well in twenty-four hours, during

A SIMPLE DRAWING-ROOM.

much of it as possible, for I found, and find still, that it is most useful to be able to enamel old and poor wood, and to make it new and beautiful to behold. At the same time I do not advise any one to buy new enamelled goods in any shape or form. The best enamelled furniture, and we should never buy any other, is as expensive as really good wood, and this latter is a far more satisfactory investment in every way. At the same time, if only inexpensive things can be had, I ad-vise my readers to buy plain wooden articles ready for painting, which they can do at most of our larger shops, and to either paint them

which the newly painted object must be protected from dust; then a second coat of enamel can be given, and the work is com-plete. The great secret in all successful painting is to see that each coat is really hard and dry before the next is put on, and that the last is quite hard before the table or chair, or whatever it may be, is taken into use. Very few ordinary people in these days can afford to buy good arm-chairs, and even when they can, I have very grave doubts about their being absolutely satisfactory possessions. That they are luxuriously com-fortable, none can deny for a moment. But they collect dust in a really desperate manner; they harbour moth cruelly, and are most certainly the reverse of hygienic possessions. If we must have them, I should as a rule have them put into petticoats, as in the illustration. These can always be washed, always renewed; in glazed chintz they are even bearable in a London house, while in cretonne in the country they remain clean for months, even if the male inhabitants of the house dare to sit upon them in their work-a-day garments: a habit which reduces to chaos

very much to the fore. Then in after-years I have had similar chairs aspinalled blue and creamy-white; now I prefer the natural tan-coloured cane or basket-work. If one sits by the fire, the enamel smells and becomes sticky, and it also soon becomes shabby; whereas one can ill-treat the natural cane as one will, the poor thing never for one moment resents the treatment. The cushions for these chairs must be of some good hard-wearing tapestry, and must be firmly fastened by strong twine to the chairs themselves in

A SITTING-ROOM CORNER.

all our most cherished possessions, if we once allow it to be formed. A capital chair for any one is the ordinary basket chair that years and years ago I used to have, despite the fact that in those days I had to have them made for me, and that there were none of the improvements that now make them quite as luxurious as a really good upholstered chair. I do not now advise these chairs to be enamelled; my first possessions in this line had to be painted, and I persuaded our carriage-builder to make me some "shiny paint" for the purpose, and this was a deep dark black: the use of black and gold was then

several places; and these should completely fill the back and seat of the chair. The fixed cushions can be supplemented by one of the down pillows, encased in plain silk, which have now entirely taken the place of chair-backs. These silk covers should be made as pillow-cases are, to button and unbutton, for "Liberty" silk washes most beautifully if washed at home. I cannot say what would be the result if the fabric were intrusted to the ordinary laundress, but any one possessed of sense can wash this silk, and it renews its youth in the home wash-tub in the most satisfactory manner possible.

In the small room the tables need cost only a very few shillings, as they can always be draped in cloths. These can be in plain serge-edged ball-fringe, in linen-edged torchon lace or in silk and woollen brocades. Several firms keep these square table-cloths ready trimmed for immediate use; and where possible, it is best to have several sent to one's own house and see the effect of different patterns and colours in the room itself, before making the final selection. In one's own house one naturally sees that the fireplace and mantelpiece are all they ought to be, but sometimes in a hired house one has to contend with an old and ugly erection. If in any way possible, a slow-combustion stove must be had; it saves its cost in one winter in the difference between the consumption of coal it incurs and that enforced by the use of the old-fashioned wide-mouthed grate; but if we cannot alter the grate, we can mitigate its drawing tendencies by having the bottom lined with a sheet of tin, and the back and sides surrounded by fire-bricks. Then the hideous mantelpiece must be covered with my own pattern, the "Gentle-woman" drapery, which is so largely used, and still more largely copied by those who have not the grace to even mention from whence they got the idea. This drapery is kept by several firms ready made, and as they make it in quantities, and far more cheaply than any one can make it at home, I will not waste space here by describing the oft-described over again. I am printing a third photograph as a guide to what can be done with the recessed part of the room, which is found in our specially designed sitting-room; and I think several hints can be taken from this for the many rooms which are so often divided by a species of arch. In this special room I had a series of brackets placed up each side to hold china; and so successful was the effect, that I have had them copied elsewhere, and many, many people have done the same. Nowadays one would eliminate the large loose cover on the sofa, also the tambourine, as naturally one does not want to accumulate more dust than one can help, and fewer ornaments altogether are desirable in small houses; at the same time the arrangement as a whole is satisfac-

tory, and the long book-case on the wall may give a hint to any one who may be in want of something to hold superfluous literature that they have no regular place for.

In the perfect room, we shall undoubtedly use nothing save matting and rugs, and the plain, patternless, string-coloured Indian matting, of about 2s. 10d. a yard, is the kind to have. This should fit the room in the way an old-fashioned carpet used to, and the rugs should be placed by some one who understands how they should look. As a rule, they are arranged in idiotic straight lines, and, in consequence, are not the success they most undoubtedly are when put down by a master hand. As regards decorations, if our home is in the country, or in so remote a suburb as to hint at country ways and ideas, then nothing can improve on the chintz or floral effect; but if it be in a large town, we must remember the inevitable dirt, and while we must never for one moment be afraid of bright real colour, to the discarding of grays and drabs and similar terrible decorative crimes, we must recollect that smuts are inevitable, and that dirt has to be legislated for by something more than the mere brush and duster of the housemaid, or even of the housewife herself. Let there be definite colour in the room, and then it will always give the visitor a cheery welcome, whose first words will undoubtedly be: "Dear me! how pretty your room always looks, to be sure!"

One last word here before we climb upstairs to the bedrooms; and that is: Never be without flowers and growing plants of some kind or other, as on these last touches depends much of the success of one's rooms. Now, flowers are so cheap there is no reason whatever why we should be without them; and if we resolutely refuse to burn the pernicious and poisonous gas, we can indulge in growing ferns and plants. These, by the way, must never be bought from "men in the street": if they are, they will speedily die, for they have, as a rule, been raised in a hot-house hurriedly for sale, and their journey through the cold and often windy streets to one's house sign their death-warrant at once and for ever.

Taken at Her Word.

By EGLANTON THORNE.

THE door of Zion Chapel, Peckham, had for more than a week a large poster attached which informed the passers-by that on the evening of tne fifteenth instant Mrs. Blessington Tripp would in that building address a public meeting on the subject of Woman Suffrage. The women who attended the services at Zion Chapel were mostly of a meek and quiet spirit, inclined to despair rather than desire social changes ; but amongst them even were to be found a few ardent souls fired by a sense of the wrongs of womanhood and eager to claim the rights which the wicked arrogance and brutal strength of men had withheld from them through ages of oppression.

These hailed with joy the opportunity of receiving inspiration from the eloquence of Mrs. Blessington Tripp, whose name was well known to all interested in the movement as that of one of the most fearless champions of the cause of her sex. And women who felt no interest in the question of Woman Suffrage were nevertheless so wrought upon by the name and fame of Mrs. Blessington Tripp as to experience considerable curiosity as to her personal appearance and power as an orator. Now that the appointed evening had come, numbers of women were gathered in the little chapel. There were women shabby and women smart, women old and women young, women of subdued, chastened demeanour, and women whose air of rampant self-assertion boded ill for any of the other sex who should dare to oppose them.

Punctually to the hour, Mrs. Blessington Tripp, a portly dame on the further side of forty, robed in black silk, with a liberal display of white lace on her bust and shoulders, stepped on to the platform. She was a good-looking woman in her way, with bright, alert dark eyes, and an abundance of black hair set off by one of the tiniest and most fashionable of bonnets. Showy rings sparkled on her hands, which were plump and white, and of which she made graceful and effective use for the illustration of her words. Her manner was perfectly self-possessed and even confident, and once launched upon her subject she spoke with a force and fluency which produced a marked impression on her hearers.

It was somewhat curious, however, that, while urging her sisters to consider public questions in a large and impersonal manner, she seemed to think that every trivial fact concerning herself, every personal detail she could drag into her address, must have for them peculiar interest. Incidents in the life of the late Blessington Tripp, showing his fervent attachment to his wife and profound belief in her powers, were related ;

opinions respecting herself, expressed by friend or by antagonist, were freely quoted : and stories were told of individuals in high places, who had rashly dared to argue the question of Woman Suffrage with Mrs. Blessington Tripp, and had been forced to retire worsted from the field. Finally she made a touching allusion to her daughter and only child, Cassandra Tripp.

" People ask me," she said, " what are my views with regard to my daughter. Should I like to see her," they asked, " battling for her rights on equal terms with men?" "Most certainly," I reply. " I have no belief in the so-called " chivalry " of men towards women. What we demand from them is not chivalry but justice. My daughter must fight for this with the rest of her sex. With all my heart I desire that she should fight, that she should struggle, that she should face contumely and reproach, if need be, rather than that she should become the willing slave of a man, rather than that she should sell her birthright of freedom and equality for the mess of pottage which man, her would-be oppressor and tyrant, offers her. My prayer for my daughter is that she may follow in the steps of her mother, braving scorn and persecution as she battles for the right, never despairing but pressing boldly onward to the goal of her sex's emancipation from the fetter's which man's selfishness and greed have fastened upon it, lifting up the fallen, supporting the weak, encouraging the timid, treading down her enemies, sweeping away the powers that oppose her, and winning at last her rightful position as the recognized equal, if not the superior of man."

Vehement and prolonged applause followed this burst of eloquence. With a few more passionate words Mrs. Blessington Tripp brought her speech to a close and sat down, looking heated but elate. A vote of thanks to her was proposed, seconded, and passed in due form, and the speakers who took part in the proceedings vied with each other in the lavish use of laudatory phrases to express their admiration of Mrs. Blessington Tripp's oratory. Then the meeting broke up, and, after lingering till she had extracted the last drop of adulation from her admirers, Mrs. Blessington Tripp went home.

She and her daughter dwelt in rooms above a chemist's shop, in a quiet street, not far from the British Museum. Here the girl spent many hours alone, her mother's public duties taking her frequently from home. When Mrs. Blessington Tripp came in hot and tired from her evening's engagement, she found Cassandra, all unwitting of the future her mother had sketched for her, awaiting her coming, with a dainty little supper on the table in anticipation of her arrival.

Cassandra, despite her formidable name, was a slight, pretty, simple girl, past twenty but looking younger than her years. She was fair of complexion and had the colourless face of a girl reared in London. Her features were cast in a more delicate mould than those of her mother ; she had soft, wistful blue eyes, and a rare, sweet smile that was very attractive. Some of Mrs. Blessington Tripp's admirers thought it a pity that her daughter was so weak and insipid looking ; but they had not noted perhaps the firm, though sweet curves of the little mouth, nor the somewhat audacious line of the chin. They said they feared Cassandra would never rise up and follow in her mother's steps. Cassandra, for her part, had no intention of doing so. She was a modest, shy girl, and no idea could be more repugnant to her than that of being thrust upon a public platform with hundreds of people staring at her. She dressed simply and tastefully in a style that was utterly feminine. No stiff, stand-up collars, no mannish waistcoats or neckties were effected by her. She was wise, for such would have ill-suited her pretty, flower-like face.

"Come at last, mother," she exclaimed in a sweet, clear voice, as her mother entered, "how tired you must be ! It is such a warm night. Did you have a good meeting ?"

" Oh, delightful ! most delightful ! The chapel was crowded. And such enthusiasm, such applause, and such kind appreciation of my efforts ! I feel quite cheered."

"That is a good thing," said Cassandra placidly, "now you will be glad of your supper. Let me take your bonnet and cloak. See, I have your slippers here."

"You are a good child, Cassandra," said Mrs. Blessington Tripp, dropping into a chair with a sigh of satisfaction. " I don't think I am very tired. It has been so gratifying. When people listen as they did to-night, I feel equal to anything. I wish you had been with me, Cassandra. You should have come."

To have shortened the illustrious name she had bestowed upon her daughter would have been contrary to the principles of Mrs. Blessington Tripp. Her intimate friends

called the girl "Cassie";
but to the mother she was
always Cassandra.

Cassie did not echo her
mother's wish. She stood
silent, her face wearing a
demure expression; but the
corners of her mouth
twitched as if ready to
break into a smile and
there was no sign of regret
in her demeanour.

"Why did you not go
with me?" asked her
mother. "You know I al-
ways like to have you with
me. What have you been
doing with yourself whilst
I have been away?"

"I have been spending
the evening with Miss Winthrop," said Cassie quietly.

Miss Winthrop was a
maiden lady, living a somewhat lonely life in her own
house in a neighbouring
square. She was afflicted
with failing eyesight, which
threatened total blindness
at no distant date, and
Cassie, for whom the old
lady had a warm affection,
was in the habit of visiting
her pretty frequently and
reading to her, by way of
relieving the monotony of
her life.

Mrs. Blessington Tripp
was satisfied for the time;
but a few minutes later she
asked with some sharpness, "Was Miss
Winthrop alone?"

"No," said Cassie, dropping her eyes,
"her nephew, Mr. Theodore Winthrop, was
there."

"What!" exclaimed her mother excitedly,
"that man! Do you know that he is the
editor of the *Weekly Satirist*, a paper which
constantly misrepresents and ridicules my
views?"

"I did not know that it ridiculed your
views," replied Cassie; "but I sometimes
read it to Miss Winthrop and it always
makes me laugh. She thinks it does a great
deal of good by showing up the absurdities
which get linked to things which are in
themselves worthy of honour. She says
that many a good cause is marred because
its leaders have no sense of humour, and

She awaited her mother, with a dainty little supper.

persist in pushing things to ridiculous
lengths."

"Oh, she talks in that way, does she?"
grimly observed Mrs. Blessington Tripp,
who was herself destitute of a spark of
humour; "I always thought Miss Winthrop
a weak, foolish, old woman. Let me tell
you, Cassandra, that there are subjects
too solemn for laughter, and the rights
and wrongs of women form such a subject."

"Oh," said Cassie, looking a little blank,
"but there can be no harm in laughing over
the question of whether women should have
the vote, can there? For it is quite certain
that there are lots of women who would not
know what to do with the vote if they had
it. I should not, for one. I was saying to
Miss Winthrop only to-day that I do not

want the vote, for I should never know to whom I ought to give it."

"Be silent, Cassandra; be silent, I command you;" exclaimed her mother, rising from her seat and extending her hands in a tragic, imploring manner. "To think that I should live to hear a daughter of mine speak in such a manner!"

"Why, mother!" exclaimed the girl, astonished at this display of agitation, "I only spoke the truth." I *don't* want the vote, and I *should not* know what to do with it if I had it."

"Be quiet, be quiet," her mother implored her, "you do not know what you are saying. Oh, that I should hear such words from you, Cassandra! But you shall be taught better, my poor child. In future you must accompany me to all my meetings. I have been wrong not to insist upon it before. I have neglected my own vineyard. But now I will see that you are trained in right principles."

Cassie lifted her head and opened her lips as if to protest; but on second thoughts she refrained, and busied herself with the preparation of her mother's cocoa. She was a thoroughly domesticated girl, and one who would have made a good wife of the old-fashioned home-loving order, as Mrs. Blessington Tripp would sometimes grudgingly admit.

"I will not have you go so often to Miss Winthrop's," she said a few minutes later; "I do not wish her to infect your mind with her antique, narrow-minded notions."

"Oh, mother! when she is almost blind, and she says my visits are such a comfort to her!" remonstrated Cassie.

Mrs. Blessington Tripp relented; for she had a kind heart, and could pity her neighbour's infirmity.

"No doubt they are," she reflected. "Well I do not want to be unkind to poor Miss Winthrop. You may visit her still; but I shall write and ask her to excuse you from reading the *Weekly Satirist*. I will not have your judgment deluded by its blatant conservatism.

Cassie made no objection. She had the gift, so rarely bestowed on women, of knowing when to be silent. She remembered that her mother did not do everything that she resolved to do. Nor was this last resolve carried out, as it happened The morrow brought Mrs. Blessington Tripp news of moment, concerning the cause she had at heart,—news which demanded that she should take prompt and vigorous measures to foil the designs of an enemy. The occupation and excitement which ensued drove from her mind all fears for Cassie, who continued to read the *Weekly Satirist* to Miss Winthrop, and formed by its perusal a decided opinion as to the wit and cleverness of its editor.

She had almost forgotten her mother's objection to the paper, and one evening having borrowed from Miss Winthrop a particularly spicy number of the *Satirist*, sat reading it in her mother's presence. Mrs. Blessington Tripp would never have noticed what her daughter was reading—for she was seated at her desk, deep in the composition of an article on "Woman's Rights" for a weekly journal—had not Cassie, who from nervous excitement was less self-controlled than usual, suddenly burst out laughing. Mrs. Blessington Tripp glanced round severely, wondering that Cassandra should so forget herself as to disturb her mother's important meditations. Her glance fell on the paper in Cassie's hand and grew instantly doubly severe.

"What are you reading, Cassandra?"

"Oh, nothing, mother," said Cassandra, blushing guiltily and pushing the offending paper away.

"Bring it to me," said her mother. Theoretically Mrs. Blessington Tripp held that every full-grown woman should be allowed perfect freedom of action and be responsible to no one for her conduct; but practically she expected from her daughter, twenty-one years of age, the unquestioning obedience of a child.

Cassie brought the paper to her mother. As Mrs. Blessington Tripp had seen, it was a copy of the *Weekly Satirist*. "What are you laughing at?" she asked. Cassie pointed to one of the columns. Her mother glanced at the paragraph and her brow darkened as she read the following :—

"If we may believe the words of certain advocates of the measure, the refusal of the Franchise to women would be fraught with danger to the Empire. Only the other day, a voluble, but not too wise declaimer, speaking on this question, declared that if the Government did not grant the just demands of women the women of this country would rise *en masse* and sweep the Government away."

"Cassandra," she said, severely, as she pointed to the passage, "was this what moved you to mirth?"

"Yes, mother," said Cassie deprecatingly,

"I could not help laughing. It really is very funny, is it not?"

"I fail to see the fun." The tones of Mrs. Blessington Tripp grew tragic in their intensity. "Cassandra, do you **know** that the words which this detestable editor ridicules are the words of your mother!"

"Oh, mother! You do not mean it. You surely did not say that?"

"I did say it, and I see no reason to be ashamed of my words. No, indeed, I am proud of them!" And Mrs. Blessington Tripp rose from her chair and began to pace the floor, her eyes flashing, her ample bust heaving, her clenched hands and passionate movements betraying strong excitement. "We will rise; we will agitate; we will make our power felt; we will show that we women are not to be for ever despised, oppressed, and ground under the heel of men. We will put forth our strength and show what women can do if they choose. And that detestable editor — that mean, base——"

"Mother, he is *not* detestable."

"Cassandra, are you going to defend such a reptile?"

"He is *not* a reptile," protested Cassie, with a sound of tears in her voice. "Mr. Theodore Winthrop is the editor of the *Weekly Satirist*."

"I am aware of that," said her mother angrily, "and I say that he is a mean, despicable, scurrilous writer. Do you dare to contradict me, Cassandra?"

Cassie did dare.

"I know Mr. Theodore Winthrop, mother," she said, falteringly, "and he is not what you say. He is a perfect gentleman, and one of the kindest of men. I am sure that if he had known it was you who said that, he would not have written so."

"You surprise me very much, Cassandra. Why should you care to defend this editor?"

"Because he is my friend," exclaimed the girl passionately; "because — because — mother—I have wanted to tell you and I have not dared: but—he has—he has—asked me to be his wife!"

"Cassandra!"

"It is true, mother. He only spoke to me yesterday, and he is coming—he is coming to-night to speak to you."

At that moment a double knock resounded on the house door.

"If that is Mr. Theodore Winthrop," said Mrs. Blessington Tripp, controlling herself by a supreme effort, and speaking with coolness, "I have my answer ready for him. You cannot suppose, Cassandra, that I

"Bring it to me," said her mother.

would suffer you to become the slave of a man who despises your sex ? "

" Not a slave, mother," said Cassie, tremulously, " and I am sure that Mr. Winthrop does not despise women."

" He despises them so much that he wishes to keep them for ever under the foot of man," said her mother.

The entrance of the little maid-servant with a card interrupted her words. The name on the card was that of Mr. Theodore Winthrop. Mrs. Blessington Tripp said no more ; but with her most belligerent air marched out to receive the unwelcome suitor.

Cassie clasped her hands and looked around her in despair. Oh, how she hated the cause and all pertaining to it ! Was that horrid question of Woman Suffrage to come between her and the greatest happiness her life had ever offered her ? She waited with her ears astrain to catch the least sound from the adjoining room. All too soon she heard the door open and her lover's steps retreat along the passage and down the stairs. Mrs. Blessington Tripp came back into the room, flushed and triumphant.

" It is all right, Cassandra," she said cheerfully, " I have sent him away. I assured him that I would never give my daughter to an opponent of the emancipation of our sex. He had a great deal to say, but I would not listen."

" Mother ! "

" My dear, you may trust me to know what is best for you. You need not fear that he will come again. He quite understands. He is really a very gentlemanly man. If only he were enlightened——"

But here she became aware that she was addressing empty space. Cassie, with a sob, had rushed away to her own little room.

Mrs. Blessington Tripp, with little compunction, settled down to finish her article for the newspaper. If she felt any uneasiness as to the state of her daughter's affections, the thousand and one interests connected with the cause, which hourly crowded on her attention, soon drove it from her mind.

Cassie on the following day looked paler than usual, and when the evening came she excused herself on the plea of a headache from accompanying her mother to the meeting at which she was to speak.

Mrs. Blessington Tripp accepted the excuse and went off to fulfil her engagement, little suspecting that Cassandra was solaced in her absence by a letter from the editor of the *Weekly Satirist*. We will not divulge the contents of that letter ; but we will steal a

few lines from the reply which Cassie wrote tremblingly ere her mother returned. " I will wait patiently, hoping that my mother's mind may change. If it does not I will think of what you say, and try to do whatever you think best, only do not ask too much of me, for you know I'm not strong-minded like mother."

" Thank heaven ! " her lover murmured when he read these last words.

After this, poor Cassie was taken to most of the meetings addressed by her mother. Stale beyond endurance became to her the story of her own sex's wrongs. She wearied of hearing constantly the same old arguments. She seemed to know beforehand everything she was likely to hear. Yet one evening words uttered by her mother, though not new, came home to Cassie's mind with quite fresh significance.

" This is an individual question," said Mrs. Blessington Tripp, " and every woman should answer it for herself. No one has any right to influence her decision. The Bible says that children should obey their parents ; but it nowhere says that grown-up men and women are bound to obey their parents. I contend that every woman has a right to decide as she will, this or any other question which affects her personal or collective life. Women should be permitted to develop their lives in the way that seems to them best."

Cassie listened with astonishment which rapidly developed into delight. Were these indeed her mother's sentiments ? If so, why should not she, Cassandra Tripp, decide for herself the question of her marriage ? Her mother could never say she was wrong to do so.

Had Mrs. Blessington Tripp glanced at the daughter who sat behind her on the platform, keeping as much out of sight as possible, she would have been surprised to see how Cassie's face had lightened, what a colour suddenly glowed in her cheeks, and how bright her eyes had become But she could not well look in that direction. She finished her speech and sat down, well satisfied with her performance, and little thinking what she had done.

Cassie seemed unusually animated as she and her mother travelled homeward. Of late her spirits had been uncertain, her mood often grave and a sad wistful look had crept into her eyes. Her mother even had observed it, and it had occurred to her that Cassandra was perhaps fretting about that horrid editor. But to-night she could dismiss that care from her mind, for Cassandra was looking happy

'E gave me 'alf a soverin."

again. Her daughter was, after all, too sensible a girl to give her heart to one of the avowed foes of her sex's liberty.

Thus dreamed Mrs. Blessington Tripp, and for a fortnight there was nothing to disturb this pleasing illusion. Then came some days of stirring excitement connected with the cause. A three days conference of workers for Woman Suffrage was held in London. Mrs. Blessington Tripp, as one of the chief promoters of the movement, was wholly absorbed in the business of the conference. Immediately after breakfast each day she left her home and did not return to it till late at night. Cassie only went to one of the meetings, domestic duties keeping her at home. Mrs. Blessington Tripp hardly realised how much of the comfort of her life was due to this good daughter who looked after the material necessities to which she

herself could give no thought. Each evening when she came home wearied out by the day's excitement and fatigue, she found Cassie awaiting her with a light, dainty meal, prepared for her refreshment.

But on the third night, though supper was spread for her as usual, Cassie was not there. Her mother felt a momentary sense of surprise ; but concluded that Cassie had been weary and had gone to bed as she had so often begged her to do. She had put ready all that her mother could possibly want. Nothing was forgotten.

Mrs. Blessington Tripp said to herself that she was glad Cassie had been so sensible as to retire early for once ; yet none the less she felt that her daughter's absence made a lack. She wanted to tell Cassie about the grand meeting which had closed their conference and the perfect "ovation" which had been accorded to herself. But that must wait till to-morrow.

Mrs. Blessington Tripp had seated herself at the table when she perceived a letter lying beside her serviette. To her surprise she saw that it was addressed to her in Cassandra's hand-writing. With some misgiving she took it up, opened it and read the following words :—

"Dearest Mother,—You will be very much surprised, and at first I am afraid, annoyed, at what I have done ; but surely you will forgive me when you think it over, for you will see that I have only acted on the principles which I have heard you lay down. You say that every woman should have full liberty to develop her life as she will. You say that a woman should assert her independence and claim her right to decide for herself every question affecting her individual life. That is precisely what I have done. I feel that life can offer me nothing better than the love of Theodore Winthrop. United to him as my husband and friend, my life will develop in the best possible way. I desire no rights that he will not lovingly accord me, for although he is not of your way of thinking on certain subjects, he is a good, true man, and I can confide my happiness to him without the shadow of a fear. By the time you read these lines I shall be his wife. We are to be married this morning by special license, and then we shall go to Paris for a fortnight's visit. When we return to London, I hope that you will not withhold from me your forgiveness. Indeed, mother, you should forgive me, for I am only acting in the spirit of your teaching. It is not easy for me to do this. Till now, I have always obeyed you, and I would much rather my marriage should take place with your approval ; but since that cannot be, I think I am right in taking the matter in my own hands. Please believe that although I thus act in opposition to your wishes,

"I am, ever,
"Your loving daughter,
"CASSANDRA TRIPP."

For a few moments Mrs. Blessington Tripp was motionless from dismay. Then she sprang up and dashed at the bell-rope with the idea of summoning someone to her aid. But ere she pulled the rope, she remembered that it was midnight, and that the people sleeping on the floors above and below might resent being roused from their first sleep, because her daughter had run away to be married. Besides, how could they help her ? What was to be done ? Absolutely nothing. By this time, the pair were married and in Paris. Mrs. Blessington Tripp could only sink helplessly into a chair and relieve her feelings by ejaculating from time to time—" Infatuated girl ! Infatuated girl ! Deliberately to give herself into bondage ! But she will live to repent it. Yes, she will live to repent it."

Later, Mrs. Blessington Tripp roused the poor tired, little maid-of-all work from her slumbers, and learned from her that Miss Cassandra had left home only half an hour later than herself. "I thought she was a goin' to the meetin' too," the girl explained, "for I saw she 'ad 'er best 'at and frock on, till I found she 'ad packed a box to take with 'er. A gentleman came in a cab and took 'er away, and 'e gave me 'alf a soverin, which made me think it was something more than ordinary. Miss Cassie, she laid the cloth and did the flowers before she went, and she told me just everythink I was to put out for your supper, and I promised 'er I wouldn't forget nothink."

Mrs. Blessington Tripp went back to the dining-room and sat down by the table, which, with its pretty decorations bore evidence of Cassie's taste and skill. She pushed the dishes from her, leaned her elbows on the cloth, bowed her head upon her hands, and then the redoubtable daunt-less champion of her sex burst into tears.

" I thought I could trust Cassandra," she sobbed, utterly illogical, as even advanced women are apt to be when greatly perturbed, " she always seemed such a good child."

Yes, it was amazing that it should be Cassandra, the meek, docile, obedient daughter, as she had always appeared, who had done this. Somehow, in spite of her brave words Mrs. Blessington Tripp had never realised that Cassandra was a woman who might choose to assert her independence and take her own way through life. She had been urging the daughters of other women to act thus ; she was astonished and aggrieved that her own daughter should take her at her word. That Cassandra should forsake her, that Cassandra should marry in defiance of her wishes, cut her to the heart.

There was much bitterness in the tears she shed ; but ere they had ceased to flow she saw there was nothing for it save to forgive her daughter. She could not take back the words she had uttered. She could not so discredit her profession as a public speaker. So she sensibly resolved to make the best of what she could not alter, and in the end found the best very good indeed. If Cassandra ever repented her marriage as her mother had prophesied, she kept the fact carefully hidden in her own bosom. There was never any appearance of repentance, nor of any cause for it.

Several years have passed since Cassandra's wedding, and the question of Woman Suffrage is still unsettled. Mrs. Blessington Tripp works as prominently for the cause as ever. But it is observable that the *Weekly Satirist* no longer treats the subject in its most caustic manner ; but has adopted a judicious and neutral tone in debating the question. There are persons intimate with the editor who playfully account for this change by saying that he is afraid of his mother-in-law. It is more probable that he is actuated by a desire to please his gentle, little wife, and spare her the annoyance of maternal reproaches. But Mrs. Blessington Tripp is convinced that the arguments she has so often launched at the head of her son-in-law has gone home, and though too proud to own it, he is secretly convinced that the position of those who oppose Woman Suffrage is wholly untenable.

FRENCH FASHION-LAND

By Marie A. Belloc

SHAKEN by revolutions, torn by internal dissensions, and woefully vanquished in the only great war of modern times, the fair land of France still keeps in the world of Art and of Letters a strange, almost uncanny supremacy, a supremacy which embraces much that is great, and even more that is infinitely little.

The fair ladies who adorned the Court of the good Queen Charlotte sent to Paris for their clothes, and now, on the eve of a new century, republican France, though lacking the prestige of a court, still sets the fashions to Europe, finding also her wealthiest patrons and the most zealous assimilators of her modish decrees in America.

Both the woman who takes an egotistical view of clothes, and she who regards them from the æsthetic and historical point of view, must find a stroll through the modern fashion-land of Paris profoundly enlightening and interesting. It is there, in the quarter bounded on the one side by the Opera, on the other by the Tuileries Gardens, that the whole world of dress comes for inspiration, for models, and for advice. Into this main artery flow thousands of tributary streams. One whole quarter of the city is de-

A WORTH TEA-GOWN.

Serial rights for America reserved.

voted to the making of artificial flowers, in another the great wholesale and retail ribbon dealers ply their trade ; and there is scarce a house, even in the more fashionable quarters of Paris, that does not contain a workwoman who is connected with a great dressmaker or milliner.

Although he has many rivals, each with their train of faithful patrons, and, it may be added, imitators, the present head of La Maison Worth is still king of fashion-land. As most people are aware, the founder of the house was, during the major portion of his long life, the greatest artist in dress the world has ever known. Although of English extraction, he early settled in Paris, and to him and to his untiring efforts the Court of the Empress Eugénie owed not a little of its modistic brilliancy. M. Worth was the first dressmaker who ventured, and indeed insisted, on imposing his personal taste on his clients. Endless were the stories told of this eccentric genius. On one occasion an American lady gave an order for a scarlet opera cloak for her daughter, a sallow blue-eyed Transatlantic belle, who was at that time making no little sensation in Paris. Worth realized that the colour would not suit the young lady, but he also knew from bitter experience that it was not easy to change the mind of a determined and clear-headed American woman. Accordingly, when the garment was sent home it was found to be reversible; pale bright blue velvet, trimmed with old point lace, on the one side, scarlet crêpe de chine on the other; the invoice running, " One cloak, pale blue velvet and lace, 2,000 francs; one scarlet ditto, no charge."

Those interested in French industry owe a debt of gratitude to the late Charles Worth. Not only did he indirectly benefit French trade, but he actually revived many of those small but important industries which had gone under during the Revolution, and which had not been reinstated even under the brilliant First Empire. To take but one example : under his auspices the French lace trade was re-organized. At the time of Napoleon's marriage to the beautiful Eugénie de Montijo, France was ransacked for two deep flounces of Alençon lace, and those that finally figured on the imperial bridal gown did not match!

In one matter La Maison Worth greatly differs from its rivals. The latter—Félix, Paquin, Rouff—to mention but a few whose names are now world-famous, are luxurious and beautiful in all their appointments, the greatest artists of the day having collaborated in the decoration of their ante-chambers and fitting-rooms. Not so No. 7, Rue de la Paix; indeed, one notable Transatlantic authority on the art of dress declared that La Maison Worth impressed her as might a great bank. The House relies on its reputation, and does not spoil its patrons by offering them fine painted ceilings, Doric columns, and boudoirs lined with mirrors. It has been said, and truly, that each one of the leading six dressmaking houses in Paris is presided over by a man or woman of such individual taste that the initiated can at any moment recognise with certainty any given garment as by Worth or Rouff, Félix or Paquin.

Then we come to that more important question, who makes the fashions? who decrees that the feminine world shall lengthen its skirts, narrow its sleeves, return to the paniers, or, as was suggested the other day, herald the new century by adopting pantaloons as the only wear? M. Jean Worth will tell you one thing, M. Paquin another. Under the Third Empire the world looked to the beautiful Empress for new sartorial ideas, just as in this country the Princess of Wales can make or mar a new fashion. In modern France the matter is practically settled by a committee, partly taken from the leading houses, and partly from the great manufacturing centres, to whom the question is of vital importance, as it affects the tem-

AN EVENING CLOAK : WORTH.

A GARDEN PARTY TOILETTE : WORTH.

the leading dressmaking houses have in their employment a number of intelligent and refined women whose only business it is to attend the great receptions, the private views, the plays of the moment—in a word, all those centres where the wealthy and great French world congregates. Each house has its own staff, not only of dress designers, but also of embroiderers who can be trusted to turn out various forms of trimming of which the designs will not be given to a rival or competitor. Worth, and doubtless every leading Paris house, always orders each year a number of lengths of Court brocades made specially and exclusively to its order, as often as not copied from some mediæval or eighteenth-century piece of material picked by M. Jean Worth in his wanderings among the curiosity shops of Paris.

As to the fashions of the moment, M. Worth, following in the footsteps of his father, who first introduced several harmonies of colour now universally worn, devotes most of his attention to the great question of tints. His chief delight is the designing of picture gowns — that is to say, of costumes that are for all time. It is to La Maison Worth that Jan Van Beers sends all his sitters, and a glance at any feminine portrait done by "Le Meissonier des Dames," proves conclusively that it is possible to design a costume which, while having about it nothing peculiar or eccentric, will yet remain dateless.

M. Worth has studied his subject exhaustively, and he can discuss the modes of the future with almost as much authority as those of the past; accordingly, it is a relief to hear from his lips the authoritative announcement that the crinoline may be safely regarded as one of the nightmares of the nineteenth century. "The love of the modern woman for athletics, though perhaps to be deplored from the æsthetic point of view, has made any revival of the crinoline impossible," he says, smiling; "besides, latter-day modes have a tendency to become more

porary prosperity of the silk and cloth trades.

In one matter the great Paris houses set an example to Anglo-Saxon commerce; they are always open to receive a suggestion from outside, and to adapt themselves to any passing whim of the moment. It used to be whispered at one time that a well-known French doctor's wife doubled her pin-money by turning her love of dress to practical use. Even a rough sketch of a really original costume will always receive the respectful attention of a great dressmaker, and a new idea for hats is positively welcomed. Artists who have seen their dreams of fame vanish, but who have to face the problem of making a livelihood, often in France become designers of new fashions; again, all and more utilitarian, while at the same time even those women who live for dress no longer slavishly follow one fashion : the lady of the twentieth century will realize that it is her duty to look her best under all circumstances, and not to follow the blind dictates of fashion."

Some of the most charming of the newer Worth gowns are moulded over the figure, falling out in flounces near the edge of the skirt. To the same house is due the revival of the charming and graceful Princess form. One new model is buttoned all down the back, with a series of little tabs from side to side curiously suggestive of the vertebral column. It is significant that even the more practical tailor-made gowns are so close-fitting that the usual place of fastening is no longer possible, and every Frenchwoman now wears her skirt buttoned in front: a curious and not very practical mode that will probably disappear as suddenly as it came in.

Certainly next in point of interest to Worth is the famous Félix establishment. The founder of the house was hairdresser to the Empress Eugénie, and this even before her marriage. The present M. Félix is the third head of the dressmaking house. Like M. Jean Worth, he is quite absorbed in his business, devoting most of his own time to the designing of costumes. "Félix" prides itself on a certain rigid sobriety of taste and originality of cut and line; accordingly, M. Félix's theories on the dress of the future may be summed up in the answer he lately gave to one inquiring of him as to the probable duration of certain exaggerated modes of the moment: "Believe me, every new fashion that is exaggerated and non-practical is bound to disappear in a very short time. Without knowing it, the great modern emporium renders a service to good taste; in its desire to produce novelties and to exaggerate whatever may be the mode of the hour, it throws upon the market a number of models which have only to be seen to be, as it were, discredited by every woman of taste." M. Félix went on to say that, in his judgment, women will not ultimately be hampered with long walking skirts that sweep the ground, or with sleeves that practically cover the hand, as do all the smarter sleeves of 1899. In this connection a visitor to M. Félix's beautiful salons, where he has, by the way, a special department devoted to the day and evening gowns of young girls, might well venture to recall the days when the crinoline—most inartistic and cumbersome of modes—dwelt in our midst for something like twenty years.

Laférière and Doucet are peculiarly

A LACE AND CHIFFON BALL DRESS.

French, although they dress many prominent Londoners; while La Maison Rouff has many clients in St. Petersburg. Russian women are very fond of dress, and every Paris house has a number of fitters who can be sent off at a moment's notice to St. Petersburg or to Moscow. Many Englishwomen also patronize Rouff. The house not only does no advertising, but it is one of the few in Paris where the journalist whose business is the description of dress finds it almost impossible to obtain an entrance, so fearful are the principals of the business lest their new models should become known to the outside world. Rouff devotes special attention to all the so-called small accessories of dress. It is there that the newest buttons, the most fantastic linings, and so on, are to be found.

M. and Mme. Paquin, though their business was founded comparatively recently, can probably boast of a larger *clientèle* than can any of their rivals; the fact that they are the only great Paris dressmaking house which has opened a London branch speaks for itself. M. Paquin's one wish is to achieve originality, he is, above all things, an innovator, and on more than one occasion he has dared to go in advance of the fashion, successfully imposing some new mode on the world of dress. Thus, to take but one example: when cycling became a craze, he and Mme. Paquin turned their attention to becoming cycling costumes, and for a while

THE SKIRT OF 1899: WORTH.

they were practically the only great dressmakers who supplied their fair patronesses with well-cut and elegant knicker-bocker costumes; indeed, as long ago as 1895, the wife of a leading Paris artist declared that the only place in Paris where a modest, becoming and practical cycling dress could be found was at Paquin's.

Although every Paris house will turn out tailor-made costumes, it is a curious fact that in Paris a London house, namely Red-fern's, is incontestably first as regards women's tailor-made costumes; and in this connection it may be added that many of the Paris Redfern's most profitable orders come to it from London and from New York. This establishment in the Rue de Rivoli is quite as palatial as the London branch. Very interesting from every point of view is the "Royal" drawing-room, lined with photographs of those Royal and Imperial personages who have patronized the establishment. Even Red-fern's, however, is strongly influenced by the modistic atmosphere of Paris, and a Redfern gown hailing from the Rue de Rivoli has not much in common either as regards cut or style with one turned out by the London house. This is probably owing to the fact that not only Frenchwomen, but those who choose to dress in Paris, become accustomed to a certain style, and insist that even their tailor-made frocks shall to a great extent follow whatever may be the passing fashion of the

190

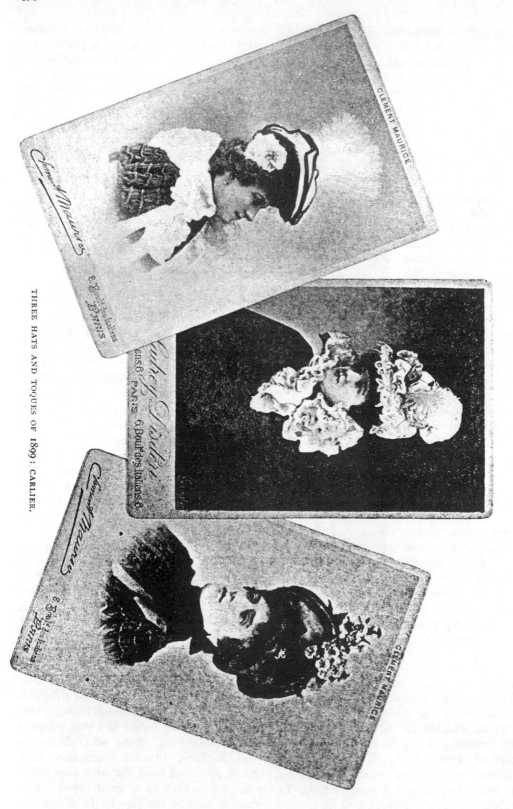

THREE HATS AND TOQUES OF 1899 : CARLIER.

SILK RECEPTION DRESS: WORTH.

edge of the skirt. Those happy in the possession of the long lace shawls and scarves which formed part of every trousseau during the early Victorian era, may now bring them out and wear them. Soft flexible materials will replace the satins and stiff silks which have so long had their day; gauzes, muslins, chiffons, and the more delicate gossamer laces will be seen in the evening.

The new colour is a grey blue, a soft dove colour, singularly becoming to many women hovering on the borderland between youth and middle age. Black and white will remain as much in favour as ever, a favourite combination being soft white silk draped with black lace. Every exaggeration is to be avoided. The most marked novelty of the moment is a sleeve, closely wrinkled down the arm, and widening at the wrist so as to cover half the hand, while out of this flat frill falls a full ruffle of lace, from which the tips of the fingers alone emerge.

Individual as are each and all of the leading Paris dressmakers, they cannot claim the same startling originality as can certain of the Paris milliners. Although it is fairly easy to distinguish a Paris gown from one made in any other city in the world, it is quite impossible to mistake a really successful Paris hat. Millinery is in Paris a fine art, and the fact that even the simplest little bonnet made in the "studios" of Virot, Carlier, and Marescot, is priced at over one hundred francs—that is four pounds—while more elaborate head-gear will run up to two and three hundred francs, proves that there is a large and indeed increasing circle of women who are willing to pay almost as much for a hat as they would have done some years ago for a gown.

Notwithstanding the fact that a hat turned out by one of the leading millinery establishments is probably often excessively dear at the price asked for it, it would be a mis-

hour. To give an example of what is meant, it may be stated that at the present time all the Paris Redfern gowns are being made either with the over-skirts which are now seen on English evening gowns and more elaborate afternoon dresses, or in the long floor-sweeping Princess shape which has very little affinity with what we in this country style a tailor-made costume.

As to the modes of the moment, we may expect to see during the next year not only the over-skirts which have now become firmly established in public favour, but also long clinging Princess robes which will be welcomed by the tall and slim. The sobriety of these garments will, however, be relieved by long sashes, knotted in front and falling to the

192

take to suppose that the mere name Virot or Carlier, to quote the two leading houses, counts for as much as it would probably do in any other city than Paris. The best French artificial flowers are exceedingly expensive, as has often been proved to those who have attempted to copy a good French model hat. Then, again, feathers are very costly. There are in Paris eight hundred wholesale houses dealing with nothing but feathers, and these in their turn employ ten thousand workpeople.

Each of the leading millinery establishments have their straw model shapes made each season to their own order, and it is quite curious, when going from one to the other, to note the thousand and one subtle differences existing between each famous *Maison de Modes*. It need hardly be said that a very large foreign business is done by these houses; four times a year hundreds of English, American, and German buyers come to Paris solely and simply to invest in model hats. As an actual fact, however, the model hat once safely ensconced in London or New York remains unique; something like it will be offered to the unsuspecting client, but the original shape is rarely if ever really copied; accordingly only a general resemblance to the original is attained.

The French lady, even with a comparatively modest dress allowance of say one hundred pounds a year, will give as much as five to eight pounds for a hat twice a year, but she will be tried for her head-gear as carefully as she is for her gowns. When ordering a new hat or bonnet, the shape of her head is elaborately measured, and Madame Carlier—for a woman is at the head of this great business—would never dream of offering to sell right off the stand one of her model hats or bonnets to a French client. English and American women passing through Paris will buy ready-made head-gear literally by the dozen, giving, when of an extravagant turn of mind, an order for a couple of hundred pounds' worth. Not so the French woman, who, before ordering even a garden-hat, will indulge in interminable discussions on straws, shapes, and colours; while if, when the hat is finally finished, she should feel that she made a mistake, no French milliner worthy of the name would compel her, or even try to persuade her, to purchase the failure.

When the foundation is to be of wire or stiffened muslin, the shape is actually made up in the work-rooms; this makes it impossible for a really new hat or toque shape to become common during the first season of its inception. As a rule, the French hat

A MUSLIN DRESSING GOWN: WORTH.

must bear some relation to the gown with which it is to be worn; this is, perhaps, one reason why so many Frenchwomen so constantly wear black. Unless she is very wealthy it would be difficult for a French lady to acquire many successful costumes, taking the word costume in its wider sense; this is why it so often happens that a Frenchwoman, after extreme youth, rings the changes on black and white, grey and mauve; it is thus that she compasses the difficult feat of appearing at any moment almost as well dressed as do those of her friends who spend their thousands for her hundreds of francs.

Probably most people who pay a flying visit to Paris imagine that fashion-land is closed to any but the very wealthy. The

A SUMMER FROCK : WORTH.

Louvre and the Bon Marché count rich English people among their most profitable clients. The reason for this is not far to seek. The pretty London heiress, unless belonging to a very "smart" set, spends the proceeds of the handsome cheque given her by a kind father in purchasing half a dozen or more Paris gowns, made in one of the great shops which hang out so many attractive lures to the visitor, rather than on, say, three frocks from Worth or Paquin.

The Frenchwoman of even very modest means has an invincible distaste for wearing anything which has become the cloak, the blouse, the bonnet, or the gown of " Madame Tout le Monde"; accordingly the theory that the well-dressed Frenchwoman longs to be up-to-date is quite a false one. On the contrary, the young Frenchwoman would far rather wear a Worth, Rouff, Paquin, gown for two seasons than be dowered with three inferior costumes in the same space of time; and even the girl enjoying what would be considered on this side of the Channel a very handsome dress allowance contents herself with quite few clothes. But then it must be remembered that her tailor-mades will have cost her from sixteen to twenty-five pounds, her afternoon dresses from twenty pounds to thirty pounds; her hats, of which she will probably only have two each year, will range from five pounds to eight pounds; she will be measured for her gloves, and the only item for which she will pay less than her English sister is foot-gear.

It should be added in this connection that very few Frenchwomen cannot, when put to it, turn out a simple frock; and an expensive model dress will serve in a very literal sense as model not only to the happy possessor of the garment in question, but also to her friends. This thoroughness extends to underclothing. A Frenchwoman will patronize the same "lingère" for a life-time, being fitted for each of her under-garments, while even French servants generally have their stays made to order.

Certain economic facts of course underlie, to a great extent, the widely different methods pursued by French and English women in this all-important matter of clothes. As all the world knows, France enjoys, or suffers under, a very strict Protectionist *régime*. Cheapness, in the London sense of the word, is unknown in Paris, where everything "made in Germany" is heavily taxed. To take one example: the endless variety of cotton materials which can be purchased in the United Kingdom for a few pence a yard cannot be found in France, their only substitute being strong unornamental linens, which begin at about fourteen-pence a yard. Thus it will be seen that the Frenchwoman, whatever her rank in life, is accustomed to spend a good deal of money on dress, and this whether her purse be deep or shallow.

This state of things brings about a curious sense of responsibility in all those employed in French fashion-land. Even in the great cosmopolitan emporiums the purchaser is not tempted, save by eyegate, to purchase a hundred and one useless little etceteras for which he or she may have no real use. True, scarce a week passes but some exceptionally cheap line is offered to the patrons of each large establishment, Bon Marché, Louvre, or Printemps; but if the chance is not at once taken, the bargain, whether it be in the shape of a hat, a mantle, a parasol, or a gown, of which of course some thousands of duplicates are offered, will have given place to some other "occasion," and be no longer on sale, save at a considerably enhanced price. As an actual fact these "occasions" are really often sold under cost price, the theory being that the purchaser will almost certainly be tempted to purchase something else in the establishment.

Another curiously French trade method, which does not seem to have been copied elsewhere, is that of allowing purchasers, even those who have no running account, to buy goods as it were on approval. Thus an extravagant woman is tempted to purchase far more than she would otherwise do, secure in the knowledge that if she changes her mind she can always within a reasonable time have the purchase money returned in full if the goods are or appear new and unworn. The leading houses, though not following closely the methods of their more popularity-hunting rivals, will almost invariably consent to take back a costume if when finally completed it does not meet with the

THE NEW SKIRT: FRONT VIEW.

approval of the purchaser. Again, taking the delicate question of misfits: not only will any mistake be rectified, but a new skirt or bodice, as the case may be, will be supplied without any astonishment or annoyance being expressed.

In one matter the denizens of French fashion-land are far more fortunate than their British brothers and sisters. Even now, on the eve of the twentieth century, the credit system, which obtains nearly all over the world, has scarcely touched French retail trade; and when some years ago a leading house threatened to post a list of those among its customers who had been in debt to the firm for upwards of ten years—a threat which, by the way, was never carried out—three-fourths of the defaulters were foreigners.

WHAT · WE · WOMEN · OWE · OUR · QUEEN.

BY THE HON. MRS. HENRY CHETWYND.

IN May our gracious Queen celebrated her eightieth birthday, and in June she entered upon the sixty-third year of her long and beneficent reign; and still she fills the first place in our hearts. Much has been said regarding the great advances made in the arts, in commerce, and in manufacture, during Her Majesty's rule, but not so much of the benefits to women. To-day women have the right of possession; fifty years ago a woman's earnings belonged legally to her husband, who perhaps earned nothing, and spent her property in drink. Besides all this improvement, there are many things we owe our Queen to which it is important to call attention. All high stations give an example,

From a photograph by Hughes & Mullins, Ryde, I.W
HER MAJESTY THE QUEEN IN THE DRESS WORN DURING THE STATE JUBILEE PROCESSION, JUNE 22, 1897.

which, filtering down, affects millions out of sight; and the example given by our Queen has affected so many, and done so much good, that one reason for our loyalty and reverence for Her Majesty's character is the gratitude we owe her for showing what a daughter, a wife, and a mother, should be.

As a daughter the Queen was a pattern to all, especially to those who, in these latter days, are too apt to forget the reverence and devotion due to a mother. As a wife, every one acknowledges that the highest example was given by the Queen of what wedded life should be; and this example was shown under many difficulties which, but for the great unselfishness and the intuition that two very noble natures had of their respective positions, might have been insurmountable. Love taught the lesson. On the one hand, there was the self-restraint which made it possible to work incessantly in the shadow, and, whilst conscious of intellectual power above the average, to go without open recognition, and to suffer misconceptions and want of appreciation in silence. On the other hand, there was the full recognition from the wife, who understood her husband and his position together with a whole-souled, wifely devotion.

As a mother, how much the Queen's example has altered the relations between mothers and their children! Fifty years ago, what did a fashionable mother know of her children, either when they were infants in the nursery, or later, when they were in the schoolroom? Nurses and governesses had it all their own way. Sometimes they were good; sometimes they were bad—and too often engaged upon the recommendation of some fashionable friend, who wanted to get rid of them. The mother saw her babies once a day, sometimes not even that, and accepted as gospel whatever she was told—was perfectly satisfied if the children had pretty manners, were tolerably graceful, could play a little, dance a little, and speak a little French.

The Queen's views of motherhood altered all this. When it became known that all the details of the nursery were her especial care; that every spare moment was spent with her children; that sanitary regulations were insisted upon; that a high character and high standard was required of the nurses and governesses; that time was not to be wasted, every honest effort being instantly recognised; and that no public or other duties neutralised the Queen's sense of true motherhood;—she at once set an example which was largely followed. Other mothers felt ashamed of neglected duties, and good wives and careful mothers became the fashion: something higher and better come into vogue.

There is also another matter which strikes all those privileged to know anything of Her Majesty's surroundings, and that is how completely the law of kindness prevails. It is well known that no one would venture to repeat an ill-natured story or a scandal to the Queen, and if you meet those whose lives in a measure touch hers, the same thing strikes every one; for how genuinely and unaffectedly they silence ill-nature, and take the kindest view of every action capable of being construed in two ways. It is not too much to say that sympathy with the poor and the highest interpretation of our duties in all the relations of life have received from the Queen's example an impetus and an inspiration which makes our womanhood something to be respected, and of which no handful of silly "new" women can deprive us.

From a photograph by Maull & Fox.

THE HON. MRS. HENRY CHETWYND.

"TIRED OUT."

TOQUE IN STEEL AND SILVER.
WHITE TIP, BUNCH OF
PURPLE HYDRANGEAS ON
LEFT SIDE.

HAT OF FINE WHITE STRAW,
TRIMMED WITH THICK
RUCHE OF SMALL
FLOWERS, RAISED ON
LEFT SIDE.

PICTURE-HAT OF CRINOLINE STRAW. PASTE
AND JET BUCKLE, WHITE OSTRICH-TIPS,
AND VELVET STRINGS.

TOQUE OF PINK TULLE.
WHITE OSTRICH-TIPS,
JET BUCKLE.

LARGE DRAWN CHIFFON HAT
IN BLACK. BLACK
FEATHERS AND CHIFFON
STRINGS; BUNCH OF PALE
GREEN POPPIES UNDER
BRIM ON LEFT SIDE.

FANCY HAT IN CHIFFON, TRIMMED
WITH LACE, BUCKLE, AND
OSTRICH-FEATHERS.

Madame Louise's.

LARGE HAT, FANCY STRAW.
FEATHERS, VELVET LOOPS
THROUGH STRASS BUCKLE.
RED ROSES RESTING ON HAIR
AT BACK.

PICTURE - HAT IN WHITE CHIFFON,
TRIMMED WITH LARGE PINK ROSES.
BLACK VELVET ROSETTE ON HAIR.

TOQUE OF BLACK SEQUINNED
NET. VELVET LOOPS,
WINGS, AND CACHE
PUYERS OF PINK ROSES.

MORNING OR SEASIDE SAILOR.
WHITE NET WINGS, EDGED
WITH BLACK RIBBON.
WHITE OSPREY.

SAILOR SHAPE IN WHITE STRAW.
NET RUCHING," EDGED WITH
BLACK CHIFFON. WHITE
OSPREY.

TOQUE. WINGS OF WHITE TULLE
STUDDED WITH SILVER, WHITE
OSTRICH - TIP, BUCKLE, AND
CHIFFON ROSETTES.

Round the Shops in September.

By MRS. M. THORNEYCROFT.

AS the extreme heat lessens more people go in for bicycling, and the machines taken down into the country or to the seaside are utilized more than was the case in July and August. Our neighbours across the Channel have designed several new things in the way of bicycle costumes, coolness being chiefly aimed at. The very latest is a skirt in strong white coutil, the hem lined with white leather to keep it down. The chemisette accompanying this skirt is white *linou*, with collars and cuffs in starched *linou*. The short bolero is cut to form a small heart in the centre, the back being tight-fitting and loose somewhat at the bottom, and the high-draped *ceinture* is in China blue taffeta. A Panama straw hat, coming well over the face, is trimmed with tufts of white silk muslin and covered with a plain veil in China blue silk muslin. The costume is completed with shoes in milky-white morocco, fine white silk stockings, having a rosy tint, and gloves in Saxe, rather large and just meeting the wrist, the interior part of the hand being pierced.

A country hat of French design is a capeline draped very full with black maline tulle, a large *chou* bow in black velvet *comête* holding up an immense butterfly in black and white feathers of a Japanese design

Underneath the hat is a demi-wreath of cream velvet *comête* ribbon. Cabriolet hats in waterproof linen are being worn at the French watering-places. This shape is most becoming to a young face, as it comes well forward. This shape of skirts is being changed in Paris. They are now much narrower, and sometimes have the appearance of a sack, shaped to fit the person at the top. They go out slightly from the ankles, but that is all, and they are long all round. A tulip turned upside down exactly represents the shape of these new skirts. They are the reverse of athletic, and more adapted for carriage exercise than for walking. Pockets are no more effectable in these new skirts than in those they superseded ; accordingly, in order that some receptacle may be at hand for handkerchief and purse, satin bags similar to those that used to hang over the arms of our great grandmothers are once again quite generally seen. Some weeks ago *Punch* suggested that the lengthening trains of ladies' dresses would again afford occupation to Paris *gamins* and London street-boys, who would be employed to hold them up, at least when madame crossed the road. But trains have not come in, although dresses are still long.

Among the Cowes' costumes, I noticed a fine cream serge with spear-head-shaped appliqued pieces of orange linen, worked in cream flax thread. These appeared at the foot of the skirt, and on a smaller scale on the coat fronts. The waistcoat, or vest, was of white tucked chiffon, set in between tulle loops in several tucks. There was a bow of the yellow *panne* and a little tulle under the brim at one side, and in front a large bunch of white and grey orchids, with green leaves. The flowers

Tho " Swift."

sling-like fronts of shot orange taffetas. The white satin straw sailor hat had a high crown, and was trimmed with a band of orange *panne*, and the garniture was composed of *panne* bows, mixed with flat white were very lovely and perfectly transparent.

For real autumn wear some of the costumes made this year for Scotland can hardly be surpassed. A good one is of light *tobal* cloth. The skirt fastens at the side and that seam is accentuated by appliqued

little coat the basques were trimmed to correspond, and the fronts were of velvet,

The " Parisian."

darker cloth, piped with lighter cord, and set in by gold thread in a conventional design of scrolls and leaves. On the smart

with a similar applique of cloth and tinsel. The back of this coat formed a **V**, and the basques were shortened over the hips, and in front fell in rounded tabs. There was a high collar, and the coat could be worn open, when it turned back to show revers one of black cashmere which was particularly original in shape and treatment. At the back it was on the lines of a

The "Brighton."

to the waist matching the cloth. The top of the revers were shaped in two small leaf-like points. *A propos* of smart coats, I saw bolero, but the fronts were in two long points reaching almost to the knees. All seams were narrowly piped, and the wrists

204

and entire coat were bordered by rows of tiny, wavy tucks, and lined with pink and gold broché. A hood gave becoming width to the shoulders, and was piped with green velvet, and there were foliated revers, and a high collar of white satin edged with

find seats for lady shop assistants already in use. Now that the Royal Assent has been given to the bill piloted through Parliament by Sir John Lubbock and the Duke of Westminster, many leading employers are not waiting for it to come into force (on

The "Blanche."

green velvet, and richly embroidered with a border and groups of flowers worked in gold and art shades of blue and green silk French knots, mixed in with others in cream silk.

Going into a large West End establishment the other day, I was agreeably surprised to

January 1st next) before doing what has so long been necessary and yet left undone. Earl Wemyss and Sir J. Blundell Maple fought against this measure to the last, but they were borne down by the public opinion generated through the Women's League formed in May last, by Mrs. Creighton. The

Duchess of Westminster, Adeline Duchess of Bedford, Lady George Hamilton, Lady Knightley of Fawsley, Lady Battersea, Mrs. Carl Meyer, Mrs. A. Cameron Corbett, Mrs.

was instituted by lady customers. It can only be watched and rendered truly effective by them. Let it be once understood in a district that ladies will not shop where seats

The " Ena."

Wynford Philipps, Mrs. W. S. Caine, Miss Bradley, and many other well-known philanthropic women joined the League. We may therefore fairly say that this important reform

are not both provided and used, and they will be forthcoming.

And now I am writing of grievances, I may as well notice that the drapers themselves have one. In the matter of damaged gloves, the retailers are caught in a cleft stick. There is, I hear, a growing inclination on the part of a certain set of customers to bring back damaged gloves for exchange, or to damage gloves by trying them on in the shop. At the same time wholesale houses are more determined than ever to keep returns within narrow limits. Hence the poor retailer has often to choose between losing a customer and paying for damages himself. Moreover, whereas gloves used formerly to be worn comparatively loose and easy, and were made of coarser materials than those now used, the reverse has been for some time the case. "You will find it decidedly cheerful," one draper remarked to another, "after you have tried a few pairs of gloves on some woman who had no notion of taking any of them, to hear the next lady customer say, "Oh! I don't want any of those gloves, they all look as if they had been tried on.""

It is a gross (and rather an unladylike) mistake to insist upon buying gloves two sizes too small. A good glove should fit easy, and will then last longer and look its best to the end. There are also different ways of putting gloves on. In the interests of all concerned I will here transcribe the rules for

PUTTING ON GLOVES.

1. Open and turn back the gloves to the thumb, and powder lightly.

2. Put the fingers in their places, not the thumb, and carefully work them on with the first finger and thumb of the other hand until they are quite down. *Never press between the fingers.*

3. Pass the thumb into its place with care, and work on as the fingers.

4. Turn back the glove and slide it over the hand wrist, *never pinching the Kid,* and work the glove into proper place by means of the lightest pressure, always allowing the Kid to slide between the fingers.

5. In finishing, care should be taken in fastening the first button.

I took a stroll to Islington last month and was much struck by the excellence of arrangements and really wonderful combinations of moderate price and good quality exhibited by some of the leading shops in that suburb. Roberts' and Rackstraws' are household names with many of us, and on this occasion I shall say no more except that I made my own purchases

at one of those establishments with the usual satisfaction. I made a longer stay with Jones Brothers, not as a customer on this occasion, but as interested in the stock shown by this celebrated firm, who are re-building a part of their already very extensive premises. The costumes sketched for this article are on sale at this establishment in the Holloway Road. Nothing could be neater and more ladylike than their large selection of smart cycling costumes in tweeds and coatings. The latest improvements in the cycling skirt are here on view, and the price of a first-rate costume is from under two pounds. I selected for illustration a model styled "Swifts."

I was here shown an exquisite French model costume in fawn poplin cloth, lined throughout with rich cerise-coloured silk. The bodice, opening on the left side, was arranged with cerise satin and appliqueé and edged with silk ruching. An equally effective, but not so rich looking costume was the one called by the firm "Parisian." This is a perfect, tailor-made gown made up in all the newest shades of cloth. The coat, beautifully braided, and lined with silk, can be worn either open or closed. Four and a half guineas did indeed seem to be a low price for costumes so unexceptionable. A cheaper costume, equally excellent in its way is the "Brighton," which only costs two and a half guineas. It looks very well in black, but is also made in all colours and consists of a handsomely braided tailor-made coat and skirt, the coat being silk-lined.

Of mantles suitable to the season, Messrs. Jones Brothers are showing a large variety. A stylish shape is the "Blanche," a Velour du Nord cape, richly beaded and trimmed with lace having a frill of silk. It is lined with satin and priced from under two pounds. The "Ena," at three guineas, is a more elaborate rich appliqué silk mantle, handsomely beaded and braided in a novel design. This mantle is silk-lined, with pleated silk frills and ruché ribbon at the neck.

The evenings are beginning to draw in and already Paris models are being shown of dresses for evening wear in the season now commencing. The following may be noted: Dress in black tulle, studded with fine steel *paillettes,* forming "Greek" round the border over white taffeta. This tulle forms peplum, falling loose back and front the whole length of the dress; sleeves in black tulle draped and bordered with the same Greek trimming. The same design borders the square *décolleté*. In the interior is a drapery of white tulle. Across the corsage is a long trailing branch of pinks in all their natural shades coming from the left shoulder and finishing at the waist. Another toilette is in rose-silk muslin, with light Pompadour impressions placed over rose taffeta, which is veiled with rose-silk muslin. Large *entre-deux* of white blonde slightly undulating are placed in the form of application, and form tablier in the front passing round the dress to form two Greek Vandykes on either side, then crossing at the back to the waist. These *entre-deux* are framed with two small gatherings of rose-silk muslin. The corsage in *muslin de soie* is framed with *entre-deux* of blonde, and held down at the waist by a corselet in draped rose taffeta, covered with ladders of ribbon to match. On the shoulders are thick tufts of roses, demi-long sleeves, tight-fitting and pleated.

ALL FAT PEOPLE

Can be CURED by taking

Trilene Tablets

(Regd.)

For a few weeks. They will safely REDUCE WEIGHT and CURE CORPULENCY PERMANENTLY. They are small, agreeable, harmless, and never fail to Improve both Health and Figure without change of Diet.

AN ENGLISH COUNTESS writes:
"Your Trilene Tablets act admirably."

Send 2s. 6d. to Mr. F. Wells, The Trilene Company, 70, Finsbury Pavement, London.

SAMPLES OF TESTIMONIALS.

"87, Alexandra Road, Norwich.
"GENTLEMEN,—I have had some boxes of your Tablets for my wife, and she has derived great benefit from them.
"Yours faithfully, J. R. CANHAM."
Illustrated Family Novelist, Nov. 30th, 1895, says: "A great many women who are plump by nature worry about their Stoutness. However, there are some perfectly safe remedies for *Embonpoint,* among them being the Trilene Tablets, which are not only safe, but absolutely beneficial to the general health, and speedily produce the desired effect."

"1, Letterstone Road, Fulham, S.W.
"SIRS,—I found myself decreased and better for your treatment, and can get about more freely.
"Yours sincerely, F. E. GODDEN."
"6, Brighton Terrace, Hull.
"Mrs. JOHNSON has much pleasure in saying she has derived great benefit from your Tablets."

"3, Castle Road, Deal.
"Mrs. J. PEARSON is glad to say she is much thinner."
"Convalescent Home, New Brighton, Cheshire.
Miss S. J. PRITCHARD says: "They have done me much good. I am 21 lb. lighter already."
"486, Market Street, Whitworth, near Rochdale.
Miss GRINDROD writes: "Have had one 2s. 6d. box of Trilene Tablets, and am 5 lb. lighter."
"Claremont House, Shrewsbury.
"DEAR SIRS,—I have nearly finished your Tablets, and cannot speak too highly of them. They do me good in many ways, being a valuable tonic and bracer-up of the nervous system, and being of a gouty tendency, they have also done me good in that way. I am very much thinner.
"Yours truly, (Mrs.) K. M. ANNAND."

"Bretton West, near Wakefield.
"Miss L. LANGFIELD has taken a box of Tablets, and is already 7 lb. lighter."

"25, Windsor Terrace, Penarth, Cardiff.
Miss M. FLAVELL says: "I have lost 2 st., and am much better in health."

"2, Chariot Street, Hull.
Mr. JUBB, Chemist, says: "My customers speak highly of your Tablets."
"Windsor Hotel, Merthyr Vale, South Wales.
Mr. J. THOMAS writes: "When I started the Tablets I weighed 17½ st., and have got down to 14 st. 9 lb."
Extract from *Bury and Suffolk Times,* June 15th, 1894: "Miss ATHERTON sings and dances as piquantly as ever, and is a marvel of agility, considering how much flesh she has put on of late. Her friends should induce her to take a course of Trilene Tablets, about which I hear wonderful things. One portly acquaintance of my own, by merely a few weeks' use of these little Tablets, has reduced his bulk perceptibly. I am assured the tablets are harmless and tasteless, and that the Trilene Company, in Finsbury Pavement, London, are doing an enormous and ever-increasing trade."

"West Cornforth, Ferryhill.
Mr. WM. USHER says: "A sister of mine, who was 17 st., was greatly reduced by your Tablets to 15 st."
"'Aspern,' 29, King's Hall Road, Beckenham.
Miss S. WOODHOUSE writes: "I have much pleasure in stating that your Tablets are really a Safe Cure for Stoutness; they have cured me, and I am a perfect figure now."
"131, Victoria Street, London, S.W.
Mrs. ARTHUR WEGUELIN (the "Society" Celebrity) writes: "By simply taking the Trilene regularly, and without change of diet, I have lost 1 st. 4 lbs. in four weeks."

THE TRILENE COMPANY, 70, FINSBURY PAVEMENT, LONDON.

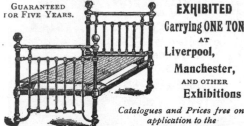

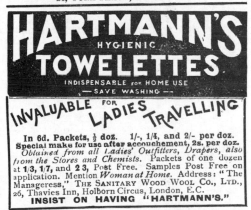

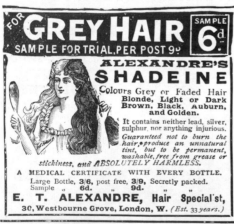

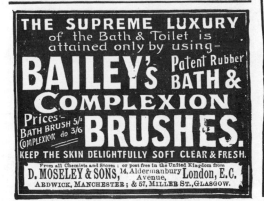

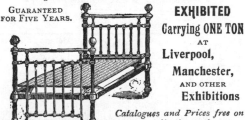